CHILD LANGUAGE AND CHILD DEVELOPMENT 7
Series Editor: Li Wei, University of Newcastle

Childhood Bilingualism
Research on Infancy through School Age

Edited by
Peggy McCardle and Erika Hoff

MULTILINGUAL MATTERS LTD
Clevedon • Buffalo • Toronto

Library of Congress Cataloging in Publication Data
Childhood Bilingualism: Research on Infancy through School Age/Edited by Peggy
McCardle and Erika Hoff.
Child Language and Child Development
Includes bibliographical references and index.
1. Bilingualism in children. 2. Language acquisition. 3. Literacy. I. McCardle, Peggy D.
II. Hoff, Erika. III. Series.
P115.2.C49 2006
404'.2 083–dc22   2005021286

British Library Cataloguing in Publication Data
A catalogue entry for this book is available from the British Library.

ISBN 1-85359-870-4 / EAN 978-1-85359-870-8 (hbk)
ISBN 1-85359-869-0 / EAN 978-1-85359-869-2 (pbk)

Multilingual Matters Ltd
UK: Frankfurt Lodge, Clevedon Hall, Victoria Road, Clevedon BS21 7HH.
USA: UTP, 2250 Military Road, Tonawanda, NY 14150, USA.
Canada: UTP, 5201 Dufferin Street, North York, Ontario M3H 5T8, Canada.

Typeset by Archetype-IT Ltd (http://www.archetype-it.com).
Printed and bound in Great Britain by the Cromwell Press Ltd.

Contents

Introduction

ERIKA HOFF and PEGGY McCARDLE

Many children in the United States and around the world grow up exposed to more than one language. For these children, bilingualism is a fact of life – not an option. Despite its prevalence, however, the phenomenon of bilingual development is neither well described nor well understood. This gap in scientific knowledge creates a practical problem for those who must assess and educate children from bilingual environments without adequate information on the normative course of bilingual development or the educational practices that best serve bilingual children. The current lack of information exists in part because bilingual development is a relatively new field of scientific study and in part because much of the early research in the area – particularly in the US (Hakuta, 1986) – focused on the question of whether bilingualism is good or bad for a variety of linguistic and cognitive outcomes. For children growing up in bilingual environments, the more relevant questions concern the nature of children's language learning experiences in bilingual environments, the course and processes of language and literacy development in two or more languages, and the relation of educational programs to academic outcomes in children exposed to more than one language.

In order to further research on these questions, a workshop on childhood bilingualism was convened in Washington, DC in April 2004, sponsored by the National Institute of Child Health and Human Development (NICHD) and the Office of English Language Acquisition (OELA) and Office of Special Education and Rehabilitation Services (OSERS) of the US Department of Education, with support from the American Federation of Teachers, the International Reading Association, and the American Speech-Language-Hearing Association. International leaders in the fields of bilingual development, language development, and adult bilingualism were brought together to take stock of current knowledge and to identify important areas in which new work is needed in the field of childhood bilingualism. (A summary document of that meeting is available at http://www.nichd.nih.gov/crmc/cdb/Childhood-Bilingualism_2005.pdf).

This volume is a product of that workshop. Its goal is to describe the current state of the science in the field of childhood bilingualism and to propose a research agenda for the future. The papers are organized into four major parts. Part 1 (Processing Two Languages) addresses speech perception and word recognition processes in infants exposed to two languages; Part 2 (Learning Two Languages) addresses oral language development in children exposed to two languages; and Part 3 (Literacy in Two Languages) addresses biliteracy. Part 4 (Perspectives on Childhood Bilingualism from Related Fields) provides commentary on studies of bilingual development from two leading scholars, one in adult bilingualism and one in the cross-linguistic study of first language acquisition. The final Part 5 (Closing Comments) provides commentary on the politics and science of bilingual practices and a summary of the issues and directions that emerged during the workshop and the discussions it stimulated.

In Part 1, papers by Werker and colleagues, Vihman and colleagues, and Fernald focus on infants and on describing the processes by which children exposed to two languages come to perceive speech sounds and recognize words in the languages they are learning. Werker *et al.* ask how infants exposed to two languages master the phonological systems of each. Their findings suggest not only that bilinguals and monolinguals follow different paths in phonological development, but also that there may be differences among infants with bilingual exposure (perhaps related to degree of exposure) in the degree to which they develop two separate systems. Fernald provides a methodological critique of speech perception research, making the point that children in bilingual environments typically hear accented speech and thus the phonetic properties of the target languages to which they are exposed differ from the phonetic properties of the target language that monolingual children are likely to hear. Vihman *et al.*, using behavioral and Event Related Potential data, report evidence that both word recognition and automatic word processing may develop differently in monolingual and bilingual children.

In Part 2, papers by Genesee and by Eilers and colleagues describe what might be termed the cognitive and social psychology of childhood bilingualism. Genesee argues that the study of what he terms bilingual first language acquisition (BFLA) is necessary both to provide data on BFLA to language and education clinicians who work with bilingual children and to enable scientists to develop a truly comprehensive theory of language acquisition. Genesee points out the many methodological difficulties that vex this area of research, including the definitional problem of what constitutes bilingual first language acquisition (e.g. if you are exposed to a second language at the age of two years does that make you a bilingual first language learner or a very young second language learner) and the ever-present problem of heterogeneity. Notwithstanding these difficulties, Genesee provides a comprehensive report on what we know about the course of bilingual first language acquisition and the communicative competence of young bilingual children. Eilers and colleagues describe the varied and complicated social circumstances surrounding childhood bilingualism in the Spanish–English bilingual community of South Florida, and they identify social and curricular variables that influence maintenance of Spanish during the acquisition of English proficiency in first and second generation Hispanics.

In Part 3, two papers take very different approaches in discussing studies of the development of literacy in bilingual children. August and colleagues discuss early reviews of studies of bilingual education programs and then report a longitudinal study of literacy outcomes for 5th grade children from Spanish-speaking homes with three different instructional situations: English only, Spanish only, and bilingual Spanish and English. Like Genesee, they point out difficulties inherent in designing studies to examine phenomena of bilingual development, and they present data that illustrate benefits and limitations of the three instruction situations their team studied.

Bialystok presents a model of the influence of bilingualism on literacy development and reports three studies of 6-year-olds, each of which compared a group or groups of bilingual children to monolingual children in terms of literacy and literacy related abilities. Bialystok compares alphabetic languages with the same and different writing systems and with a non-alphabetic language. Using these comparisons she addresses the roles of phonological awareness and decoding in the development of literacy in bilingual students and how language proficiency can influence reading outcomes. The important conclusion that emerges from the findings of these studies is that the consequences of bilingualism for literacy depend on the nature of the writing systems and the degree of bilingualism.

Two recurring themes in the papers in these first three sections of the issue are that the population of bilingual children is extremely heterogeneous and that the findings with respect to the consequences of bilingualism are quite varied. These papers go further and suggest that these two phenomena might be systematically related. The parameters of variation within the bilingual population, such as age and amount of exposure to each language, dominance, and the typological relation between the two languages, might have systematic effects that explain the varied findings in the literature on bilingualism. Bilingualism appears not to be a monolithic phenomenon whose effects researchers must try to pin down. Rather, bilingualism is an umbrella term for a variety of language experiences and competencies. The variables that describe the heterogeneity in the bilingual population are also variables which affect both language and literacy acquisition.

Part 4 includes brief discussions by language researchers who, at the workshop, were asked to think about how their areas of research could inform and enhance our thinking about the study of childhood bilingualism. Kroll brings findings from the study of adult bilingualism to bear on the topic of childhood bilingualism, pointing out that in adult bilinguals the two languages interact. Thus, two monolinguals in one brain is not the end state of bilingual development. Waxman's cross-linguistic research points out the complexity of the task facing children who acquire two different systems for encoding meaning in sound sequences and suggests specific areas for future research.

The concluding Part 5 contains commentary by Crago and a research agenda. Crago compares policies and approaches to bilingualism in the US and Canada, two nations in which she has lived, conducted research and trained researchers and clinicians who deal with bilingual children. She challenges us all to think more broadly and more creatively about research approaches, both in terms of the way we study bilingualism, the way that we implement the findings of such research, and the way that we support (both financially and in terms of collaboration) the research infrastructure.

The workshop goals were to bring together researchers from different disciplines and areas of study within bilingualism and language development, to examine the state of the science, and to develop a research agenda. The research agenda in this volume is drawn both from that April 2004 workshop and from other sources; it is offered in the hope it will stimulate additional rigorous, high quality, well-designed studies to explore the complex puzzle of bilingual language acquisition and its influences on literacy.

References

Hakuta, K. (1986) *Mirror of Language: The Debate on Bilingualism*. New York: Basic Books.

Chapter 1

Bilingual Speech Processing in Infants and Adults

JANET F. WERKER, WHITNEY M. WEIKUM and KATHERINE A. YOSHIDA

Adults are highly adept at processing their native language. They use phonological (sound) properties to effortlessly segment sentences, phrases and individual words, correctly detect morphological markers, and distinguish words that are phonetically similar such as *bad* vs. *dad*. All of these functions are performed rapidly and automatically when *listening* to speech. Furthermore, *viewing* speech has also been shown to play an important role, as adults are adept at extracting and processing the visible concomitants of spoken language that are available in the movements of the lips, tongue, jaw, face, head and neck. Considerable research has shown that the ease with which adults process their native language has its roots in listening to and observing speech in the infancy period (Werker & Tees, 1992). The resulting efficiency of phonological processing is essential for successfully understanding the meaning of the language being spoken and for recovering the underlying speaker intent.

As effortlessly as adults are able to process a native language, attempting to learn a second language (L2) is difficult. Finding boundaries between significant phonological units, pulling out and distinguishing individual words, and properly encoding morphological markers can all be very challenging tasks. Together, these difficulties in phonological perception of an unfamiliar language, or an L2 acquired late in life, summate to make the task of listening for meaning in the L2 considerably more taxing than it is in the first language (L1; for a review, see Sebastián-Gallés & Bosch, in press).

Our present understanding of how speech develops and is processed is largely based on the results of studies examining monolingual adults and infants. However, as the populations of bilinguals in North America grow, the study of bilingual language acquisition has become an increasingly important focus. As noted, individuals may face unique challenges in acquiring their L2, and such challenges will differ depending on whether

1

the L2 was learned in infancy or in adulthood. Any differences found between early and late bilinguals are also theoretically interesting as they inform on a number of issues, including the question of whether or not there are sensitive periods for learning of the sound properties, and whether or not the L2 acquisition process is the same or different later in life.

In this chapter, the findings of several studies that are beginning to address the question of phonological processing in bilinguals are reviewed. We begin with an examination of phonetic categories in adult and infant bilinguals, and examine the role that perception of these phonetic categories plays in associative word–object learning. This is followed by an overview of the ability to recognize languages on the basis of factors such as rhythmicity and visual information. We conclude with a reconsideration of what it means to grow up bilingual, and how studies of bilingual speech processing can not only help inform linguistic and psychological theory, but also inform policy makers.

Throughout this chapter, we will refer to those who acquired their two languages from an early age as 'bilingual first language acquisition' (BFLA; e.g., de Houwer, 1995). In all cases, when we talk about bilingual infants we, of course, are using a shorthand for bilingual-learning infants. In studies reported from our lab, we assessed adult language dominance (proficiency in each language) using a questionnaire developed by Alain Desrochers (2003). To ensure that the bilingual infants in our studies have had relatively equal exposure to each of their languages, we required that they have a minimum of 30% and a maximum of 70% input in each language as determined by a parent report scale designed by Bosch and Sebastián-Gallés (1997a).

Adult Phonetic Perception: Monolingual and Cross-linguistic Studies

Among the hallmarks of adult L1 speech perception is the ability to easily perceive just those acoustic/phonetic differences, in individual consonants or vowels, that signal a potentially meaningful distinction in the native language. For example, when presented with equally spaced stimuli on /ba/ to /pa/ voicing continuum, adult English speakers show a very sharp perceptual category boundary. They label all of those stimuli up to approximately +25 msec in voice onset time[1] (VOT) as /ba/ and all of those with longer VOTs as /pa/. Their ability to discriminate stimuli from along the continuum is predicted by their labelling performance (Liberman *et al.*, 1967; Repp, 1984). Perception of phonetic continua is language-specific: adults have difficulty discriminating those phonetic differences that are not used to convey meaningful distinctions in their native language. For example, the Japanese language does not contrast the consonants /r/ and /l/, and Japanese speakers have difficulty perceiving the difference between them (Goto, 1971; Miyawaki et al., 1975). Similarly, Hindi has a contrast between a front (dental) /d/ and a /D/ that is produced with the tongue curled over with the tip pressed against the roof of the mouth (retroflex), whereas in English a /d/ is produced at the alveolar ridge, between the two Hindi phones. Adult English speakers have difficulty discriminating the two Hindi sounds (Werker et al., 1981). Although performance on non-native phonetic distinctions improves with training (Lively et al., 1993; McClelland et al., 2002), there is conflicting evidence as to whether their performance ever reaches the level of a native speaker (e.g. Flege, 1991; Polka, 1991; Sebastián-Gallés & Soto-Faraco, 1999).

Privileged processing of native phonetic contrasts has its roots in perceptual experience in infancy. In the first several months of life, infants appear able to discriminate both native and non-native phonetic distinctions equally well (e.g. Streeter, 1976; Trehub, 1976; Werker et al., 1981). In the second half of the first year of life, however, their discrimination performance begins to change. By 6 months of age they show language-specific organization of vowel categories (Kuhl et al., 1992; Polka & Werker, 1994), and by 10–12 months of age they show poor discrimination of difficult non-native consonant distinctions (Werker & Lalonde, 1988; Werker & Tees, 1984). Moreover, their performance on native contrasts is not only maintained, but also sharpened (Polka et al., 2001). Recent studies have demonstrated that both these types of changes – improvement and decline – could occur through statistical learning. In an artificial language learning study, Maye et al. (2002) showed that infants change their phonetic categories on the basis of the distributional characteristics of the input. Further, in a study that tracked the frequency of heard phonemes in English, Anderson, Morgan, and White (2003) demonstrated that frequency of exposure impacts the age at which infants stop discriminating non-native phonetic distinctions. Thus by simply listening to the speech spoken around them, infants are able to tune their phonetic categories to more closely match those required for contrasting meaning in the adult language.

Infant Phonetic Perception: Bilingual and Cross-linguistic Studies

There has been considerable cross-linguistic speech perception research with infants (for reviews, see Aslin et al., 1998; Saffran et al., in press), but to our knowledge there have been only two studies examining phonetic perception in BFLA infants. The results of both studies reveal differences from those typically found with monolingual infants. In one study, Bosch and

Sebastián-Gallés (2003) examined vowel perception in Catalan and Spanish monolingual and Catalan–Spanish bilingual infants. The two languages are similar in many dimensions, but they differ in their vowel inventories: Spanish has only five vowels whereas Catalan has seven. Bosch and Sebastián-Gallés took advantage of this fact to compare the three groups of infants on their ability to discriminate a vowel distinction /e/-/ɛ/ which is used in Catalan, but not in Spanish. Monolingual Catalan infants discriminated their native distinction at 4-, 8-, and 12-months, as predicted. Monolingual Spanish infants discriminated the Catalan distinction at 4-months, but not beyond. The bilingual infants showed a surprising pattern, discriminating the Catalan /e/-/ɛ/ at 4- and 12-months, but not at 8-months. These results suggest that the developmental trajectory of age-related changes in speech perception in bilingual learning infants may be unique.

The other published study of phonetic perception in BFLA infants compared English, French, and French–English bilingual infants on their ability to discriminate the /b/ – /p/ voicing distinctions as implemented in both English and French (Burns *et al.*, 2003). The English infants were tested in Vancouver, British Columbia, while the French and bilingual French–English infants were tested in Ottawa, Ontario, with the assistance of Alain Desrochers at the Université d'Ottawa. To test the question of whether or not infants distinguish both the English and French contrasts, three stimuli that span the English and French boundaries were created: A French /ba/, an English /pʰa/ and a /pa/ stimulus with acoustic values intermediate between those of the /ba/ and the /pʰa/. The /pa/ has a relatively short VOT (+28 msec), but no aspiration. Crucially, this intermediate stimulus was labelled as [pa] by French adults and [ba] by English adults. A mock representation of the stimuli is shown below.

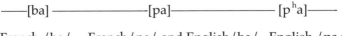

——[ba] ————————[pa]———————— [pʰa]——

French /ba/   French/pa/ and English/ba/   English /pa/

Infants of 6 to 8, 10 to 12, and 14 to 17 months were habituated to the central exemplar [pa], and then given two test trials, a change to [ba] and a change to [pʰa]. Discrimination of the French boundary was indicated by a recovery of looking time to [ba], whereas discrimination of the English boundary was indicated by a recovery to [pʰa].

At 6 to 8 months of age, the English monolingual and French–English bilingual infants showed the same pattern. Both groups were better able to discriminate the French ([pa] to [ba]) than the English ([pa] to [pʰa]) distinction, but, as expected, both groups performed similarly. By 10 to 12 months of age, the English infants discriminated only the English contrast, while the bilinguals showed marginal, but not significant, recovery to both changes. Testing infants of 14 to 17 months revealed that although the English and French infants continued to discriminate only their native contrasts, the bilinguals showed two distinct patterns. Half of the bilingual infants behaved like monolinguals, recovering significantly to the change in only one of the languages. The other half of the infants showed significant recovery to both the English and the French (recovered to a change to [ba] as well as to a change to [pʰa]).

These data suggest that there may be more than one pattern to bilingual phonetic perception. Specifically, it appears that although some bilinguals may show dominance for one of their languages, it may be possible to maintain equal facility in each. Determining factors, such as maternal language or amount of exposure, that predict the conditions under which a dominant language may emerge in infancy and/or the conditions under which the phonetic systems of two languages can be equally dominant, is an important goal for the future.

Adult Phonetic Perception: Bilingual Studies

The data on adult phonetic perception are similarly complex, with some indicating two sets of phonetic categories, one for each language (e.g. Grosjean, 1989), and other studies yielding evidence of only a single, summary representation averaging the values of the phonetic distinctions used in each language (e.g. Caramazza *et al.*, 1973). More recent research continues to address this question. Two factors that have received much attention are age of acquisition and acoustic/phonetic distance of the phonetic categories in the two languages.

Perhaps the best-known example of L2 phonetic acquisition is that of native speakers of Japanese who later acquire English. Japanese is a language with only one liquid, an /r/ that falls in between the English /r/ and /l/. Japanese late learners of English have been shown to have great difficulty with both production and perception of these English-specific phones (e.g. Best & Strange, 1992; MacKain *et al.*, 1982; Miyawaki *et al.*, 1975). Although training can improve performance (e.g. McClelland *et al.*, 2002), late learners of English seldom achieve native-like levels of proficiency. The differential acoustic/phonetic distance between the Japanese liquid and the respective English liquids helps to mediate perceptual performance: The Japanese liquid in fact is closer to the English /l/ than the /r/, and when auditorily exposed to English /r/-/l/-contrastive minimal pairs, native speakers of Japanese were able to correctly identify more of those tokens containing the more distant /r/ than those with /l/ (Flege *et al.*, 1996).

There are many other examples highlighting the influence of acoustic/ phonetic distance on phonetic perception in late bilinguals. French mono-linguals typically produce the phonemes /p t k/ with VOT values that are much shorter than those produced by monolingual English speakers. Flege (1987) showed that French speakers acquiring English have difficulty forming new English categories, perhaps due to their similarity and resulting perceptual conflation. Indeed, French L1 speakers initially produced the English L2 phonemes with their L1 VOTs. As the French L1 speakers became more proficient in English, their VOTs shifted away from the L1 value towards that of the L2, resulting in an intermediate value. That is, the French natives began to produce the stops with longer VOTs than do monolingual French speakers. In this case, even though separate L2 catego-ries were not created, the L1 phonemes shifted towards those of the L2, resulting in a 'compromise' category. The impact of such an intermediate category on speed and efficiency of processing is an area for further study.

The effect of acoustic/phonetic distance may itself be mediated by age of acquisition. An examination of native speakers of Spanish, a language with similar VOT values to those of French, revealed that only those who had acquired English in adulthood displayed compromised VOT values (Flege, 1991). Those who were exposed to the L2 as children were able to produce stops with values in different ranges for both English and Spanish, indicat-ing the presence of separate categories for the phones in each language.

In a series of studies, Sebastián-Gallés and her colleagues reported that when bilingual Spanish–Catalan speakers were tested in basic discrimina-tion tasks, their performance was relatively similar to that of the Catalan monolinguals (Diaz *et al.*, 2004). However, when the tasks were more difficult, performance differences could be seen even in those bilinguals who had acquired their second language before age 6. One example comes from a gating task, where participants are presented with the first segment of a word (e.g. 50 ms long), and asked for an identification decision, then a longer segment (e.g. 60 ms) is presented, and so forth, until the entire word is presented. Here, early Spanish-dominant bilinguals required more gates before they could accurately label (in a forced-choice task) pseudowords containing Catalan-specific phones (Sebastián-Gallés & Soto-Faraco, 1999). In another study, when asked to decide whether a given token from along the Catalan-specific /e/ – /ɛ/ continuum was a better example of the first vowel in the Catalan words /Pera/ or /pɛra/, the Catalan-dominant bilingual listeners succeeded, but the Spanish-dominants failed to differentiate along the continuum (Pallier *et al.*, 1997). These studies indicate that even though they had learned Catalan at an early age, the Spanish-dominant bilinguals did not form separate categories for the L2 vowels.

Some of the strongest evidence suggesting that even early bilinguals may show language dominance comes from an implicit task: repetition priming. In the repetition priming task, subjects are asked to make lexical decisions on auditorily presented stimuli. A priming effect is observed whereby faster decision times are recorded to the second presentation of a word than to its first (Slowiaczek & Pisoni, 1986). Pallier *et al.* (2001) used the repetition priming task with Catalan–Spanish bilinguals, and compared Spanish-dominant to Catalan-dominant individuals. Both groups were tested on their sensitivity to Catalan-specific minimal pairs such as / Pera/ and /pɛra/ and only the Spanish-dominant listeners showed the repetition priming effect. These results indicate that the two phones are actually represented lexically as homophones, as the minimal pairs did not prime the Catalan-dominants. Thus, although early bilinguals may perform equally to monolinguals on some basic perceptual tasks, dominance may none the less be evident when the phonetic detail is necessary for lexical tasks.

We extended this repetition priming experiment to Cantonese–English bilinguals, who were compared to English monolingual controls. Similarly to the Spanish-dominants, the English L2 speakers showed significant repetition priming in response to only the L2-contrast specific minimal pairs, indicating that they had trouble discriminating the L2-specific contrast. The English monolinguals experienced no such difficulties (Yoshida & Werker, 2004). We are in the process of analyzing data from the same English-specific contrasts in a simple discrimination task in order to ascertain whether this context may ease discrimination for the L2 speakers. Stimuli were created by retaining only the first CV syllable from the words used in the repetition priming task. They were presented in pairs, and subjects were asked to make a 'same' or 'different' judgment (AX discrimination) in response to the paired syllables. Both accuracy rates and reaction times were recorded. Preliminary analyses indicate that the bilinguals may be discriminating the L2-specific contrast syllables with accuracy rates analogous to those of the monolinguals. Taken together, these studies confirm that although bilinguals may be equally facile in some aspects of phonetic perception, some differences in deeper processing of their two native languages may be evident in other tasks.

Monolingual and Bilingual Infant Lexical Perception

The above studies raise the question of whether infants who are acquiring two languages from birth will also show subtle differences in how they use phonetic detail in word segmentation and associative word learning tasks. Across the first year of life, infants become tuned to many properties of the native language in addition to phonetic detail, all of which are important for successful word segmentation and word learning. As one example, by 9–10 months of age English monolingual infants show a preference for listening to words that correspond to the dominant, Strong–Weak stress pattern (words such as *DOCtor* rather than *guiTAR*; Jusczyk *et al.*, 1993). The knowledge of native stress patterns influences infants' ability to segment words from continuous speech. When presented with the same two words over and over (e.g. *dog* and *cup*), infants of 7 months will subsequently show a preference for listening to passages that contain those words over passages with two equally common, but not recently presented words (e.g. *feet* and *bike*; Jusczyk & Aslin, 1995). At this age, English infants can also pull out bisyllabic words, but only if the stress is on the first syllable. If the case of Weak–Strong words like *guiTAR*, 7 month English infants show recognition of only *TAR*. By 10 months, however, English infants can recognize both the more common Strong–Weak words as well as the less frequent WS words.

Recently, Polka and Sundara (2003) compared monolingual to bilingual infants of 7 months learning either Québécois French or English or both. French is an ideal comparison to English as it does not have alternating stress. Instead, most syllables are of equal stress, with the final syllable being a bit longer. Polka and Sundara found differences between English and French monolingual infants: the English infants segmented only the Strong–Weak words, but the French infants were better at segmenting words that conformed to the French form. Furthermore, results of their ongoing work suggest that bilingual learning French–English infants are able to segment both types.

It is also of interest to compare the approaches of bilingual and monolingual infants in learning phonetically similar words. One method for studying the earliest steps in word learning is the word-object associative learning 'Switch' task. In this task infants are habituated to two word–object pairings, and then tested on their ability to detect a 'switch' in the pairing. An initial study using this procedure showed that monolingual infants as young as 14 months are able to successfully learn to associate phonetically dissimilar nonsense words with objects (Werker *et al.*, 1998). However, if the words are phonetically similar and differ in only the initial consonant, infants of 14 months fail to learn new word–object associations in this task (Stager & Werker, 1997) even though they can perform successfully when tested with well-known words such as *ball* and *doll* (Fennell & Werker, 2003a). This difficulty in learning phonetically similar words is short-lived, as infants succeed by 17 months of age (Werker *et al.*, 2002).

Importantly, once they are able to access phonetic detail in this task, the native language phonetic categories guide word learning. At 17 and 20 months of age only Hindi-learning infants are able to learn to map minimally different words differing in a Hindi-specific (non-English) distinction to two different objects (Werker, Ladhar & Corcoran, in preparation). Similarly, English and Dutch learning infants can only learn to map minimally different words using the vowel distinctions that are phonemic in their native language (Dietrich *et al.*, 2004).

To ascertain whether bilingual-learning infants are equally able to use phonetic detail in associative word-learning as are monolingual infants, Fennell tested bilingual learning infants of 14, 17 and 20 months of age on their ability to learn the phonetically similar nonsense words *bih* vs. *dih*. Surprisingly, although the monolingual learning infants were able to succeed in this task at 17 months of age (Werker *et al.*, 2002), the bilingual learning infants did not succeed until 20-months (Fennell & Werker, 2003b; in preparation). One interpretation of these results would be that bilinguals are 'delayed'; however, the pattern of data obtained supports a more nuanced explanation. Among the bilinguals who did succeed at both 17 and 20 months, the size of the increased looking time to the Switch trial was greater than typically seen in our studies with monolinguals. Further research is required to understand this data pattern more completely, and to determine whether the difference in age of acquisition is predictive of later performance. But, as with the research on phonetic discrimination, the research on associative word learning indicates that the pattern and trajectory of acquisition may be unique in BFLA infants.

Recognizing the Native Language

The majority of research on bilingual speech processing has focused on perception and use of phonetic detail. There are, however, other phonological characteristics that distinguish languages. For example, languages contain rhythmical properties that are influenced by stress and syllable form. As previously noted, in English there are strong syllables and weak syllables such as in the word *doctor* where the stress is on the first syllable (the strong syllable). Stress is signalled in English by intensity, duration, and the fullness of the vowel. The syllable *doc* is louder, longer, and has a more fully pronounced /o/ than the syllable *tor*. In 'stress timed languages' such as English, there is a relatively equal beat from one strong syllable to another. Other languages, such as French, have relatively equal beats between each syllable. This class of languages is sometimes called 'syllable timed'. When there is a stress difference, it is signalled primarily by duration, with a duration increase in the last syllable of an utterance

(Abercrombie, 1965; Pike, 1945). These rhythmical characteristics thus provide more global information that allows discrimination between languages and recognition of the native language. In the final section of this paper, we turn to a series of studies examining language discrimination and preference in bilingual-learning infants, and complement these auditory-based studies with new work investigating the role visual speech plays in language recognition.

Discrimination and Recognition of Native Language

The ability to recognize one's native language using auditory information is present at birth. Moon *et al.* (1993) showed that 2-day-old infants discriminate and prefer the sounds of their native language. Recognition of the native language appears to be based, at least in part, on the rhythmical properties of the native language as infants are better able to discriminate two languages from different rhythmical classes than from the same (Mehler *et al.*, 1988; Moon *et al.*, 1993), even when the language samples are low-pass filtered to remove phonetic and lexical information (Nazzi *et al.*, 1998; Ramus *et al.*, 2000). For example, newborns and 2-month-olds can discriminate languages from two different rhythmical classes [e.g., stress vs. syllable timed languages such as French vs. English (Mehler *et al.*, 1988) and English vs. Spanish (Moon *et al.*, 1993) and stress vs. mora timed languages such as English vs. Japanese (Nazzi *et al.*, 1998) and Dutch vs. Japanese (Ramus *et al.*, 2000)]. However, infants of this age fail when tested on two languages from the same rhythmical class (e.g. two stress timed languages such as English vs. Dutch, Nazzi *et al.*, 1998).

These early language discrimination abilities may be particularly useful in bilingual environments: infants exposed to multiple languages could potentially use rhythmicity to segregate the input into the language from which it was derived. By 4–5 months of age, both monolingual (Nazzi *et al.*, 2000) and bilingual (Bosch & Sebastián-Gallés, 2001) infants are able to discriminate the native language from another language in the same rhythmical class. There is, none the less, an important difference between the way bilingual and monolingual infants show their recognition of the native language. When tested in an orientation latency procedure, monolingual infants orient faster to sentences in their native language (Nazzi *et al.*, 2000), whereas bilingual infants orient faster to the unfamiliar language (Bosch & Sebastián-Gallés, 1997b). It is not known why bilinguals orient differently to the presented native language, but this result stimulates interesting speculation for the development of language recognition abilities in these infants. Specifically, these findings once again point to the possibility that the very process of language acquisition is unique in BFLA infants.

Currently, we are investigating whether there are differences from birth in the way bilingual infants process languages. Werker, Burns and Moon (in preparation) are comparing newborn infants who were exposed to only English prenatally to those who were exposed to both English and Tagalog approximately equally throughout gestation. Crucially, English and Tagalog are from different rhythmical classes. English is generally characterized as a stress timed language, whereas Tagaolog exhibits a combination of syllable and mora-timed characterics (Bird _et al._, 2005). The critical question will be whether bilingual newborns who have been exposed to both English and Tagalog prenatally choose to listen equally to both languages.

As evident from the above review, the study of speech perception preference in early BFLA infants is itself only in its infancy, but this work is already beginning to chart how the listening biases present in early infancy may help direct attention to the key properties of the language or languages the infant is required to learn.

Recognition of the Native Language using Visual Speech Information

Speech processing involves not only the auditory signal, but also the visual information provided by the speaker. It has been well documented that the ability to process conversational speech is significantly enhanced when the speaker is visible (e.g. Gagne _et al._, 1994; Helfter, 1997; Summerfield, 1991). Visible information about the shape of the articulators influences the 'heard' phoneme (McGurk & MacDonald, 1976). For example, when presented with an auditory /ba/ and a visual /ga/, participants often perceive the intermediate phoneme, /da/. This 'McGurk' effect is language-specific with different influences across different languages (Massaro _et al._, 1995; Werker _et al._, 1992). In illustration, in their work, Werker _et al._ (1992) found that when presented with an auditory /ba/ and a visual /tha/, English speakers showed visual capture and perceived /tha/, whereas Québécois French perceived /da/. This is in agreement with Québécois French phonology: there is no /th/ phoneme at all, and the /da/ is produced with the tongue close to the same interdental position (at the back of the front teeth) as the English 'th' is often articulated.

Hardison (1999, 2003) has recently begun to explore the role of visual information in L2 learning. An influence from the L1 was found when the auditory and visual information were mismatched. However, when matching auditory and visual information were given, learning of L2 phonetic distinctions was enhanced. The information conveyed by visual speech has recently been shown to be even richer than first surmised, with rhythmicity playing a key role. The rhythmical head movements that accompany speech convey information about pitch and amplitude, and significantly facilitate speech intelligibility (Munhall *et al.*, 2004).

Given the detailed information provided by visual speech, it is possible that visual speech may, on its own, enable recognition of the native language. In collaboration, we have recently begun to explore the role of visual speech information in language discrimination by both monolinguals and bilinguals. To examine this question, adults were tested on their ability to visually distinguish different languages. Silent video clips containing two different languages were shown to adults. If the adults' native language was one or both of the languages represented in the clips, they were able to correctly (significantly better than chance) discriminate the languages. However, if the adults' native language was not one of the languages in the silent video clips, they performed at chance (Soto-Faraco *et al.*, under review). Interestingly, bilinguals who knew only one of the 'seen' languages, and had acquired it as an L2 later in life, did not perform as well as native speakers of that language. Indeed, in many cases, the L2 participants did not perform significantly better than chance (Weikum *et al.*, 2005).

It is not yet known why the L2 speakers were less able than the native speakers to use visual information to distinguish and detect languages. Since this population of bilinguals acquired their L2 later in childhood, lack of experience could be responsible for the differences in performance. Use of visual speech information is known to increase with both age (McGurk & MacDonald, 1976) and pronunciation accuracy (Desjardins *et al.*, 1997; Siva *et al.*, 1995). Currently, we are conducting additional experiments to try to more fully answer this question.

Infants are also sensitive to visual speech information and can use it to match heard and seen speech (Kuhl & Meltzoff, 1982, 1984; Patterson & Werker, 1999, 2003). Moreover, when the auditory and visual information are in conflict (e.g. visual /ba/ and auditory /ga/), the infants' 'heard' percept may be influenced by what they see (Burnham & Dodd, 2004; Desjardins & Werker, 2004; Rosenblum *et al.*, 1997).

We recently began testing 6-month-old infants' visual language discrimination abilities. The preliminary results suggest that infants can discriminate languages on the basis of visual speech alone. In fact, infants as young as 4 months of age show a similar pattern of results (Weikum *et al.*, 2004). Currently, we are testing infants growing up in a bilingual French–English environment from birth. The findings from this study will provide insight into the mechanisms used by infants when selecting potential communication partners and acquiring their native language(s). Moreover, this study will help reveal, in another domain of speech processing, whether bilingual infants simultaneously use the same sources of information to master their native languages as do monolingual learning infants.

Summary

This paper has sought to review bilingual acquisition in light of the question of whether bilingual infants show the same or different developmental trajectories for phonological acquisition as do monolinguals and whether adult bilinguals perceive speech similarly or differently to monolinguals. Overall, we have shown that bilingual acquisition influences all aspects of speech processing. This is evident in phonetic perception studies with adults, in lexical processing studies with adults, and even in studies of adult and infant visual speech perception. Investigations of bilingual development in infancy reveal that from the very earliest days, there are differences in the ways in which BFLA infants attend to the phonological structures of the languages they are exposed to, and use that structure to acquire each of their native languages. In almost every study reviewed, the bilinguals showed a developmental trajectory different from the monolingual infants.

We would like to suggest that the unique developmental trajectories shown by BFLA infants may be optimally suited for the linguistic challenges the simultaneous bilingual faces. A bilingual child needs to be open to learning more than one language. This may, in some cases, require retaining perceptual flexibility for a longer period in infancy before native phonetic categories are set. Or, it may require listening to and watching language differently – perhaps noting who speaks what, and when, and developing a phonology, or set of phonologies accordingly. Furthermore, when using phonetic knowledge to guide word learning, the bilingual child is faced with the additional challenge of having to map two labels to the same object. This in itself could lead to a different attentional weighting when mapping sound on to words. In future research, it may be useful to move beyond documenting differences in how bilinguals perceive speech, to investigate phonological use from the functional perspective of bilingual speakers. The phonological processing required to optimize use of two languages on a regular basis may have unique requirements compared to those for processing a single language. By focusing on these unique requirements, together with careful, developmental work with different types of populations of bilingual learners, we may be better positioned to fully understand not only the challenges and successes of bilingual acquisition, but also more about how the human mind is designed for optimally adjusting to its linguistic and cultural environment.

In summary, the research to date indicates that the developmental trajectory is different for BFLA infants, and the use of phonological information remains distinct even in fluent adult bilinguals. The exciting challenge for future work is to build on these findings to better understand how and why bilingual speech processing is unique.

Acknowledgement

This work was supported by grants to J.F. Werker from the Social Sciences and Humanities Research Council of Canada, The Canada Foundation for Innovation, The Canada Research Chairs Program, and the Human Frontiers Science Foundation. C.T. Fennell and T. Burns both contributed significantly to the work on bilingual first language acquisition in infants.

Notes

1. Voice onset time refers to the interval between the release of the closure and the onset of the vibrations of the vocal cords, i.e. voicing.

References

Abercrombie, D. (1965) *Studies in Phonetics and Linguistics*. London: Oxford University Press.

Anderson, J. L., Morgan, J.L. and White, K.S. (2003) A statistical basis for speech sound discrimination. *Language and Speech* 46 (2–3), 155–82.

Aslin, R.N., Jusczyk, P.W. and Pisoni, D.B. (1998) Speech and auditory processing during infancy: Constraints on and precursors to language. In D. Kuhn and R. Siegler (eds) *Handbook of Child Psychology* (5th ed. Vol. 2, pp. 147–98). *Cognition, Perception and Language* (W. Damon, series editor), New York: Wiley Press.

Best, C.T. and Strange, W. (1992) Effects of language-specific phonological and phonetic factors on cross-language perception of approximants. *Journal of Phonetics* 20, 305–30.

Bird, S., Fais, L. and Werker, J.F. (2005, May) The phonetic rhythm / syntax headedness connection: Evidence from Tagalog. Poster presented at the Acoustical Society of America meeting, Vancouver, Canada.

Bosch, L. and Sebastián-Gallés, N. (1997a) Infant bilingual language questionnaire. Unpublished instrument, Universitat de Barcelona, Barcelona, Spain.

Bosch, L. and Sebastián-Gallés, N. (1997b) Native-language recognition abilities in four-month-old infants from monolingual and bilingual environments. *Cognition* 65, 33–69.

Bosch, L. and Sebastián-Gallés, N. (2001) Evidence of early language discrimination abilities in infants from bilingual environments. *Infancy* 2 (1), 29–49.

Bosch, L. and Sebastián-Gallés, N. (2003) Simultaneous bilingualism and the perception of a language-specific vowel contrast in the first year of life. *Language and Speech* 46, 217–43.

Burnham, D. and Dodd, B. (2004) Audio-visual speech integration by prelinguistic infants: Perception of an emergent consonant in the McGurk effect. *Developmental Psychobiology* 44, 204–20.

Burns, T.C., Werker, J.F. and McVie, K. (2003) Development of phonetic categories in infants raised in bilingual and monolingual environments. In B. Beachley, A. Brown, and F. Conlin (eds) *Proceedings of the 27th Annual Boston University Conference on Language Development*. Cascadila Press.

Caramazza, A., Yeni-Komshian, G.H., Zurif, E.B. and Carbone, E. (1973) The acquisition of a new phonological contrast: The case of stop consonants in French–English bilinguals. *Journal of the Acoustical Society of America* 54 (2), 421–8.

De Houwer, A. (1995) Bilingual language acquisition. In P. Fletcher and B. MacWhinney (eds) *Handbook of Child Language* (pp. 218–50). London: Blackwell.

Desjardins, R., Rogers, J. and Werker, J.F. (1997) An exploration of why preschoolers perform differently than do adults in audiovisual speech perception tasks. *Journal of Experimental Psychology: Human Perception and Performance* 66, 85–110.

Desjardins, R. and Werker, J.F. (2004) Is the integration of heard and seen speech mandatory for infants? *Developmental Psychobiology* 45 (4), 1–17.

Desrochers, A. (2003) Fluency assessment questionnaire for English–French bilinguals. Unpublished instrument, Cognitive Psychology Laboratory, University of Ottawa, Ottawa, Canada.

Diaz, B., Baus, C., Costa, A. and Sebastián-Gallés, N. (2004, September) The relationship between perception and production in L2 categories. Poster presented at the Architectures and Mechanisms for Language Processing (AMPAP) meeting, Aix-en-Provence, France.

Dietrich, C., Swingley, D. and Werker, J. (2004, November) *Phonetic Information in Infant Word Learning*. Paper presented at the Boston University Conference on Language Development, Boston, USA.

Fennell, C.T. and Werker, J.F. (2003a) Early word learners' ability to access phonetic detail in well-known words. *Language and Speech* 46 (2–3), 245–64.

Fennell, C.T. and Werker, J.F. (2003b, May) Bilingual infants' attention to fine phonetic detail in a word learning task. International Symposium on Bilingualism, Tempe, Arizona.

Fennell, C.T. and Werker, J.F. (in preparation). Bilingual infants' attention to fine phonetic detail in a word learning task.

Flege, J.E. (1987) The production of 'new' and 'similar' phones in a foreign language: Evidence for the effect of equivalence classification. *Journal of Phonetics* 15, 47–65.

Flege, J.E. (1991) Age of learning affects the authenticity of voice onset time (VOT) in stop consonants produced in a second language. *Journal of the Acoustical Society of America* 89, 395–411.

Flege, J.E., Takagi, N. and Mann, V. (1986) Lexical familiarity and English-language experience affect Japanese adults' perception of r and l. *Journal of the Acoustical Society of America* 99 (2), 1161–73.

Gagne, J.P., Masterson, V., Munhall, K.G., Belida, N. and Querensguessar, C. (1994) Across talker variability in auditory, visual, and audiovisual speech intelligibility for conversational and clear speech. *Journal of the Academy of Rehabilitative Audiology* 27, 135–58.

Goto, H. (1971) Auditory perception by normal Japanese adults of the sounds 'L' and 'R'. *Neuropsychologic*, 9, 317–23.

Grosjean, F. (1989) Neurolinguists, beware! The bilingual is not two monolinguals in one person. *Brain and Language* 36, 3–15.

Hardison, D.A. (1999) Bimodal speech perception by native and nonnative speakers of English: Factors influencing the McGurk effect. *Language Learning* 49, 213–83.

Hardison, D.A. (2003) Acquisition of second-language speech: Effects of visual cues, context, and talker variability. *Applied Psycholinguistics* 24, 495–522.

Helfter, K.S. (1997) Auditory and audio-visual perception of clear and conversational speech. *Journal of Speech, Language and Hearing Research* 40, 432–43.

Jusczyk, P.W. and Aslin, R.N. (1995) Infants' detection of sound patterns of words in fluent speech. *Cognitive Psychology* 29, 1–23.

Jusczyk, P.W., Cutler, A. and Redanz, N.J. (1993) Infants' preference for the predominant stress patterns of English words. *Child Development* 64, 675–87.

Kuhl, P.K. and Meltzoff, A.N. (1982) The bimodal perception of speech in infancy. *Science* 218, 1138–41.

Kuhl, P.K. and Meltzoff, A.N. (1984) The bimodal representation of speech in infants. *Infant Behavior and Development* 7, 361–81.

Kuhl, P.K., Williams, K.A., Lacerda, F., Stevens, K.N. and Lindblom, B. (1992) Linguistic experience alters phonetic perception in infants by 6 months of age. *Science* 255, 606–8.

Liberman, A.M., Cooper, F.S., Shankweiler, D.P. and Studdert-Kennedy, M. (1967) Perception of the speech code. *Psychological Review* 74 (6), 431–61.

Lively, S.E., Logan, J.S. and Pisoni, D.B. (1993) Training Japanese listeners to identify English /r/ and /l/. II: The role of phonetic environment and talker variability in learning new perceptual categories. *Journal of the Acoustical Society of America* 94, 1242–55.

Mackain, K.S., Best, C.T. and Strange, W. (1982) Categorical perception of /r/ and /l/ by Japanese bilinguals. *Applied Psycholinguistics* 2, 369–90.

Massaro, D.W., Cohen, M.M. and Smeele, P.M.T. (1995) Cross-linguistic comparisons in the integration of visual and auditory speech. *Memory & Cognition* 23, 113–31.

Maye, J., Werker, J.F. and Gerken, L. (2002) Infant sensitivity to distributional information can affect phonetic discrimination. *Cognition* 82, B101–B111.

McClelland, J.L., Fiez, J.A. and McCandliss, B.D. (2002) Teaching the /r/-/l/ discrimination to Japanese adults: behavioral and neural aspects. *Physiology & Behavior* 77, 657–62.

McGurk, H. and MacDonald, J. (1976) Hearing lips and seeing voices. *Nature* 264, 746–48.

Mehler, J., Jusczyk, P., Lambertz, G., Halsted, N., Bertoncini, J. and Amiel-Tison, C. (1988) A precursor of language acquisition in young infants. *Cognition* 29, 143–78.

Miyawaki, K., Strange, W., Verbrugge, R., Liberman, A.M., Jenkins, J.J. and Fujimura, O. (1975) An effect of linguistic experience: The discrimination of [r] and [l] by native speakers of Japanese and English. *Perception & Psychophysics* 18, 331–40.

Moon, C., Cooper, R.P. and Fifer, W.P. (1993) Two-day-olds prefer their native language. *Infant Behavior and Development* 16, 495–500.

Munhall, K.G., Jones, J.A., Callan, D.E., Kuratate, T. and Vatikiotis-Bateson, E. (2004) Visual prosody and speech intelligibility: Head movement improves auditory speech perception. *Psychological Science* 15, 133–37.

Nazzi, T., Bertoncini, J. and Mehler, J. (1998) Language discrimination by newborns: Toward an understanding of the role of rhythm. *Journal of Experimental Psychology: Human Perception & Performance* 24 (3), 756–66.

Nazzi, T., Jusczyk, P.W. and Johnson, E.K. (2000) Language discrimination by English-learning 5-month-olds: Effects of rhythm and familiarity. *Journal of Memory & Language* 43, 1–19.

Pallier, C., Nosch, L. and Sebastiàn-Gallès, N. (1997) A limit on behavioural plasticity in speech perception. *Cognition* 64, B9–B17.

Pallier, C., Colomé, A. and Sebastián-Gallés, N. (2001) The influence of native-language phonology on lexical access: Exemplar-based versus abstract lexical entries. *Psychological Science* 12, 445–8.

Patterson, M.L. and Werker, J.F. (1999) Matching phonetic information in lips and voices is robust in 4.5-month-old infants. *Infant Behavior & Development* 22, 237–47.

Patterson, M.L. and Werker, J.F. (2003) Two-month-old infants match phonetic information in lips and voice. *Developmental Science* 6 (2), 191–6.

Pike, K. (1945) *The Intonation of American English*. Ann Arbor: University of Michigan Press.

Polka, L. (1991) Cross-language speech perception in adults: Phonemic, phonetic and acoustic contributions. *Journal of the Acoustical Society of America* 89 (6), 2961–77.

Polka, L., Colantonio, C. and Sundara, M. (2001) A cross-language comparison of /d/-/eth/ perception: Evidence for a new developmental pattern. *Journal of the Acoustical Society of America* 109 (5), 2190–2201.

Polka, L. and Sundara, M. (2003) Word segmentation in monolingual and bilingual infant learners of English and French. *Proceedings of the 15th International Congress of Phonetic Sciences, Barcelona, Spain* (pp. 1021–24).

Polka, L. and Werker, J.F. (1994) Developmental changes in perception of non-native vowel contrasts. *Journal of Experimental Psychology: Human Perception and Performance* 20 (2), 421–35.

Ramus, F., Hauser, M.D., Miller, C., Morris, D. and Mehler, J. (2000) Language discrimination by human newborns and by cotton-top tamarin monkeys. *Science* 288 (5464), 349–51.

Repp, B.H. (1984) Categorical perception: Issues, methods, findings. In N.J. Lass (ed.) *Speech and Language: Advances in Basic Research and Practice* 10 (pp. 243–335). New York: Academic Press.

Rosenblum, L.D., Schmuckler, M.A. and Johnson, J.A. (1997) The McGurk effect in infants. *Perception and Psychophysiology* 59, 347–57.

Saffran, J.R., Werker, J.F. and Werner, L.A. (in press) In R. Siegler and D. Kuhn (eds) The infant's auditory world: Hearing, speech, and the beginnings of language. *Handbook of Child Development*. New York: Wiley Press.

Sebastián-Gallés, N. and Bosch, L. (in press) Phonology and bilingualism. In J.F. Kroll and A.M.B.D. Groot (eds), *Handbook of Bilingualism: Psycholinguistic Approaches*. Oxford: Oxford University Press.

Sebastián-Gallés, N. and Soto-Faraco, S. (1999) Online processing of native and non-native phonemic contrasts in early bilinguals. *Cognition* 72, 111–23.

Siva, N., Stevens, E.B., Kuhl, P.K. and Meltzoff, A.N. (1995) A comparison between cerebral-palsied and normal adults in the perception of auditory-visual illusions. *Journal of the Acoustical Society of America* 98, 2983.

Slowiaczek, L.M. and Pisoni, D.B. (1986) Effects of phonological similarity on priming in auditory lexical decision. *Memory and Cognition* 14, 230–7.

Soto-Faraco, S., Navarra Ordono, J., Weikum, W.M., Vouloumanos, A., Sebastián-Gallés, N. and Werker, J.F. (under review). Discriminating languages by speechreading.

Stager, C.L. and Werker, J.F. (1997) Infants listen for more phonetic detail in speech perception than in word learning tasks. *Nature* 388, 381–2.

Streeter, L.A. (1976) Language perception of 2-month-old infants shows effects of both innate mechanisms and experience. *Nature* 259, 39–41.

Summerfield, Q. (1991) Visual perception of phonetic gestures. In I.G. Mattingly (ed.) *Modularity and the Motor Theory of Speech Perception* (pp. 117–37). Hillsdale, NJ: LEA.

Trehub, S.E. (1976) The discrimination of foreign speech contrasts by infants and adults. *Child Development* 47, 466–472.

Weikum, W.M., Vouloumanos, A., Werker, J.F. and Navarra Ordono, J. (2005, March) Bilingual Visual Language Discrimination. *5th International Symposium on Bilingualism, Barcelona, Spain.*

Weikum, W.M., Werker, J.F., Vouloumanos, A., Navarra Ordono, J., Soto-Faraco, S. and Sebastián-Gallés, N. (2004, November) When can infants start discriminating languages using only visual speech information? Poster presented at the Boston University Conference on Language Development, Boston, USA.

Werker, J.F., Burns, T. and Moon, E. (in preparation) Bilingual exposed newborns prefer to listen to both of their languages.

Werker, J.F., Cohen, L.B., Lloyd, V.L., Casasola, M. and Stager, C.L. (1998) Acquisition of word-object associations by 14-month-old infants. *Developmental Psychology* 34 (6),1289–309.

Werker, J.F., Fennell, C.T., Corcoran, K.M. and Stager, C.L. (2002). Infants' ability to learn phonetically similar words: Effects of age and vocabulary size. *Infancy* 3, 1–30.

Werker, J.F., Gilbert J.H.V., Humphrey, K. and Tees, R.C. (1981) Developmental aspects of cross-language speech perception. *Child Development* 52, 349–53.

Werker, J.F., Ladhar, N. and Corcoran, K.M. (in preparation) Perceptual categories established in infancy direct word learning: A cross-linguistic study.

Werker, J.F. and Lalonde, C.E. (1988) Cross-language speech perception: Initial capabilities and developmental change. *Developmental Psychology* 24 (5), 672–83.

Werker, J.F., McGurk, H. and Frost, P.E. (1992) La langue et les lévres: Cross-language influences on bimodal speech perception. *Canadian Journal of Psychology* 46, 551–68.

Werker, J.F. and Tees, R.C. (1984) Cross-language speech perception: Evidence for perceptual reorganization during the first year of life. *Infant Behavior and Development* 7, 49–63.

Werker, J.F. and Tees, R.C. (1992) The organization and reorganization of human speech perception. *Annual Review of Neuroscience* 15, 377–402.

Yoshida, K.A. and Werker, J.F. (2004, August) Contextual effects of bilingual contrast processing. Poster presented at the 28th meeting of the International Congress of Psychology, Beijing, China.

Chapter 2

When Infants Hear Two Languages: Interpreting Research on Early Speech Perception by Bilingual Children

ANNE FERNALD

Studies exploring fundamental issues in child language acquisition now number in the thousands, and the majority of these focus on aspects of linguistic competence that develop over the first three years of life (see Clark, 2003). However, children learning more than one language are poorly represented in this literature. Although most people in the world grow up in multilingual environments (Grosjean, 1982), only about 2% of basic research on language development includes children learning two languages (Bhatia & Ritchie, 1999). And given the strong applied emphasis in this area, the focus has been primarily on school-aged children, with little attention to bilingual learning in the early years. Only recently have researchers interested in the early stages of learning begun to explore speech processing by infants growing up with two languages, bringing new perspectives and experimental paradigms to the study of bilingual development. The goal in this commentary is first to contrast three major traditions in basic research on early language development along two key dimensions – how they characterize and measure *language competence* at different ages in their studies, and the extent to which each is concerned with features of the *early language environment* that might influence the child's emerging linguistic abilities. I then focus on recent investigations of speech perception by infants in monolingual environments, outlining some of the challenges we face in extending this research to infants in multilingual environments. Since a number of recent findings show that infants hearing two languages perform differently in speech perception experiments than do infants hearing only one (see Werker, Weikum and

Yoshida, Chapter 1 this volume; Vihman, Lum, Thierry, Nakai and Keren-Portnoy, Chapter 3 this volume), it is essential to understand the strengths and limitations of these experimental paradigms in order to make sense of the results. In particular, studies using speech perception paradigms with infants define *language competence* very narrowly and pay little attention to details of the *early language environment* that might influence infants' performance in such tasks, factors which make it difficult to interpret group differences between children growing up in monolingual and bilingual environments.

Different Measures of Competence and Linguistic Input in Research on Early Language Development by Monolingual Children

The three most influential paradigms in current research on early language learning differ not only in their favored questions and methodologies, but also in how they conceptualize children's language competence and dimensions of the linguistic environment thought to contribute to this competence. The first and oldest paradigm (e.g. Brown, 1973) relies on detailed observations of children's speech productions as well as the parental speech that constitutes the early language input to the child (see Clark, 2003; Tomasello, 2003). As the child moves from one-word to more complex utterances, growth in competence is observed in productions that increasingly approximate adult models in terms of their phonological, semantic, syntactic and pragmatic appropriateness. Such descriptive studies may be motivated by different theories about the factors that drive language learning, but they typically share two basic methodological principles relevant to this discussion. First, they are high in ecological validity, using naturalistic data and drawing on a diverse array of outcome measures for assessing language competence. And second, they are also concerned with fine-grained analyses of the language the child hears as well as what the child produces (e.g. Gallaway & Richards, 1994). An important goal of observational studies of early language input is to examine how children's developing linguistic competence may be influenced by aspects of the speech they are exposed to in everyday interactions (e.g. Hoff, 2003; Huttenlocher *et al.*, 1991; Pine & Lieven, 1997).

A second predominant paradigm uses experimental methods to investigate how children figure out what novel words refer to (e.g. Woodward & Markman, 1997). Here the measure of competence is typically defined in terms of a forced-choice behavior by the child, who might choose between familiar and unfamiliar objects when asked *Which one is the dax?* Because selection of the most appropriate referent is the correct response, such dependent measures are plausibly related to behaviors that children use spontaneously to reveal their understanding of language and thus seem reasonably valid. Experiments in this tradition define 'language input' in a very restricted sense, in terms of the linguistic cues manipulated as the independent variable. For example, when choosing between a solid object and a substance, does the child make a different choice when asked to find *the dax* as opposed to *some dax*? Other than that, the language background of the child has been relevant in only a few cross-linguistic studies, as when generalizations made by Japanese- and English-learning children were compared in a word-learning task (e.g. Imai & Gentner, 1997). While studies in this tradition are high in experimental control, they are lower in ecological validity than are naturalistic studies, and the issue of language input is rarely relevant.

The third major approach in research on early language learning is the field of infant speech perception, which has gained in influence through the work of Jusczyk (1997), Kuhl (2000), Saffran (2003), Werker (1995), and others. This research explores how infants develop sensitivity to regularities in the ambient language months before they are able to find meaning in speech or to speak themselves. Thus investigators cannot use response measures that require skill in comprehension or production and their methodological options are limited. The experimental procedures in this area all in one way or another test the ability of the infant to discriminate one type of speech sound from another based on perceptual properties or higher levels of organization among the stimuli. For example, auditory preference procedures might be used to compare infants' overall listening time to type A stimuli versus type B stimuli (e.g. French vs. English, or infant-directed vs. adult-directed speech) to determine whether infants at a certain age can distinguish between them. The dependent measure is a listening bias or preference, operationalized as longer mean listening time to one or the other sets of stimuli across trials; thus the measure of 'competence' in this procedure is captured by a single difference score. Other methodologies employ different but comparable response measures, including conditioned head turns (Kuhl, 2000) or dishabituation (Stager & Werker, 1997) to changes in sound from one category to another.

These kinds of measures have been used in hundreds of studies to document developmental changes in infants' awareness of the structure of speech sounds on phonological and other levels (see Aslin *et al.*, 1998), so there is no doubt as to their utility. But it is important to note that the relation between infants' phonological knowledge and their performance on such experimental measures – i.e. small mean differences in attention to one stimulus type over another – is not straightforward. Moreover, in some studies researchers find a significant preference for the more familiar stimulus type (e.g. Jusczyk & Aslin, 1995), while in others the less familiar type is preferred (e.g. Saffran *et al.*, 1996), a difference not always easy to make sense of. The point here is that the connection between an infant's phonological competence and a single measure of listening time in an auditory preference experiment seems much less transparent and ecologically valid than does the connection between a child's lexical knowledge and the ability to speak or respond appropriately to familiar words. And this point may be particularly noteworthy in relation to studies of infants growing up in multilingual environments.

Extending Research on Early Speech Perception to Infants Learning Two Languages

Before discussing recent efforts to extend this research to investigations of bilingual learning in infancy, a few of the major findings with monolingual infants will illustrate how productive this paradigm has been. Studies using auditory preference and other measures of discrimination show that infants in monolingual environments can distinguish between the ambient language and another language they have never been exposed to as long as the two differ in their basic rhythmic structure (e.g. Nazzi *et al.*, 2000), suggesting that even very young infants are attentive to prosodic features characteristic of what will be their native language. Infants also start early to absorb detailed information about regularities at the segmental level in the speech they are hearing, and begin to 'specialize' in their native language over the first year. While young infants can initially discriminate speech sounds not present in the native language, their performance in distinguishing non-native contrasts declines by the end of the first year as they become more proficient in categorizing those phonemes used in the ambient language (e.g. Werker, 1995; Kuhl, 2000). Note that in all of these cross-linguistic studies with monolingual infants, language input is represented in the independent variable in terms of a simple dichotomy between 'native' speech sounds (i.e. from the one language the infant has been exposed to) versus 'non-native' speech sounds (i.e. from some language the infant has never heard before).

While infant speech perception research has focused almost exclusively on infants in monolingual environments, a few recent studies have included children learning two languages from infancy, referred to as 'bilingual first language acquisition' (BFLA) (e.g. de Houwer, 1995). Two questions have motivated these studies. First, if monolingual infants show a listening bias for the one language they are familiar with (e.g. Nazzi, *et al.*, 2000), do BFLA infants show biases for *both* languages they are hearing?

And second, given that monolingual infants appear to lose sensitivity to non-native speech contrasts over the first year (e.g. Werker & Tees, 1984), do BFLA infants *maintain* the ability to discriminate speech sounds in more than one language? Working in Barcelona with infants learning either Spanish or Catalan as their first language, or both languages simultaneously, Bosch and Sebastián-Gallés (1997) tested 4-month-olds on their responsiveness to the language spoken by the child's mother (either Spanish or Catalan) and to English, unfamiliar to all the infants. Monolingual infants were significantly faster to orient to speech sounds in the maternal language than to speech in English. In contrast, BFLA infants oriented more slowly to speech in the maternal language than to English speech, and were slower overall to orient to either language than were monolingual infants, an unexpected pattern of results.

In a later study, Bosch and Sebastián-Gallés (2003) tested infants across the first year on their ability to discriminate the vowel distinction /e/-/ɛ/ which occurs in Catalan but not in Spanish. As predicted, monolingual infants learning Catalan could make this distinction at 4, 8, and 12 months, while those learning Spanish discriminated the Catalan distinction only at 4 months and not at later ages. However, BFLA infants exposed to both Catalan and Spanish responded inconsistently, discriminating the Catalan /e/-/ɛ/ at 4 and 12 months but not at 8 months. In other recent research comparing monolingual and bilingual infants in standard speech perception tasks, Werker *et al.* (Chapter 1 this volume) and Vihman *et al.* (Chapter 3 this volume) also report unexpected findings. For example, Burns *et al.* (2003) examined discrimination of French and English speech contrasts by infants learning either French or English, or both languages simultaneously. Consistent with previous findings, monolingual infants lost the ability to make the non-native discrimination over the first year, but retained the ability to discriminate speech sounds in the language they were learning (see Werker, 1995). If early and consistent exposure to a particular language accounts for this effect, one might expect that children hearing two languages would maintain their ability to make discriminations in both languages. However, Burns *et al.* found that half the French/English bilingual children at 14 to 17 months of age made only one distinction, but not both. Werker *et al.* (this volume) also describe another recent study in which bilingual children were delayed relative to monolinguals, in that children exposed only to English could discriminate an English speech contrast at an earlier age than did BFLA children exposed both to English and to another language at the same time.

Interpreting Discrepant Results from Speech Perception Experiments with Monolingual and Bilingual Infants

According to Kuhl (2000), research on the early development of speech perception abilities indicates that infants in monolingual environments become increasingly specialized in a particular system of speech sounds, making a 'neural commitment' to the phonological system of their native language by the end of the first year. This view leads to the prediction that infants in bilingual environments would show specialization in two different languages over the same period. However, when compared with monolingual infants in standard speech perception experiments, it appears that BFLA infants are relatively *less* able to distinguish the sounds in their two languages either from each other or from those in a third unfamiliar language (Bosch & Sebastián-Gallés, 1997, 2003; Vihman *et al.*, this volume; Werker *et al.*, this volume). If increasing specialization in the native language as shown by differential listening and discrimination is interpreted as 'progress' in phonological development by monolingual infants, then how should we interpret the negative results found in some studies when bilingual infants are tested in the same experimental procedures?

Given the additional challenges BFLA infants face in learning two different language systems simultaneously, there are several reasons why they might perform differently than monolingual infants in speech perception tasks assessing listening biases. One possibility is that BFLA infants hear less speech in either language than monolingual infants hear in the single language they are exposed to, and this reduction in language-specific input might result in slower development of speech perception skills. Although no studies have investigated whether the amount of early linguistic input influences speech perception abilities in infancy, studies at later ages show that the amount and quality of language heard by the child are correlated with measures of lexical and syntactic growth (e.g. Hoff, 2003; Huttenlocher *et al.*, 1991). There is also some evidence that individual differences in speech perception abilities by monolingual infants predict differences in later vocabulary growth (Tsao *et al.*, 2004). That is, monolingual infants who for whatever reason performed less reliably in a vowel categorization task at 6 months of age tended to be somewhat slower in lexical development a year later, as compared to infants who were more successful in the experimental procedure. If BFLA infants performed less well overall than monolingual infants in this particular speech perception task (as they appear to do in other such tasks described earlier) would this difference also predict slower vocabulary growth later in either or both of the languages they are learning? There is no research on this question, but this prediction might seem plausible if the rather erratic performance of bilingual infants in speech perception studies to date is interpreted in terms of 'failure' or 'delay'.

In interpreting what appear to be negative findings in speech perception studies with infants exposed to two languages, it is crucial to keep in mind the two questions about experimental paradigms in this research tradition that were outlined earlier. First, how is *linguistic competence* operationalized in such research and how clearly are the experimental measures linked to children's knowledge of language? And second, if the linguistic environment of the child is relevant to the research question, how adequately is *early language experience* characterized and assessed? Regarding the measure of competence, early speech perception studies all necessarily rely on indirect measures that involve differential listening to different sets of speech stimuli, reflecting the child's recognition of one set as more familiar or novel than the other. In many auditory preference experiments, one could gloss the child's listening bias as 'I find this engaging because I've heard it before', while in habituation studies the listening bias is in favor of more novel stimuli. But in either case, the infant is comparing sounds that are more familiar with sounds that are unfamiliar or relatively novel. Thus when monolingual French-learning infants are presented with speech samples from both French and Russian, the choice is between highly familiar speech sounds and speech sounds never heard before (Mehler *et al.*, 1988).

Given that speech perception experiments assess phonological competence by asking infants to discriminate between speech stimuli designed to be very familiar or novel to the child, the task demands may be inherently different for bilingual and for monolingual infants. Here is where the issue of language input becomes a crucial consideration. In studies with BFLA infants, the language background of the child is typically described in terms of the percentage of time the child hears each of the two languages spoken in the family, based on parental report. For example, the criterion for the BFLA classification in a particular study might be that a child hears Spanish no more than 60% of the time and English at least 40% of the time. This is a difficult measure to assess in any case, even with newly developed parental questionnaires that attempt to provide more detailed descriptions of both qualitative and quantitative features of children's linguistic environments (e.g. Marchman *et al.*, 2000).

A fundamental problem here is that because the *sounds* of the speech heard by the infant are not captured by questionnaire data, the characterization of the input as 60% Spanish and 40% English is an idealization that could be quite misleading. In reality, the child may hear 40% Spanish from a native speaker (e.g. the mother), 20% English from a native speaker (e.g. the father or daycare provider), with the additional 40% of the input consisting of Spanish spoken by native English speakers and English spoken by native Spanish speakers. These latter mixed categories are not uncommon in bilingual families, when one parent uses the language of the other, or when other bilingual relatives and neighbors speak their second language with an accent influenced by their first language. Thus at the phonological level, *four* rather than two categories are needed to characterize the sources of language input to this hypothetical child: native Spanish, native English, Spanish-with-English-phonology, and English-with-Spanish-phonology. Moreover, the latter two categories are likely to be heterogeneous with considerable variability in the speech sounds used, given that different individuals will be proficient to different degrees in speaking L2. The result is that the infant will be exposed not only to two different languages in their standard forms, but also to two classes of highly variable input in which Spanish phonology is overlaid on sentences using the lexicon and grammar of English, and vice versa.

How would such phonological diversity in the early language environment influence the performance of BFLA infants in speech perception tasks? It seems likely that experiencing heterogeneous input of this sort at the very beginning of language learning could have two consequences relevant to interpreting the results of these studies. First, it would be more difficult for BFLA than for monolingual infants to distinguish one language from another, given that bilingual infants regularly hear speech from different sources in which there is continuous variation from one language to another on the phonological level. A related point is that BFLA infants would also be less likely to perceive phonetic contrasts as categorically different if they had experienced tokens of these speech sounds on a gradient from one to the other. In the study by Bosch and Sebastián-Gallés (2003), for example, the Catalan/Spanish bilingual infants may have failed to discriminate the Catalan /e/-/ɛ/ contrast consistently because they had frequently heard these vowels pronounced incorrectly by Spanish speakers of Catalan who do not make this distinction in their native language. Thus the 'failure' of the BFLA infants to show evidence of making categorical distinctions between phonemes in the languages they are learning may reflect the fact that category boundaries are less well defined in the distributions of speech sounds they hear than in the speech to which monolingual infants are exposed. While auditory preference and discrimination tasks can reveal whether the child perceives one set of speech sounds as familiar and the other as unfamiliar, an appropriate paradigm for use with monolingual children, BFLA infants have typically had extensive experience with a wider distribution of speech sounds that may not map cleanly onto the categories experienced by the infant who hears only one language spoken by native speakers.

Conclusions

Although there is still very little research on individual differences in infants' ability to categorize speech sounds, there is convincing evidence that typically developing monolingual infants make progress in mapping out the phonological categories of the ambient language over the first year (Kuhl, 2000; Werker, 1995), and also some preliminary evidence that monolingual infants who are slower to develop such capacities may be less advanced in vocabulary learning in the second year (Tsao *et al.*, 2004). However, because infants hearing two languages face quite different challenges than do those exposed to a single language spoken only by native speakers, the bilingual child should not be viewed as 'two monolinguals in one'. Rather than distinguishing two separate systems of language-specific phonological categories by the end of the first year, BFLA infants may initially form broader categories that reflect the nature and variability of the input; and if so, it is hardly surprising that they perform differently from monolinguals in standard speech perception tests. The question of interest here is whether the apparent 'delays' in categorization abilities reported for BFLA infants are in any sense predictive of delay in later language learning, as they may be for monolingual infants, or whether such performance differences simply reflect patterns of phonological development that are inevitably different for monolingual and bilingual infants.

Before we can interpret the results of speech perception experiments with bilingual infants with any confidence, we need to consider the two questions with which we began: First, how broadly do these speech perception tasks capture the emerging *language competence* of the BFLA infant? And second, how much attention do researchers in this tradition pay to details of the child's *early language environment* that are likely to influence this emerging competence? Regarding the first question, the dependent variables used in speech perception experiments are exceedingly indirect measures of language competence that are often quite difficult to interpret. Until more is known about the test-retest reliability and predictive validity of these early listening measures in relation to traditional measures of productive and receptive language competence, we should be extremely cautious in drawing conclusions about what listening biases actually reveal about the state of children's knowledge at a particular age. Moreover, it seems unlikely that listening measures in infancy will be correlated with later language measures in the same way for bilingual and monolingual children. Regarding the second question, studies of infant speech perception have never included the detailed assessments of the child's language environment characteristic of naturalistic research on language development, although such data are especially important in research with bilingual children. Infants growing up in multilingual environments not only hear two different languages spoken with native phonology, they are also likely to hear one or both of these languages spoken with a non-native accent. Thus BFLA infants are exposed in varying degrees to non-standard as well as standard versions of each language. If research with bilingual infants were based on detailed analyses of the full range of phonetic variability in the speech they are actually hearing, rather than on idealized estimates of the percentage of input in a particular language, it would be possible to make more informed predictions about the development of phonological awareness in children who grow up hearing two languages.

References

Aslin, R., Jusczyk, P.W. and Pisoni, D. (1998) Speech and auditory processing during infancy: Constraints on and precursors to language. In D. Kuhn and R. Siegler (eds) *Handbook of Child Psychology* (5th edn, Vol. 2, pp. 147–98). New York, NY: Wiley.

Bhatia, T.K. and Ritchie W.C. (1999) The bilingual child: Some issues and perspectives. In W.C. Ritchie and T.K. Bhatia (eds) *Handbook of Second Language Acquisition* (pp. 569–643). San Diego: Academic Press.

Bosch, L. and Sebastián-Gallés, N. (1997b) Native-language recognition abilities in four-month-old infants from monolingual and bilingual environments. *Cognition* 65, 33–69.

Bosch, L. and Sebastián-Gallés, N. (2003) Simultaneous bilingualism and the perception of a language-specific vowel contrast in the first year of life. *Language and Speech* 46, 217–43.

Brown, R. (1973) *A First Language: The Early Stages*. London: George Allen & Unwin.

Burns, T.C., Werker, J.F. and Mcvie, K. (2003) Development of phonetic categories in infants raised in bilingual and monolingual environments. In B. Beachley, A. Brown and F. Conlin (eds) *Proceedings of the 27th Annual Boston University Conference on Language Development*. Somerville, MD: Cascadila Press.

Clark, E.V. (2003) *First Language Acquisition*. Cambridge, UK: Cambridge University Press.

De Houwer, A. (1995) Bilingual language acquisition. In P. Fletcher and B. MacWhinney (eds) *Handbook of Child Language* (pp. 218–50). London: Blackwell.

Gallaway, C. and Richards, B.J. (1994) *Input and Interaction in Language Acquisition*. Cambridge, UK: Cambridge University Press.

Grosjean, F. (1982) *Life with Two Languages*. Cambridge, MA: Harvard University Press.

Hoff, E. (2003) The specificity of environmental influence: Socioeconomic status affects early vocabulary development via maternal speech. *Child Development* 72, 1368–78.

Huttenlocher, J., Haight, W., Bryk, A., Seltzer, M. and Lyons, T. (1991) Vocabulary growth: Relation to language input and gender. *Developmental Psychology* 27, 236–48.

Imai, M. and Gentner, D. (1997) A cross-linguistic study of early word meaning: Universal ontology and linguistic influence. *Cognition* 62, 169–200.

Jusczyk, P.W. (1997) *The Discovery of Spoken Language*. Cambridge, MA: MIT Press.

Jusczyk, P.W. and Aslin, R. (1995) Infants' detection of the sound patterns of words in fluent speech. *Cognitive Psychology* 29, 1–23.

Kuhl, P.K. (2000) A new view of language acquisition. *Proceedings of the National Academy of Science* 97, 11850–7.

Marchman, V., Martínez-Sussmann, C. and Price, P. (2000) Individual differences in learning contexts for Spanish- and English-speaking children. Poster presented at the Conference on Developmental and Contextual Transitions of Children and Families, Head Start's Fifth National Research Conference, Washington, DC (June–July, 2000).

Mehler, J., Jusczyk, P., Lambertz, G., Halsted, N., Bertoncini, J. and Amiel-Tison, C. (1988) A precursor of language acquisition in young infants. *Cognition* 29, 143–78.

Nazzi, T., Jusczyk, P.W. and Johnson, E.K. (2000) Language discrimination by English learning 5-month-olds: Effects of rhythm and familiarity. *Journal of Memory and Language* 43, 1–19.

Pine, J M. and Lieven, E.M. (1997) Slot and frame patterns and the development of the determiner category. *Applied Psycholinguistics* 18, 123–38.

Saffran, J.R. (2003) Statistical language learning: Mechanisms and constraints. *Current Directions in Psychological Science* 12, 110–14.

Saffran, J.R., Aslin, R.N. and Newport, E.L. (1996) Statistical learning by 8-month-old infants. Science 274, 1926–28.

Stager, C. and Werker, J. (1997) Infants listen for more phonetic detail in speech perception than in word-learning tasks. *Nature* 388, 381–2.

Tomasello, M. (2003) *Constructing a Language: A Usage-Based Theory of Language Acquisition*. Cambridge, MA: Harvard University Press.

Tsao, F., Liu, H. and Kuhl, P.K. (2004) Speech perception in infancy predicts language development in the second year of life: A longitudinal study. *Child Development* 75, 1067–84.

Werker, J.F. (1995) Exploring developmental changes in cross-language speech perception. In L. Gleitman and M. Liberman (eds) *An Invitation to Cognitive Science* (Vol. 1: *Language*), pp. 87–106. Cambridge, MA: MIT Press.

Werker, J.F. and Tees, R.C. (1984) Cross-language speech perception: Evidence for perceptual reorganization during the first year of life. *Infant Behavior and Development* 7, 49–63.

Woodward, A. and Markman, E.M. (1997) Early word learning. In W. Damion, D. Kuhn and R. Siegler (eds) *Handbook of Child Psychology*, Vol. 2, *Cognition, Perception, and Language*. New York: Wiley.

Chapter 3

The Onset of Word Form Recognition in One Language and in Two

M.M. VIHMAN, J.A.G. LUM, G. THIERRY, S. NAKAI and
T. KEREN-PORTNOY

Introduction

Infants' rapid advances in the recognition of native language patterns over the first year of life have been well established for some time (Jusczyk, 1997; Vihman, 1996). These advances are primarily restricted to prosody in the first 6 months, but begin to be supplemented by familiarity with segmental sequences by 9 months (e.g. Friederici & Wessels, 1993; Jusczyk *et al.*, 1993; Jusczyk *et al.*, 1994, all showing familiarity with native language phonotactic patterns; Saffran *et al.*, 1996, showing statistical learning of segmental sequences). All of this can be taken to reflect implicit learning, the unconscious tallying of frequently heard patterns, whether prosodic or segmental.

But when do children first recognise frequently heard word forms in the absence of any experimental training or contextual support? Such recognition would constitute the first step in word learning, involving attention to form without any necessary connection to meaning. The association with meaning, and the ability to access or recall such form-meaning links at will, can be expected to be achieved somewhat later. It is only at that later stage, when lexical representations begin to be formed that are strong enough to support flexible word use, across a variety of contexts and in the absence of priming by familiar situations or verbal routines, that explicit word learning can be identified (Bates *et al.*, 1979; Vihman & McCune, 1994; McCune & Vihman, 2001; Vihman, 2002a).

In the first study to investigate the beginnings of untrained word form recognition, Hallé and Boysson-Bardies (1994) developed a list of 12 words likely to be familiar to 11-month-olds, based on early words produced by French infants (Boysson-Bardies & Vihman, 1991), and contrasted these with a list of 12 rarely occurring words of closely similar phonotactic

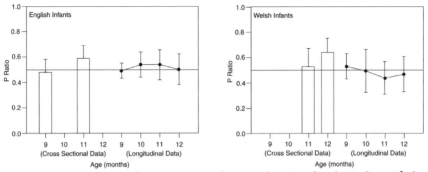

Figure 1 Comparison of cross-sectional versus longitudinal results with familiar / rare stimuli: English (left panel) and Welsh (right panel). The P(reference) ratio is a quotient of (listening time towards the familiar list) / (total listening time). P > 0.05 indicates longer orientation towards the familiar list. Error bars depict standard deviation.

structure using the Preferential Head-Turn (HT) paradigm. The 12 French infants were found to respond with longer looks to the familiar word list at 11 months. We replicated the study with English-learning children, at both 9 and 11 months (Vihman *et al.*, 2004) and with Welsh-learning children at 11 and 12 months (Vihman & DePaolis, 1999). We found the familiarity effect in children exposed to English at 11 months, just as in the case of French, but not at 9 months (Figure 1, left panel). However, the 12 children exposed to Welsh only in the home (but to both English and Welsh in the community) did *not* show the expected group effect at 11 months, although a separate sample of 12 children did show it at 12 months (Figure 1, right panel). One might want to interpret the difference between the English and the Welsh 11-month-olds by reference to the extent of English vs. Welsh heard in the larger bilingual community of North Wales. However, the sample sizes were small and an additional limitation of the study was the absence of any control over the relative familiarity of the English or French vs. the Welsh stimuli chosen for the test. Thus the results of that study had to be considered preliminary.

Finally, a study of 16 children using Event Related Potentials (ERPs) showed that word form recognition starts within 250 ms for English at 11 months (Thierry *et al.*, 2003). In response to both familiar and rare words, whether monosyllabic or disyllabic, we observed two positive (P) and two negative (N) ERP peaks in succession or, more technically, a P1-N2-P3-N4 complex. The only significant difference between the categories of stimuli was a larger peak for Familiar than for Rare words in the N2 range (around 200 ms after stimulus onset). Based on the timecourse of this effect as well as on previous observations of newborn infants (Kushnerenko *et al.*, 2002) we interpreted this modulation as Mismatch Negativity (MMN; Näätänen, 2001). The MMN is a negative modulation by a deviant stimulus within a stream of standard stimuli (oddball paradigm), in the absence of overt attention. In adults, this effect is thought to be automatic and based on the evaluation of perceptual cues. Despite the fact that there were equal numbers of familiar and rare words in our study, we interpreted the N2 modulation as an MMN because any given child could be expected to recognise only a small subset of the 'familiar' words. Thus the word-form recognition response that we observed can be taken to reflect implicit processing rather than any more or less conscious 'preference'.

The results of the French, English and Welsh head turn studies suggested that it might be possible to identify the onset of word form recognition rather precisely in the period immediately preceding the typical age of first word production (around 12 months), with possibly some differences arising from variations in ambient language exposure. Accordingly, a longitudinal study was designed to track the point at which individual infants' orientation towards the familiar list would increase with age. The design proved problematic, however. Longitudinal testing of two samples of 12 infants each, one English-, the other Welsh-learning, at 9, 10, 11 and 12 months revealed apparent carry-over effects in the test/retest situation (Figure 1, longitudinal data): We found no systematic increase in orientation towards the Familiar list with age, nor could we find clear group evidence of word recognition at any one age. Another test-retest experiment with a sample of 12 Welsh infants at 11 and 12 months yielded similar results (Vihman & DePaolis, 1999), as did a parallel study of trochaic vs. iambic English stimuli conducted with infants at 6, 9 and 12 months (Vihman, 2002b). The outcome is of some interest in itself, despite the fact that the intended findings could not be obtained, since the studies seem to show that, when infants are exposed to the same speech stimuli in the same laboratory on repeated occasions, even across three-month intervals, the memory of the previous occasion is revived or 'reinstantiated' (Hayne & Findlay, 1995; Rovee-Collier, 1997), with concomitant habituation to the stimuli.

In the present study we pursue the question of age of onset of word form recognition in the absence of training or of situational context, using HT and ERPs in parallel with each of the infants. We avoid the test/retest problem by using cross-sectional samples of monolingual English and Welsh children at 9 to12 months. In addition, we test English/Welsh bilingual children at 11 months. In what follows we will provide an answer to the first question raised above – When do children first recognise frequently heard (but untrained) word forms? – and will additionally address the question: How does bilingualism, or minority language learning in a bilingual community, affect the timing of the onset of word form recognition?

Method

Participants

A total of 64 monolingual English-learning infants, 31 monolingual Welsh-learning infants, and 16 English-Welsh bilingual infants were tested (age range 9–12 months).[1] Infants were recruited primarily through advertisements in local newspapers. Families were paid for their participation. All families completed a Communicative Development Inventory (CDI; Fenson *et al.*, 1993) in the appropriate language(s).[2]

A short language evaluation questionnaire (adapted from that of Bosch & Sebastián-Gallés) was administered to all the bilingual families. However, we found the results to be unreliable, in that the average number of hours of use reported for each language frequently failed to relate to the more detailed statements regarding interlocutors using each language and the time each reportedly spent with the infant. We therefore used the CDI reports returned for the children as an independent index of relative knowledge of each language (cf. Pearson *et al.*, 1993 for a comparable procedure for establishing language dominance). Specifically, for each child we computed an index which expressed the total words the children were reported to know *in English* over the total words known in both English and Welsh. Using this measure, a value of 1.0 would indicate that 100% of the child's lexicon consisted of English words and 0% of Welsh words. Alternatively, a value of 0.0 would indicate 100% of the child's lexicon consisted of Welsh words and 0% of English words. Children were considered to be bilingual only if the index was between 0.2 and 0.8. Using the above index four children obtained a value between 0.33 and 0.38, suggesting more knowledge of Welsh, while eight children obtained values between 0.63 and 0.78, suggesting more knowledge of English (seven children had values between 0.63 and 0.73 in the ERP sample[3]). Four children obtained scores between 0.47 and 0.59, indicating relatively balanced knowledge of the two languages (five children's values fell in this range in the ERP sample).

Stimuli

In this study, new stimuli were developed for the two languages, with careful attention to the aim of arriving at a closely similar selection of familiar words based on frequency of use according to previous parental reports, so that age of onset of word recognition could be reliably equated across language groups. A list of 33 familiar and 33 rare words was recorded by three female native speakers for each language. Based on 158 CDIs returned for English infants participating in previous studies in our laboratory and 113 CDIs returned for Welsh infants, an average of 36% of the English and 35% of the Welsh words used as stimuli were reported by parents as understood by English and Welsh infants, respectively, at age 9 to 12 months. Testing consonants and vowels separately, we ascertained that the familiar word stimuli were not different in phonemic composition from the rare word stimuli in either language. Acoustic analysis showed that there were no significant differences in loudness, pitch or duration between familiar and rare words.

Procedure

In our HT procedure the word lists were presented on a rotating basis, with 11 words of each type (familiar and rare) used in each trial, in a single voice. For bilingual infants we ran the HT procedure twice, once for each language, with a short snack and play break between procedures. Order of presentation of the two languages was counterbalanced across infants. In the ERPs for the bilingual infants we used an oddball stimulus presentation structure, including 30 of the 33 familiar words used in HT and 90 rare words of similar phonotactic structure. The oddball paradigm thus included 25% familiar and 75% rare words, departing from the 50:50 stimulus presentation format used in a previous study in our laboratory (Thierry *et al.*, 2003). This list was recorded by a single balanced bilingual speaker of English and Welsh; stimuli from the two languages were presented in separate blocks, the order of presentation counterbalanced across participants.

ERP recording and analysis

Scalp voltages were recorded from 11 Ag/AgCl electrodes applied in anatomical reference to the canthomeathal line and referenced to the left mastoid. Impedances were kept below 14 KO. The middle frontal polar electrode was the ground. Electrodes were located at left and right frontal sites (F3, F4), left, middle and right central sites (C3, Cz, C4), left and right parietal occipital sites (PO3, PO4) and over the right mastoid. A frontal polar electrode (FP1) was used to monitor eye movements. Voltages were filtered online bandpass between 0.1 and 100 Hz and continuously digitised at 1 KHz.

Recordings were digitally (zero phase shift) re-filtered band pass between 1 Hz (12 db/Oct) and 30 Hz (48 db/Oct), visually inspected for motor/eye artefacts, re-referenced to the left and right mastoid channels and cut into 1100 ms epochs starting 100 ms before stimulus onset. Remaining artefacts were rejected automatically when voltage amplitude exceeded ±100 μV. Data from 16 infants who had more than 30 artefact free trials in each condition were baseline corrected in reference to the prestimulus activity and averaged in each experimental condition.

Peak detection was performed automatically in search intervals derived from the global average of the seven recording electrodes: 100 to 200 ms for the

P1, 180 to 310 ms for the N2, 270 to 360 ms for the P3 and 320 to 480 for the N4. Peak amplitudes and latencies were then analysed over 7 electrodes using a 2 (familiarity) × 2 (language) × 7 (electrode) repeated measures ANOVA.

Results

The results are presented in three sections: first, head turn results from the monolingual infants, second, comparison of the HT results from the monolingual and bilingual infants, and finally, ERP results from the bilingual infants.

Head Turn in Monolingual English and Welsh infants

Figure 2 shows the mean and individual looking times (in seconds) for Familiar vs. Unfamiliar words at 9, 10, 11 and 12 months for the English

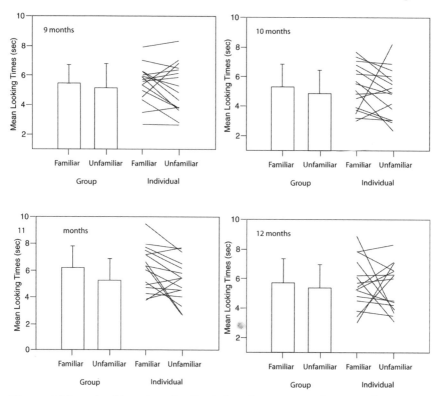

Figure 2 Mean looking time for English infants at 9 and 10 months (upper panels) and 11 and 12 months (lower panels). Mean group looking times to Familiar and Unfamiliar word lists are supplemented by individual looking times on the right of each graph. Error bars depict standard deviation. Difference signifiant at 11 months only, $p = 0.027$.

infants.[4] Based on paired samples *t*-tests, the difference in looking times to the Familiar list is significant only at 11 months (9 months: $t(15) = 1.001$, $p = 0.333$; 10 months: $t(15) = 0.950$, $p = 0.357$; 11 months, $t(15) = 2.419$, $p = 0.029$; and 12 months, $t(16) = 0.533$, $p = 0.302$).

For Welsh, the present stimuli failed to elicit significantly longer looking to familiar words at either 9 or 11 months (9 months: $t(14) = 1.303$, $p = 0.214$;

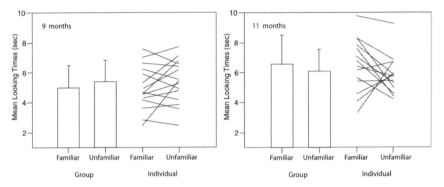

Figure 3 Mean group (left) and individual (right) looking times for Welsh infants at 9 and 11 months. Differences n.s. at both ages.

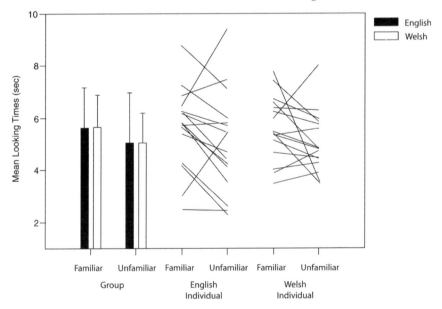

Figure 4 Mean looking times to familiar and unfamiliar words for bilingual infants at 11 months. Mean group looking times are presented on the left and individual looking times on the right

11 months: $t(15) = 1.059$, $p = 0.306$: Figure 3). The results from the 11 month-old Welsh children replicate our previous finding with a new set of stimuli and differently structured experiment (rotating word lists – each with a fixed word sequence – across trials, rather than a single list repeated in varying orders across trials).

The bilingual HT results are based on the 16 11-month-old infants who successfully completed both English and Welsh experiments. Figure 4 shows that, for the group as a whole, familiar word forms received longer looks in both languages. However, this difference in looking times failed to reach statistical significance in either language (English: $t(15) = 1.636$, $p = 0.123$; Welsh: $t(15) = 1.579$, $p = 0.135$).

Head turn findings for monolingual vs. bilingual infants

We compared monolingual with bilingual infant performance on the head turn task by looking at effect sizes (Figure 5).[5] The trend toward an increasing attentional response to the familiar words in English is apparent for ages 9 to 11 months, with a striking reversal in this trend at 12 months. We can see here that the effect size increases with each month of age to 11 months for English but then declines sharply at 12 months. The effect sizes

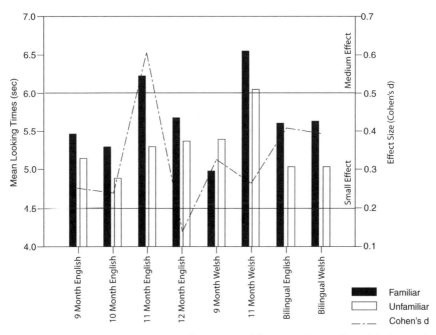

Figure 5 Effect sizes for English and Welsh monolingual and bilingual infants

associated with the bilingual infants are at a mid-point between the 10 and 11 month old monolingual English infants.

ERPs in bilingual infants

The ERP results for 16 bilingual children (aged 11 months) are shown in Figure 6. We found a main effect of familiarity on the amplitude of both the negative peaks (N2 and N4). The mean ERP peak amplitude was significantly more negative for familiar than for rare words between 180 and 310 ms (F[1, 15] = 9.43, p = 0.008) and between 360 and 490 ms (F[1, 15] = 12.45, p = 0.003) after stimulus onset. There was no effect of language on N2 or N4 amplitudes and no interaction between familiarity and language. However, the N2 elicited by Welsh words peaked marginally later than the N2 elicited by English (F[1,15] = 3.93, p = 0.066). In short, whereas at 11 months the bilingual children failed to show a behavioural response indicative of word form recognition in either language, when we measure an

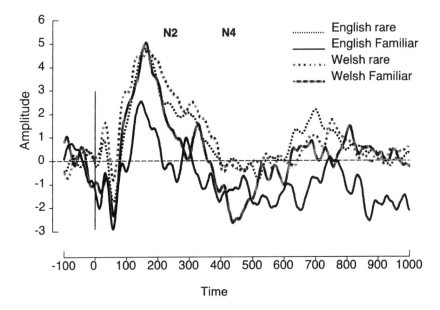

Figure 6 ERPs recorded at frontocentral electrodes for 16 English-Welsh bilingual infants (11 mos). There was a main effect of familiarity on N2 (p = 0.008) and N4 (p = 0.003) peak amplitudes but no main effect of language or interaction between familiarity and language. In addition, the N2 tended to be delayed for Welsh as compared to English (p = 0.066).

index of brain activity in children drawn from the same sample we find a significant differentiation of familiar and unfamiliar words in both languages. In addition, comparing the findings here with those we reported for monolingual English-learning 11-month-olds in Thierry *et al.* (2003), we find that the bilingual children's response tended to be delayed relative to that of the monolinguals (the N2 peaked at 210 ± 15 ms in the monolinguals and at 249 ±25 ms in the bilinguals).

Discussion

We have reviewed a number of studies of word form recognition in English and Welsh, both longitudinal and cross-sectional. Longitudinal testing failed to provide information regarding the age of onset of word form recognition due to apparent interference from infant habituation to the stimuli. The present cross-sectional study has replicated our previous finding of word form recognition for English monolinguals by 11 months, despite a changed presentation structure for the words used as stimuli. It has further revealed a decline in the size of the familiarity effect at 12 months. We infer that at this age word form alone (outside of any relevant situational context) has lost its interest for most of the children, who are typically beginning to expect words to convey meaning.

For children exposed to Welsh only in the home we failed to find word recognition by 11 months, contrary to findings for children acquiring either English or French but in agreement with our earlier, smaller-scale study (Figure 1). It is likely that this apparent delay is the effect of living in an English-dominant community: Anglesey and Gwynedd, the counties from which our infant participants are drawn, are heavily dominated by English despite the presence of a large number of Welsh speakers. We also failed to see longer looking to familiar words in either language for the bilingual infants at 11 months. However, the overall performance of the two groups (monolingual Welsh, bilingual English and Welsh) cannot be expected to be the same, given the differences in the makeup of the samples. Recall that the bilingual infants, unlike the monolingual Welsh, are a heterogeneous group, with a bipolar distribution of knowledge of their two languages (some with more knowledge of English words and others with more knowledge of Welsh). We could predict that Welsh-dominant bilingual infants would perform comparably to Welsh monolinguals while English-dominant bilingual infants might show word form recognition already at 11 months, like English monolinguals. However, our bilingual sample is not yet sufficiently large to permit inferences from the findings for subgroups of infants.

Interestingly, in contrast to the head turn findings, the ERP procedure did reveal a significant effect of word familiarity in bilingual infants drawn from the same sample at the same age. We have previously suggested that ERPs provide an insight into very rapid implicit processing of familiar stimuli (Thierry *et al.*, 2003); we expected to see a differential response to familiar vs. unfamiliar words at an earlier age on ERPs than on HT, since ERPs reflect neural processing more directly, with no requirement for a behavioural response (e.g. a head turn). Given that the bilingual infants showed a significant N2 familiarity effect in their ERPs in both languages but failed to show such an effect in either language in HT, we believe that we are seeing the expected sequence, in addition to identifying a trend for a delay in the onset of word form representation in bilinguals as well as in Welsh monolinguals. With further study we expect to see this implicit neurological response earlier in English-learning monolingual children as well – at 10 or even 9 months, as compared with the 11-month HT effect.

Beyond this, the marginal N2 peak latency difference indicated, in the same infants, a tendency for English words to be processed more rapidly than Welsh. This intriguing trend will need to be evaluated on the basis of ERP findings from our larger monolingual study in progress. Such an online processing delay in word recognition (at the millisecond level) may be interpreted in terms of the accentual pattern of Welsh (see Vihman *et al.*, in press), which gives less salience to the initial consonant than does English. A comparable difference can be seen in the salience for infants of the initial consonant in English vs. French, validated experimentally in Vihman *et al.* (2004). An additional factor that could slow word form recognition in Welsh is the mutability of the initial consonant, due to grammatically conditioned changes – e.g. *ci mawr* / ki maʊr / 'big (m.) dog'; *cath fawr* / kaθ vaʊr / 'big (f.) cat'. Further study will be needed to confirm the delay and determine whether only one or both of these factors are involved.

Finally, we obtained in this study an N4 effect that we failed to see in our previous monolingual study (Thierry *et al.*, 2003). In the present study, unlike the previous one, familiar and rare words were presented with a ratio of 1:3 in an attempt to maximise the chances of generating an oddball effect. In addition to the automatic MMN effect (Näätänen, 2001), 'explicit' or conscious reorientation of attention triggered by an oddball stimulus elicits a P3 modulation in adults. It has been suggested that the infant equivalent of the adult P3 is an inverted wave peaking later, due to a different configuration of the infantile cortex and to a lesser degree of neural maturation (see Thierry, 2005, for discussion). We hypothesise that the N4 effect observed here is an equivalent of the adult P3 wave, reflecting infant sensitivity to the lower probability of familiar words as well as providing further evidence of implicit recognition of the familiar words.

In summary, in this study the bilingual infants differed from the English-learning monolinguals in two respects: they failed to recognise familiar words at the age at which monolingual English-learning children do so (a chronological delay) and they also showed a small temporal delay in their response to the familiar words in comparison with English monolingual 11-month-olds (Thierry *et al.*, 2003). The first effect is in agreement with other recent studies of bilingual infants, who show small delays in developing word representation (Bosch & Sebastián-Gallés, 1997) and in vowel and consonant discrimination (Bosch & Sebastián-Gallés, 2003; Burns *et al.*, 2003). The tendency to show a slower neural processing response, on the other hand, recalls much earlier work with older children, in which it was shown that bilingual children and young adults are slower in rapid, relatively automatic processing tasks than are monolinguals (Mägiste, 1979).

The question of 'language learning delay' has been addressed in at least one previous study tracking lexical growth in both bilingual and monolingual infants, using the CDI only (based on children acquiring English and Spanish in Miami, Florida: Pearson *et al.*, 1993). In that study the global percentile achieved by reported word production across the ages 14 to 30 months was found to be higher in English monolinguals (using the norms reported by Fenson *et al.*, 1993, N = 33) than in either of the two languages of the bilingual infants tested (N = 24). When reported lexical production for the two languages was combined, however, the total 'double-language measure' was quite similar to that of the monolinguals. On the other hand, for comprehension the individual language percentiles of the bilingual group (N = 12, age range 8–16 months) were close to those of the monolinguals (N = 10), with the total lexicon exceeding that of the monolinguals, although the difference did not reach statistical significance. The authors caution that the comprehension figures may be overestimated for the bilinguals, since parents reported 'difficulty in knowing in which language an interchange was taking place, so understanding in both languages may have been credited on the basis of comprehension in only one' (p. 112).

In the present study, we have no way of determining the extent of the infants' capacity for word form recognition in the two languages combined. Using the head turn measure we were able to probe for only one language at a time – and on that basis our findings are not inconsistent with those of Pearson *et al.*, working with a wider age range and generally older children. The bilingual infants in our study showed what can be characterised as a 'small delay', the effect size for word recognition falling between that of 10- and 11-month-old monolinguals in English (Figure 5). The same conclusion is suggested by the fact that the familiar words in *both* languages elicited evidence of word form recognition when we used the more sensitive ERP measure. Further study is needed to establish whether or not a comparable group of bilingual infants will recognise word forms in both their languages by 12 months in the HT paradigm. Similarly, for children being raised as monolinguals in the minority language (here, Welsh) in a bilingual community we anticipate seeing only a slight delay, with word form recognition on the ERPs by 11 months and on HT by 12 months, once our studies in progress are complete. These findings, if confirmed, would again be consistent with an earlier study of Pearson and her colleagues (Pearson *et al.*, 1997), who report that 'it appears to be harder for a child to learn Spanish than English [in the United States], even within the Spanish-speaking community of Miami' (p. 47).

Acknowledgements

We would like to thank Pam Martin for helping to develop the Welsh stimuli, Dilys Hughes for recording stimuli in both languages, and Kat Barker for running the ERP experiments. We are grateful to the undergraduate students – Aimee Butler, Ruth Dyson, Charlotte Harrington, Vicky Hudson, Jenny Hughes, Athena Trigenis, Alaina Turnbull and Sarah Williams – who recruited and tested most of the bilingual infants. We are also happy to acknowledge ESRC support for this research.

Notes

1. This is the first report of an ongoing study that will be complete when 24 children have been successfully tested in each age group and for each language on both HT and ERPs. So far, we have successfully tested 20 9-month-olds, 23 10-month-olds, 21 11-month-olds and 17 12-month-olds for English. and 15 9-month-olds and 21 11-month-olds for Welsh. We have also successfully tested 16 11-month-old bilinguals for both languages in each procedure. In order to keep the sample sizes comparable to that of the bilingual group HT data from only the first 16 children tested in each age and language group are reported in this paper. The HT analyses carried out on all groups whose numbers were greater than 16 are presented in the Appendix.
2. The English CDI is that developed at Oxford (Hamilton *et al.*, 2001). The Welsh CDI was originally developed at the University of Wales Bangor by Margaret Bell; we have adapted this form to accord more closely with the usage of our participating families, with the help of Pamela Martin.
3. Although we are conducting HT and ERP experiments with each of the infants, not all of the children can be included in subsequent analyses in either case. Of the 16 children analysed for the HT findings here, 11 are also included in the ERP results. Thus the samples are heavily overlapping but not identical for the two procedures.
4. Data are reported only for those children whose looking times were greater than zero seconds for at least three out of six trials for both familiar and unfamiliar lists.
5. Effect size is the standardised difference between two means (group looking

times to Familiar vs. Unfamiliar), divided by the standard deviation of the two sets of scores (see Cohen, 1988)

Appendix A

Looking times to familiar and unfamiliar word lists in all groups seen to date in which N is more than 16.

Group	n	t statistic	p-value
9-month-olds (English)	20	0.985	0.168
10-month-olds (English)	23	1.231	0.116
11-month-olds (English)	21	1.921	0.035
12-month-olds (English)	17	0.490	0.31
11-month-olds (Welsh)	19	0.402	0.346

References

Bates, E., Benigni, L., Bretherton, I., Camaioni, L. and Volterra, V. (1979) *The Emergence of Symbols: Cognition and Communication in Infancy.* New York: Academic Press.

Bosch, L. and Sebastián-Gallés, N. (1997) Native-language recognition abilities in 4-month-old infants from monolingual and bilingual environments. *Cognition* 65, 33–69.

Bosch, L. and Sebastián-Gallés, N. (2003) Simultaneous bilingualism and the perception of a language-specific vowel contrast in the first year of life. *Language and Speech* 46, 217–44.

Boysson-Bardies, B. de and Vihman, M.M. (1991) Adaptation to language: Evidence from babbling and first words in four languages. *Language* 67, 297–319.

Burns, T.C., Werker, J.F. and McVie, K. (2003) Development of phonetic categories in infants raised in bilingual and monolingual families. In *Proceedings of the 27th Annual Boston University Conference on Language Development.* Somerville, MA: Cascadilla Press.

Cohen, J. (1988) *Statistical Power Analysis for the Behavioral Sciences* (2nd edn). Hillsdale, NJ: Lawrence Erlbaum.

Fenson, L., Dale, P.S., Reznick, J.S., Thal, D., Bates, E., Hartung, J.P., Pethick, S. and Reilly, J.S. (1993) *MacArthur Communicative Development Inventories: User's Guide and Technical Manual.* San Diego, CA: Singular Publishing.

Friederici, A.D. and Wessels, J.M.I. (1993) Phonotactic knowledge of word boundaries and its use in infant speech perception. *Perception & Psychophysics* 54, 287–95.

Hallé, P. and Boysson-Bardies, B. de (1994) Emergence of an early lexicon: Infants' recognition of words. *Infant Behavior and Development* 17, 119–29.

Hamilton, A., Plunkett, K. and Schafer, G. (2001) Infant vocabulary development assessed with a British CDI. *Journal of Child Language* 27, 689–705.

Hayne, H. and Findlay, N. (1995) Contextual control of memory retrieval in infancy: Evidence for associative priming. *Child Development* 18, 195–207.

Jusczyk, P.W. (1997) *The Discovery of Spoken Language.* Cambridge, MA: MIT Press.
Jusczyk, P.W., Friederici, A.D., Wessels, J., Svenkerud, V.Y. and Jusczyk, A.M. (1993) Infants' sensitivity to the sound patterns of native language words. *Journal of Memory and Language* 32, 402–20.
Jusczyk, P.W., Luce, P.A. and Charles-Luce, J. (1994) Infants' sensitivity to phonotactic patterns in the native language. *Journal of Memory and Language* 33, 630–45.
Kushnerenko, E., Ceponiene, R., Balan, P., Fellman, V. and Näätänan, R. (2002) Maturation of the auditory change detection response in infants: A longitudinal ERP study. *Neuroreport* 13, 1843–8.
Mägiste, E. (1979) The competing language systems of the multilingual: A developmental study of decoding and encoding processes. *Journal of Verbal Learning and Verbal Behavior* 18, 79–89.
McCune, L. and Vihman, M.M. (2001) Early phonetic and lexical development. *Journal of Speech, Language and Hearing Research* 44, 670–84.
Näätänen, R. (2001) The perception of speech sounds by the human brain as reflected by the mismatch negativity (MMN) and its magnetic equivalent (MMNm). *Psychophysiology* 38, 1–21.
Pearson, B.Z., Fernández, S.C. and Oller, D.K. (1993) Lexical development in bilingual infants and toddlers: Comparison to monolingual norms. *Language Learning* 43, 93–120.
Pearson, B.Z., Fernández, S.C., Lewedeg, V. and Oller, D.K. (1997) The relationship of input factors to lexical learning by bilingual infants. *Applied Psycholinguistics* 18, 41–58.
Rovee-Collier, C. (1997) Dissociations in infant memory. *Psychological Review* 104, 467–98.
Saffran, J.R., Aslin, R.N. and Newport, E.L. (1996) Statistical learning by 8-month-old infants. *Science* 274, 1926–8.
Thierry, G. (2005) The use of event-related potentials in the study of early cognitive development. *Infant Child Development* 14, 85–94.
Thierry, G., Vihman, M. and Roberts, M. (2003) Familiar words capture the attention of 11-month-olds in less than 250 ms. *Neuroreport* 14, 2307–10.
Vihman, M.M. (1996) *Phonological Development: The Origins of Language in the Child.* Oxford: Basil Blackwell.
Vihman, M.M. (2002a) Getting started without a system: From phonetics to phonology in bilingual development. *International Journal of Bilingualism* 6, 239–54.
Vihman, M.M. (2002b) The relationship between production and perception in the transition into language. End of award report, Economic and Social Research Council, UK.
Vihman, M.M. and DePaolis, R.A. (1999) The role of accentual pattern in early lexical representation. End of award report, Economic and Social Research Council, UK.
Vihman, M.M. and McCune L. (1994) When is a word a word? *Journal of Child Language,* 21, 517–42.
Vihman, M.M., Nakai, S. and DePaolis, R.A. (in press) Getting the rhythm right: A cross-linguistic study of segmental duration in babbling and first words. In L. Goldstein, D. Whalen and C. Best (eds) *Laboratory Phonology 8: Varieties of Phonological Competence.* New York: Mouton de Gruyter.
Vihman, M.M., Nakai, S., DePaolis, R.A. and Hallé, P. (2004) The role of accentual pattern in early lexical representation. *Journal of Memory and Language* 50, 336–53.

Chapter 4

Bilingual First Language Acquisition in Perspective

FRED GENESEE

The purpose of this chapter is to provide a brief overview of recent research on bilingual first language acquisition (BFLA). Before proceeding to that, it is noteworthy that the study of bilingual first language acquisition (BFLA) has had a remarkably long history. The first scientific report of a bilingual child is usually attributed to a publication by Ronjat in 1913 and, of course, there is the monumental, longitudinal study by Werner Leopold of his two bilingual daughters that was published between 1939 and 1949. Despite the early work of Ronjat and Leopold, further research remained sparse until the 1980s. Beginning in the late 1980s, there was an upsurge in attention devoted to BFLA, including the research by Jurgen Meisel and his colleagues in Hamburg; Annick De Houwer in Belgium; Elizabeth Lanza, in Norway; Marilyn Vihman in the US; and work at McGill University in Canada. This surge in interest can be attributed to several factors. First, there is the growing recognition that simultaneous acquisition of two, or more, languages is not uncommon. While we lack definitive statistics, it has been speculated that there may be as many or even more children who grow up bilingual as monolingual (Tucker, 1998). Therefore, the study of bilingual acquisition is worthy in its own right. Second, theories of language acquisition are currently based largely on monolingual children, but must ultimately incorporate the 'facts' of BFLA if they are to be comprehensive. While most theories do not exclude the possibility of learning two languages at the same time, they do not address it explicitly or in detail. Research on BFLA can fill this gap in our knowledge.

Third, research on BFL learners can make a unique contribution to our understanding of the human language faculty because it permits us to examine the capacity of the mind to acquire and use language and it can address issues about acquisition in general (see, for example, the work by Paradis *et al.*, 2005, on the nature of specific language impairment). The capacity of infants to simultaneously acquire two or more linguistic systems, sometimes with radically different structural properties such as Inuktitut and English, has implications for our conceptualization of the neuro-cognitive architecture of the human mind that underlies acquisition of any language. Finally, the investigation of BFLA can provide important information to speech and language clinicians and other professionals who work with bilingual children suspected of having language learning difficulties (Genesee, 2003a).

BFLA pertains to children who grow up learning two languages simultaneously. Alternative criteria have been proposed to distinguish simultaneous from successive dual language learning. De Houwer (1995), for example, has proposed the stringent cut-off of one month, while McLaughlin (1978), in an early review of bilingual acquisition research, proposed the much more lenient cut-off of three years of age. Whether children who acquire an additional language within one, two or three years of birth comprise different kinds of dual language learners is an empirical question, one that can only be answered by examining whether dual language learning that begins at different ages is different in kind or rate from that of dual language learning that begins at birth. Most research on BFLA has examined children who begin dual language acquisition at birth and has examined their development until approximately three years of age. This is the focus of this review.

A fundamental issue in these studies, and the focus of this review, is the nature and developmental trajectory of simultaneous bilingual children's language development. In question, in all cases, are the precise patterns of development of the bilingual child's two languages and the time course of development in each domain. Much of this research has been motivated by the unitary language system hypothesis according to which children exposed to two languages go through an initial stage when the languages are not differentiated (see Genesee, 1989, for a review). The most explicit formulation of this hypothesis was presented by Volterra and Taeschner (1978: 312):

> In the first stage the child has one lexical system which includes
> words from both languages . . . in this stage the language develop-
> ment of the bilingual child seems to be like the language
> development of the monolingual child. . . . In the second stage, the
> child distinguishes two different lexicons, but applies the same
> syntactic rules to both languages. In the third stage the child speaks
> two languages differentiated both in lexicon and syntax . . .

Volterra and Taeschner's hypothesis, in effect, proposed that the initial state of the developing bilingual child is essentially monolingual. It is only by the third stage, thought to occur around three years of age, that children exposed to two languages at birth can be considered truly bilingual. Volterra and Taeschner were not alone in proposing that bilingual children go through a monolingual stage, as this quote from Leopold (1978: 27) demonstrates:

> The free mixing of English and German vocabulary in many of her sentences was a conspicuous feature of her speech. But the very fact that she mixed lexical items proves that there was no real bilingualism as yet. Words from the two languages did not belong to two different speech systems but to one . . .

That BFL learners might go through an initial monolingual stage is but one instance of the more general concern that BFLA strains the child's language learning capacity, leading to delayed and even deviant forms of language development. This concern has been expressed in a number of ways; specifically, that bilingual acquisition might result in impaired cognitive, as well as linguistic, development (e.g. see Bialystok, 2001, and Cummins, 1981, for reviews); that bilingual education puts children at risk for academic failure or delay (e.g. Macnamara, 1966), and that children with impaired capacity for language learning will be impaired even further if exposed to more than one language, simultaneously or successively.

Findings from studies of BFLA are reviewed in the following sections around three general topics:

- development;
- bilingual code-mixing;
- communicative competence.

Development

Most studies on the language development of BFL learners has focused on morpho-syntactic development, with some but limited research on lexical and phonological development. In question, in most cases, is the precise patterns of development of the bilingual child's two languages and the time course of that development. Also at issue is whether the bilingual child's developing languages are differentiated or not and when in development this is evident.

Morpho-syntactic development

Contrary to the unitary language system hypothesis, it has been shown that children acquiring two languages simultaneously acquire language-specific morpho-syntactic properties of the target languages and these correspond to monolingual patterns, for the most part (e.g. Bedore, 2004; De

Houwer, 1990; Döpke, 2000a; Hulk & Müller, 2000; Juan-Garau & Pérez-Vidal, 2000; Meisel, 1989; Paradis & Genesee, 1996; Yip & Matthews, 2000; see Meisel, 2001, for a review). Paradis and Genesee (1996), for example, found that 2–3 year-old French–English bilingual children: (1) used finite verb forms earlier in French than in English; (2) used subject pronouns in French exclusively with finite verbs but subject pronouns in English with both finite and non-finite verbs, in accordance with the status of subject pronouns in French as clitics (or agreement markers); and (3) placed verbal negatives after lexical verbs in French (e.g. *'n'aime pas'*) but before lexical verbs in English (*'do not like'*). These patterns characterize the performance of monolingual children acquiring these languages.

At the same time, cross-language influences, or transfer (see Paradis & Genesee, 1996, for a definition), have been noted in some cases; for example, by Döpke (2000a) in Verb-Object word order in German–English bilingual children, by Müller and Hulk (2001) in object-drop in Dutch–French, German–French and German–Italian children, and by Yip and Matthews (2000) in relative clause, wh-in-situ interrogative, and null object constructions in a Chinese–English child (see Döpke, 2000b, for a review). Transfer has been attributed to overlap in the surface structure of the participating languages (Döpke, 2000a) and to underlying abstract properties of the languages (Hulk & Müller, 2000). Döpke (2000a), for example, reports that Australian children learning English and German simultaneously overgeneralized the -VO word order of English to German which instantiates both -VO and -OV word orders depending on the clausal structure of the utterance. Working within the Competition Model (Bates & MacWhinney, 1987), Döpke argued that these children were prone to overgeneralize S-V-O word order in German main and subordinate clauses because the -VO order is reinforced on the surface of both the German and the English input they heard. Hulk and Müller (2000: 229), have similarly argued that 'there has to be a certain overlap of the two systems at the surface level' for cross-linguistic syntactic influence to occur. Structural overlap and ambiguity in the input have also been invoked as possible explanations in phonological transfer by Paradis (1996) in a study of French–English 2–3-year-olds.

Instances of cross-linguistic transfer that have been reported are restricted. They pertain to specific aspects of the child's developing grammars and they appear to occur only under certain linguistic circumstances, as noted. In other words, transfer does not occur across all aspects of the child's developing languages. Moreover, it is usually temporary since we know from research on adult bilinguals that, in the long run, bilingual children can acquire the appropriate target language forms (White & Genesee, 1996); however, at present, there is no research on how long cross-language transfer persists and how it is resolved. Thus, instances of transfer as have been reported do not compromise the general conclusion that the morpho-syntactic systems of bilingual children are language-specific and are the same in most respects as those of monolingual children at the same stage of development.

These conclusions may not obtain in all cases since there may be mitigating circumstances that result in different patterns. For example, Paradis (1996) and Yip and Matthews (2000) have proposed that dominance (i.e. differences in relative proficiency in each language) may mitigate cross-linguistic effects so that transfer and deviation from monolingual patterns might be more pronounced in cases where exposure to or proficiency in both languages is not balanced (see also Petersen, 1988) Thus, these conclusions should be construed to pertain to the child's capacity to acquire two languages simultaneously and not to what happens in every case.

Lexical development

Research on the lexical development of BFL learners is more limited and, like that in other domains, often consists of case studies; one important exception is research by Pearson and her colleagues on a group of 27 children raised in Spanish and English in Miami, Florida (Pearson *et al.*, 1993, 1995). Pearson *et al.*, as well as other researchers, have reported that bilingual children often score lower on standardized tests of vocabulary than monolingual children when each language is considered separately (Genesee & Nicoladis, 1995; Pearson *et al.*, 1993). However, Pearson and her colleagues also found that the total *conceptual vocabulary* of bilingual children (i.e. their combined vocabulary in both languages minus translation equivalents) is the same as that of the monolinguals (Pearson *et al.*, 1993). The single language vocabulary scores of bilinguals may be smaller than those of monolinguals for a number of reasons: (1) they, like monolinguals, have limited long-term memory in early stages of development but must retain vocabulary from two languages in contrast to the monolinguals' one; (2) bilingual children's exposure to each language is less than that of monolinguals', and (3) the context for learning each of two languages is likely to be less than the total context for learning one language and, thus, bilingual children's vocabulary repertoire in each language is likely to be less than that of monolinguals. It is likely that vocabulary knowledge in each language would expand as the context for using each language expands. We know little else about the vocabulary development of bilingual children at this time.

Phonological development

When it comes to phonological development, findings are best regarded as tentative owing to the relative paucity of studies in this domain and the diversity of issues examined by existing studies. Studies with simultaneous bilingual children in the verbal stage of development indicate that they exhibit language-specific patterns of production (Johnson & Lancaster, 1998; Paradis, 1996, 2001). Maneva and Genesee (2002) also report language-specific patterns in the babbling of a French–English boy around 12 months of age at the onset of first word production. This child's babbling with his French-speaking father exhibited certain supra-segmental features that are characteristic of infants learning French, and his babbling when with his English-speaking mother exhibited English-specific patterns (cf. Poulin-Dubois & Goodz, 2001, for a study of segmental features of bilingual babbling). While language-specific in certain respects, bilingual children's phonological repertoires are not always the same as those of monolinguals' (Paradis, 2001). Similarly, studies on the early speech perception of bilingual infants indicate that while language-specific and like that of monolinguals in certain respects, their speech perception differs sometimes from that of monolinguals in other respects. For example, Polka and Sundara *et al.* (2003) report that pre-verbal bilingual French–English children in Montreal were able to segment French words from continuous French speech and English words from continuous English speech at 7½ months of age, the same age when monolingual French and English children exhibit word segmentation ability. Monolingual children could segment words only in the language to which they have been exposed. In contrast, others report different patterns of speech perception for bilinguals in comparison to monolinguals, arguing that the developmental trajectory for bilinguals is shaped in specific and significant ways as a result of their exposure to two phonological systems. Bosch and Sebastián-Gallés (2003a,b), for example, report that 8–12 month old bilingual children (Spanish-Catalan) differ from monolinguals in their perception of certain language-specific speech sounds (vowel contrasts and a voicing contrast in fricatives). As well, Fennel *et al.* (2002) report that while 17-month old monolingual children were able to attend to fine phonetic detail in minimal word pairs, bilingual children exhibited the same discrimination only later, at 20 months of age. Studies of adult bilinguals indicate that they too differ significantly from monolinguals on speech discrimination and production tasks (Sundara *et al.*, 2004). Thus, the speech perception and production skills of BFL learners appear to differ in significant ways from those of monolinguals. Much more research in BFL learners at all stages of development is needed to provide a more complete picture and explanations of the similarities and differences in BFLA and monolingual acquisition in this domain of acquisition.

Rates of development

Only qualified conclusions with respect to rate of BFLA are possible at present because the extant database is limited to case studies or small groups of children (cf. Pearson *et al.*, 1993) and, as noted, there is a paucity of research in some domains. Moreover, BFL learners are not a homogeneous group; they vary considerably in amount and consistency of language exposure. Thus, it is risky to identify normative patterns that apply to all BFL learners. The existing database does, nevertheless, make it possible to ascertain if bilingual children can acquire two languages in the same time frame as monolingual children; but not whether all bilingual children do. With these caveats in mind, published studies of BFL learners indicate that they can exhibit the same basic milestones in language development at approximately the same ages as monolingual children, and they can exhibit the same rate of language-specific grammatical development as monolingual children. In particular, bilingual children babble (Oller *et al.*, 1997; Maneva & Genesee, 2002), produce their first words and word combinations (Petitto *et al.*, 2001), and exhibit developmental patterns for specific morpho-syntactic properties of the target languages (e.g. acquisition of finite forms, use of subject pronouns) within the same age ranges as those reported for monolingual children (e.g. De Houwer, 1990; Paradis & Genesee, 1996; Yip & Matthews, 2000). They do not systematically exhibit evidence of acceleration or delay (Genesee, 2003b; Genesee *et al.*, 2004).

Child Bilingual Code-mixing

Virtually all bilingual children code-mix within and across utterances; the former is referred to as intra-utterance mixing and the latter as inter-utterance mixing. The mixed elements can be phonological, lexical, morpho-syntactic, or pragmatic, with lexical mixing often reported to be the most common form (e.g. Goodz, 1987; De Houwer, 1990), but not always (Deuchar, 1999; Meisel, 1994; Vihman, 1985). Code-mixing is controversial since it is often attributed to confusion or lack of language differentiation, as noted previously (Volterra & Taeschner, 1978; Leopold, 1978). Child bilingual code-mixing has been examined with respect to both its grammatical-structural and its functional properties; in other words, how it is structured internally and why children engage in it.

Grammatical properties

When two languages are used in the same utterance, grammatical incompatibilities between the languages can arise due to differences in word order, inflectional morphology, and syntactic sub-categorization; these in turn can result in patterns of language use that are awkward or illicit. Indeed, the commonly held perception of code-mixing (or switching) is that it is a 'bastardized' (ungrammatical) form of language and, for this reason, parents and others often discourage their children from code-mixing. Contrary to this view, it is generally agreed that adult bilingual code-mixing is usually grammatical according to the constraints of the participating languages (MacSwan, 1999; Myers-Scotton, 1997; Poplack, 1980). That bilingual children ultimately acquire grammatical constraints on their code-mixing is attested by results from studies on adults. Questions remain, however, about child bilingual code-mixing. Are there grammatical constraints on child bilingual code-mixing? What do they look like? and When in development are they evident? Evidence of grammatical constraints on the code-mixing of young bilingual children would provide important insights into their capacity to learn and use two languages at the same time since in order to code-mix in ways that respect the grammars of the participating languages the child has to have acquired the grammars of both languages and must also be able to access them simultaneously so that they can be co-ordinated during production. Evidence that the constraints are operative from the outset of two- and multiple-word productions would argue that they emerge with the advent of grammatical competence and do not require additional learning.

Research has examined grammatical constraints on intra-utterance code-mixing by bilingual children learning the following language pairs: French and German (Köppe, in press, Meisel, 1994); French and English (Genesee & Sauve, 2000, Paradis et al., 2000); English and Norwegian (Lanza, 1997); English and Estonian (Vihman, 1998), and Inuktitut and English (Allen et al., 2000). The constraint models of Poplack (1980) and of Myers-Scotton (1997) have formed the basis for most, although not all, analyses in studies on this topic (see Köppe, in press, and Meisel, 1994, for alternative analyses). The Myers-Scotton and Poplack models differ substantially in the extent to which they refer to abstract, underlying grammatical constraints with respect to system and content morphemes in contrast to surface level grammatical constraints, such as word order and bound versus open class morphemes, respectively. Despite the diversity of language pairs and analytic frameworks that comprise this body of research, all researchers have concluded that child bilingual code-mixing is grammatically constrained. The operation of constraints based on abstract notions of grammar, which are at the core of Myers-Scotton's Matrix Language Frame model, is most evident in bilingual children once they exhibit such knowledge in their actual language use (as marked by verb tense and agreement, for example), usually around 2.6 years of age and older for children learning English, while the operation of constraints that reflect surface features of grammar (such as word order) are evident even earlier in development, prior to overt marking of abstract grammatical relations in the child's language, from the two word/morpheme stage onward. Köppe (in press) has proposed a hybrid model, composed of linear, word order constraints during the early stages of production and abstract, hierarchically organized constraints subsequently. The constraints that describe child bilingual code-mixing, as noted, are essentially the same as those that describe adult code-mixing. Moreover, they appear to be operative as soon as children begin to combine words into single utterances and, by implication, emerge along with grammatical competence.

Functional properties

As reported in studies on grammatical development and on the grammatical constraints on child bilingual code-mixing, there is no evidence that child bilingual code-mixing is due to lack of neuro-cognitive differentiation of their developing languages. The question remains: why do they code-mix? Extant evidence indicates quite clearly that there are multiple explanations for child bilingual code-mixing and that, contrary to interpretations that it reflects incompetence or confusion, it reflects cognitive, communicative, and social competence.

The gap-filling hypothesis

One explanation of child bilingual code-mixing is that it serves to fill gaps in the developing child's linguistic competence (Deuchar & Quay, 2000; Genesee, Paradis & Wolf, 1995). The simplest illustration of this is the case of lexical mixing. According to the lexical-gap hypothesis, bilingual children mix words from language X when using language Y because they do not know the appropriate word in language Y. Mixing syntactic patterns might also occur in order to fill syntactic gaps in the child's knowledge of the target language (Gawlitzek-Maiwald & Tracy, 1996; Lanza, 1997; Petersen, 1988). There is considerable evidence in favor of the lexical gap explanation. First, this explanation is compatible with the general observation that young bilingual children mix more when they use their less proficient language (Genesee *et al.*, 1995a). By definition, lexical knowledge in the less proficient language is less developed than in the other language and, thus, bilingual children might be compelled to draw on the resources of their more proficient language in order to express themselves fully when using their less well developed language. While this is likely to be characteristic of code-mixing of children in the process of learning two languages, it can also be true for older bilinguals whose language development has reached maturity because lexical knowledge in both languages of the bilingual is seldom equivalent.

There is direct evidence that bilingual children are more likely to mix words for which they do not know translation equivalents than for words for which they do, regardless of whether they are using their less or more proficient language (Nicoladis, 1995; Genesee *et al.*, 1995b). Genesee *et al.* (1995b) asked two sets of parents who were raising their children bilingually to keep daily diary records of their sons' language use during a three-week period. The parents were to write down everything the children said during this period; this was feasible because the children were 1.8 and 2.0 years of age and were not producing many words. With these detailed records, it was possible to identify how often the children code-mixed and whether they code-mixed words more often when they did not know the appropriate word in the language of their conversational partner. Code-mixing in this study was defined as use of a word in the language that was not habitually used by the child's interlocutor. We found that both boys were more likely to code-mix words for which they did not know translation equivalents. This was especially true of Wayne for whom 100% of the words he code-mixed were words for which he did not know the translation equivalent. For Felix, as well, the majority (65%) of words that he code-mixed were words for which he did not know translation equivalents. Similar results have been reported in case studies of other children (Nicoladis & Secco, 2000).

In some cases, lexical mixing might not be a matter of the child not knowing the appropriate word, but an appropriate word might not exist in the target language. For example, in Quebec, the French word *'dodo'* (nap) is used primarily with children (from French 'dormir' to sleep). There is no exact equivalent in English since all such terms in English are equally appropriate with adults and children. It is not uncommon in bilingual families in Montreal where French and English are spoken for parents to use 'dodo' at all times, even when speaking English. There are many examples of adult bilinguals who mix words because an exact equivalent does not exist in the target language; for example, 'scholarity' (years of schooling), 'bourse' (fellowship or grant), 'formation' (training), and 'stage' (internship) are all French words that are commonly used by English speakers in Montreal because they have a particular meaning in Quebec. In fact, borrowing is a well documented phenomenon by which languages acquire new vocabulary; English is a particularly good example – many English words associated with food and eating are derived from French: beef, mutton, ragout, veal, and so on.

Mixing to fill gaps in children's lexical or syntactic knowledge in one or the other of their languages reflects bilingual children's competence in using all their linguistic resources in order to satisfy their communication needs. Since bilingual children grow up with others who are also bilingual, this can be an effective and appropriate strategy. When bilingual children use this strategy inappropriately with monolinguals, it is usually not because they are confused or are unable to differentiate their languages, as hypothesized by Volterra and Taeschner and Leopold. Some bilingual children may persist in code-mixing with monolinguals because they have failed to grasp that their interlocutor is monolingual; monolinguals may be rare in their day-to-day lives. A unique aspect of growing up bilingual is that children may encounter adults who are less linguistically competent than they are because the adult is monolingual.

Pragmatic explanations

Bilingual children may also code-mix for pragmatic effect – to emphasize what they are saying, to quote what someone else said, to protest, to narrate, etc. For example, when speaking English, Spanish–English bilingual children may interject expressions in Spanish in order to emphasize the importance of what they are saying in much the same way that monolinguals might repeat themselves, altering their wording slightly in order to emphasize an important detail (e.g. *'I was terrified, scared to death!'*). See Example 1 for an example of inter-utterance mixing for emphasis from a 2½ year old French–English girl in Montreal (from Goodz, 1986). For some bilingual children, one of their languages may have more affective load than the other, and they may use that language to express emotion when they speak. Mixing in order to quote what someone else said or when narrating events can be a way of rendering one's discourse more authentic if the event or material being quoted took place in the other language – for example, bilingual teenagers may use English and Spanish to describe a music video they saw in Spanish on TV; pre-school children may use English and Spanish to describe what they did at their bilingual daycare or with their bilingual friends.

Example 1 (from Goodz, 1986):

> . . . *laisse mes barrettes, touche pas papa.* **Me's gona put them back in the bag so no one's ganna took them!** [leave my barrette alone, don't touch it daddy . . .]

Language socialization

A third explanation of child bilingual code-mixing is related to socialization. Children learning two languages are exposed to the normative patterns of bilingual code-mixing in their communities and they learn these patterns at the same time as they learn the sounds, words and grammatical patterns of the languages. Acquiring appropriate community-based patterns of code-mixing is an important part of bilingual children's language socialization. Communities have different social norms with respect to appropriate kinds of mixing, when and where mixing occurs, and how often mixing is appropriate (for example, see research by Poplack, 1987, and Myers-Scotton, 1997). In an early seminal study, Poplack (1980) examined code-mixing patterns in a Puerto Rican Spanish-speaking community in New York City. She found that members of this community engaged in an especially fluent form of mixing where the same utterance could include several switches from Spanish to English and back again; see Example 2. Bilingual code-mixing can be an important marker of social identity and, in the Puerto Rican community that Poplack studied, rapid, fluent mixing served to identify the speaker as both Spanish- and English-speaking and, thus, as both Puerto Rican and American (see also Zentella, 1997).

Example 2 (from Poplack, 1980):

> **But I used to eat the** *bofe, the brain.* **And then they stopped selling it**
> **because,** *tenian, este, le encontraron que tenia* (they had, uh, they found
> out that it had) worms. **I used to make some** *bofe! Después yo hacía*
> *uno d'esos* (then I would make one of those) *concotions:* **the garlic** *con*
> *cebolla, y hacía un moho, y yo dejaba que se curare eso* (with onion, and
> I'd make a sauce, and I'd let that sit) *for a couple of hours. Then you*
> *be drinking and eating that shit. Wooh! It's like eating anchovies*
> *when they drinking. Delicious!*

In contrast, the norms regarding bilingual code-mixing are quite different among French–English bilinguals in the Ottawa region of Canada (Poplack, 1987). Generally speaking, code-mixing by bilinguals in this community, especially if they identify as 'French Canadian', is less frequent and less fluent; it is often 'flagged' to indicate that the discourse is bilingual (see Example 3). The flagged mixing exhibited by this group is not necessarily due to lack of proficiency, but, arguably, to identity issues. It is likely that this pattern of mixing reflects the desire among members of this community to identify with the French-speaking community in Canada and to set themselves somewhat apart from English Canadians. To use French and English like Puerto Ricans in New York City use Spanish and English would blur their identity. Children growing up bilingual in each of these communities learn distinct patterns of bilingual usage in order to fit into and to be fully functional members of the community. Proficiency may be an issue in second language learners, however (Genesee *et al.*, 2004).

Example 3 (from Poplack, 1987):

*Mais je te gage pare exemple . . . **excuse my English**, mais les odds sont là.*
(**But I bet you that . . . excuse my English, but the odds are there.**)

Norms in individual families can also influence child bilingual code-mixing (Lanza, 1997; Vihman, 1998). The pattern and frequency of code-mixing can vary from one family to another in the same community because some families and even individual parents within the same family are more tolerant of mixing than others. Lanza (1997) describes a bilingual family in Norway that was raising their child, Siri, bilingually. Although both parents were bilingual, Lanza observed that Siri code-mixed much less with her native English-speaking mother than with her native Norwegian-speaking father. Upon close examination, Lanza noticed that Siri's mother discouraged her from code-mixing by avoiding mixing herself, by pretending that she did not understand Siri when she said something in Norwegian, or by indicating in her reply to Siri that she wanted Siri to express herself in English. One might imagine that Siri's mother sought to encourage Siri to use only English because this was one of the few opportunities Siri got to use English; elsewhere, everything took place in Norwegian. In contrast, her father indicated that using both English and Norwegian was all right. He did this by code-mixing himself and by indicating that he understood Siri even when she used his non-native language, English. Consequently, Siri's language choice was not an issue with her father as it was with her mother.

Another example of the influence of family norms on bilingual children's language use comes from Döpke in a study of German–English bilingual families in Australia. Döpke (1992) observed that some of the bilingual families she was studying were more successful than others in promoting the use of both languages and, in particular, the minority language (German) in a community that was otherwise dominated by English. Döpke attributed the successful family's success to their adoption of explicit discourse strategies that obliged the children to use German even though they were often tempted to use English. Poplack's, Lanza's and Döpke's findings illustrate that children will differ in their style and frequency of bilingual code-mixing as well as in their preference to code-mix as a result of different norms in their homes and communities. Clearly, this aspect of mixing is socially conditioned and must be learned.

In summary, there are a number of explanations for child bilingual code-mixing: to fill gaps in the child's linguistic competence (lexical or morpho-syntactic); for pragmatic reasons or effects; and as a result of language socialization norms in their families and language community.

Contrary to early conceptualizations that code-mixing reflects incompetence and even confusion, evidence indicates clearly that it reflects bilingual children's linguistic resourcefulness and communicative competence.

Bilingual Communicative Competence

Bilingual children face the same communication challenges as monolingual children; namely, production of target-like language forms (including words and morpho-syntactic patterns) that are comprehensible to others; getting one's meaning across when language acquisition is incomplete; and use of language in socially appropriate ways. At the same time, the ability to communicate appropriately and effectively in two languages entails an understanding of interpersonal communication that exceeds that required for monolingual communication, including, among others, an understanding that not all adults or children know two languages, that mixing languages may not be appropriate or comprehensible to others, and that breakdowns in communication may be due to language choice. Examining the development of communicative competence in bilingual children provides a window into their cognitive capacities as well as their linguistic competencies because bilingual communicative competence goes beyond the acquisition of the formal properties of two language codes and includes the ability to use two languages appropriately and effectively with others. Studies of bilingual children's communicative competence also addresses the unitary language system hypothesis in so far as evidence that young bilingual children can use their languages differentially and appropriately would be difficult to reconcile with this hypothesis.

Basic pragmatic skills involving language choice develop at an early age in BFL learners. Even bilingual children in the one- and early two-word stages of development usually use their interlocutor's language as much as their linguistic proficiency allows. For instance, Genesee *et al.* (1995a) observed 2-year-old French–English bilinguals (MLU in French was 1.65 and in English 1.70) while they were interacting with their parents and found that they used more of their mother's language with their mothers than with their fathers, and vice-versa for the father's language, despite the fact that some children were more proficient in one language than in the other (see also De Houwer, 1990, and Lanza, 1997, for additional evidence). A follow-up study by Genesee *et al.* (1996) showed that 2-year-old French–English bilinguals (average MLU in French was 1.37 and in English 1.50) were also capable of using their languages appropriately with unfamiliar monolingual interlocutors. Three of the four children they examined used more of the stranger's language with the stranger than they did with the parent who spoke the same language as the stranger but was also bilingual (see also Deuchar & Quay, 2000; and Petitto _et al._, 2001). Genesee _et al._ argued that these findings indicate that bilingual children's ability to use their developing languages differentially does not simply reflect an over-learned association between speaker and language (as might occur when communicating with their parents and other family members), but an ability to make on-line adjustments to interlocutors' language preferences and/or abilities without the benefit of previous experience or learning.

Additional evidence that young bilingual children are sensitive and responsive to interlocutors' language preferences comes from a study by Comeau _et al._ (2003) of bilingual children's code-mixing. Comeau _et al._ observed six French-English bilingual 2- to 2½-year-olds while they played with an experimenter on three separate occasions. The experimenter showed a preference for one language, but varied her rate of mixing across sessions. About 15% of her utterances were mixed during the first session, 40% during the second session, and 15% again during the third and last session. All of the children mixed significantly more during the second session than the first session, and four of the children reduced their mixing rate once again during the third session. The mixing rates of three of these children fell within 4% of the experimenter's in every play session, suggesting that these children were closely monitoring their interlocutor's language choice.

Other studies have attempted to determine which cues children rely on to make their language choices. Lanza (1997, 2001), as noted previously, argues that bilingual children are sensitive to parental discourse strategies that encourage either monolingual or bilingual usage. More specifically, her observations of an English–Norwegian bilingual 2-year-old indicated that she mixed her two languages more with her Norwegian-speaking father, who often responded in English to her English utterances, than with her English-speaking mother, who often pretended not to understand when the child spoke Norwegian to her. Similar findings have been reported by Kasuya (1998) with English–Japanese bilingual children (cf. Nicoladis & Genesee, 1998). Parental discourse strategies may therefore be one way in which children learn to make appropriate language choices.

In a related vein, Comeau and Genesee (2001) examined bilingual children's ability to adjust their language use in accordance with feedback concerning the appropriateness of their language choice. More specifically, they investigated 2- and 3-year-olds' responses to requests for clarification following their use of a language not understood by their conversational partner. The question of interest was whether the children were able to respond to a clarification request by translating their utterance into their interlocutor's language. An experimenter speaking only one language played with each child for approximately one hour. The adult used the child's less developed language on the assumption that the child would be likely to use his or her more proficient language, resulting in a high number of breakdowns in communication. Each time the child used the 'inappropriate' language, the adult made up to five requests for clarification, going from non-specific to explicit (i.e. from 'What?' to 'Can you tell me that in French/English?'). Adults also requested clarification following utterances that were incomprehensible for other reasons – they were inaudible or unclear or the child used a non-adult like word.

The children switched to the appropriate language about 25% of the time following a request for clarification from the adult. Most of these language changes were made in response to the first or second requests which did not provide the reason for the breakdown. Moreover, the children virtually never changed their language when attempting to repair breakdowns that were due to reasons other than language choice. Their ability to change language only when it was appropriate suggests that young bilingual children have the ability to correctly infer the meaning of non-specific feedback regarding their language choice and to switch to their other language in response to such feedback, even if this means abandoning use of the more proficient language. This ability appeared to be more developed among the older children. A significantly higher number of 3-year-olds changed their language when they were required to do so. The 3-year-olds also favored reformulation as a repair strategy over repetition, suggesting that they understood that the form of their utterance was a possible cause of breakdowns. In contrast, the younger children used a higher proportion of repetitions.

Conclusions

As noted previously, extant evidence does not permit normative conclusions about BFLA, but it does permit conclusions about what is possible when children are exposed to two languages from birth. Keeping this qualification in mind, extant evidence indicates that children exposed to two language from birth exhibit language-specific and target-appropriate patterns of morpho-syntax from the earliest stages of verbal development, and, for the most part, their patterns of development resemble those of monolingual children acquiring the same languages. Instances of cross-language transfer of morpho-syntax have been reported, but these are linguistically circumscribed to specific aspects of the grammar and, given sufficient input, are likely to be short term, although the latter is open to empirical verification. That the morpho-syntactic development of bilingual children is not compromised by learning two languages is also evident from analyses of their intra-utterance code-mixing. Several studies have shown that child bilingual code-mixing is constrained according to the grammatical principles and restrictions that govern each language. For this to be the case, bilingual children must be acquiring the language-specific grammatical principles of the target languages and, from a processing point of view, they must be able to access both sets of grammars at the same time in order to co-ordinate them on-line during mixing. Extant evidence suggests further that this ability emerges with the onset of grammar. At the same time, and as noted, bilingual children learn socio-pragmatic constraints on code-mixing and appear to be highly responsive to the language proficiency and preferences of adult interlocutors.

The developmental pattern for phonology appears to be more complicated and is also less clear owing to the relative paucity of research in this domain. Simultaneous bilingual children in the verbal stage of development have been found to exhibit language-specific phonological patterns in their production; but these patterns are not always identical to those of monolinguals. Studies of pre-verbal BFL learners indicate similarities and differences when compared with monolinguals, but these studies are even fewer in number than those on phonological development during the early verbal stage of development. Whether differences between bilinguals and monolinguals in speech perception and production are generalizable across learners and whether they are long term are questions that remain to be answered through future longitudinal research. Equally important is whether and in what ways differences between bilinguals and monolinguals in this (or other domains) are consequential. Sundara _et al._ (2004) found that the speech production of French–English adult bilinguals differed significantly from that of monolinguals in certain respects (i.e. [dV] and [tV]) when detailed acoustic analyses were carried out, but untrained adult listeners could not distinguish differences between bilinguals' and monolinguals' versions of these sounds.

Bilingual children have been found to have smaller vocabularies in each language than monolinguals, but their combined conceptual vocabulary may be the same, suggesting that it is performance factors and not underlying abilities that account for single-language vocabulary results of bilinguals. Indeed, bilingual children's reduced vocabulary knowledge in each language can be explained in a number of ways – amount of exposure to each language, overlap in contexts of learning, and memory capacity, none of which implicate underlying deficiencies. Moreover, it would not be surprising if their vocabularies differ from those of monolinguals, even into adulthood, because vocabulary knowledge is determined by learning context and the contexts for learning two languages seldom overlap completely. We currently have no evidence concerning other aspects of bilingual children's lexical knowledge – e.g. its underlying organization or long-term development (see Nicoladis, 2002, for an example of research that goes beyond the issues that have been reviewed here).

Findings from studies of bilingual communicative competence also indicate that BFLA is well within the capacity of typically developing children. BFL learners use their developing languages differentially and appropriately early in development – in the two-word and even one-word stages of development. Findings that young bilingual children are responsive to the language proficiency and preferences, including rates of code-mixing, of unfamiliar as well as familiar interlocutors, indicate that they have the capacity to adapt their language use online in accordance with their conversational partners' usage. In other words, their ability to use their two languages appropriately is not simply a matter of associating a language with a speaker, as might suffice with familiar interlocutors.

Research by Comeau et al. indicates further that they can change languages in response to feedback that communication has broken down because of their language choice even when such feedback is implicit and does not specify either the source of the breakdown or the nature of the modification that is called for. Bilingual children can demonstrate these abilities even when using their less developed language, which arguably increases the communicative demands on them. Children raised bilingually exhibit a range of communication skills that are particular to bilingual communication, indicating that they can accommodate the additional demands of communicating in two languages from early in development. In this regard, code-mixing has been shown to be a communicative resource that bilingual children use to fill lexical or syntactic gaps in their linguistic competence and for pragmatic and language socialization reasons. In an early study, Genesee et al. (1975) compared bilingual and monolingual school-age children's sensitivity to the communicative needs of interlocutors with different communication needs – some could see and some were blindfolded and could not see a game that the children were describing. The bilingual children outperformed the monolingual children by providing the blindfolded interlocutors with the specific kinds of information they needed, indicating that bilingual children might even acquire superior communication skills in certain respects as a result of the additional communicative challenges they face (see Bialystok, 2001, for evidence of cognitive advantages in bilinguals).

In short, there is no evidence that the development of linguistic and communicative competence is systematically compromised by simultaneous exposure to two languages in typically developing children during the period of primary language acquisition, other things being equal. However, in the world of dual language learners, things are seldom equal. As noted previously, BFL learners are a heterogeneous group but, at present, we have scant empirical evidence and, thus, understanding of the impact of this heterogeneity on their language learning. Studies on the relationship between input and learning outcomes in BFLA would be a welcome addition (see Pearson _et al._, 1999 for an example of such a study). Research on children at different ages of onset of dual language exposure (e.g. during the first vs. the second year) would provide valuable evidence concerning early effects of age and, in particular, whether there is a critical age at which one can distinguish second language learning from BFLA. There is little evidence on BFLA in children who are at risk for language delay or impairment (see Paradis _et al._, 2003, for an example). Evidence concerning the language development of these populations has important practical implications (e.g. should such children be encouraged to learn two languages) as well as theoretical implications (e.g. is impairment fundamental to the language learning capacity and, thus, likely to be evident in any language). Clearly, there is much more to be learned about BFLA.

References

Allen, S., Genesee, F., Fish, S. and Crago, M. (2000) _Grammatical Constraints on Early Bilingual Code-mixing: Evidence from Children Learning Inuktitut and English._ Paper presented at the Boston University Conference on Language Development.

Bates, E. and MacWhinney, B. (1987) Competition, variation, and language learning. In B. MacWhinney (ed.) _Mechanisms of Language Acquisition_ (pp. 157–94). Hillsdale, NJ: Lawrence Erlbaum.

Bedore, L. (2004) Morphosyntactic development. In B. Goldstein (ed.) _Bilingual Language Development and Disorders in Spanish-English Speakers_ (pp. 165–87). Baltimore: Brookes.

Bialystok, E. (2001) _Bilingualism in Development: Language, Literacy, & Cognition._ New York: Cambridge University Press.

Bosch, L. and Sebastián-Gallés, N. (2003a) Simultaneous bilinguals and the perception of a language-specific vowel contrast in the first year of life. _Language and Speech_ 46, 217–43.

Bosch, L. and Sebastián-Gallés, N. (2003b) Language experience and the perception of a voicing contrast in fricatives: Infant and adult data. In M.J. Solé, D. Recasens and J. Romero (eds) _International Congress of Phonetic Sciences_ (pp. 1987–90). Adelaide, Aus. Casual Productions.

Comeau, L. and Genesee, F. (2001) Bilingual children's repair strategies during dyadic communication. In J. Cenoz and F. Genesee (eds) _Trends in Bilingual Acquisition_ (pp. 231–56). Amsterdam: John Benjamins.

Comeau, L., Genesee, F. and Lapaquette, L. (2003) The modeling hypothesis and child bilingual code-mixing. _International Journal of Bilingualism_ 7, 113–26.

Cummins, J. (1981) The role of primary language development in promoting educational success for language minority students. In _Schooling and Language Minority Students: A Theoretical Framework_ (pp. 3–49). California State University, Los Angeles: Evaluation, Dissemination and Assessment Center.

De Houwer, A. (1990) _The Acquisition of Two Languages from Birth: A Case Study._ Cambridge, MA: Cambridge University Press.

De Houwer, A. (1995) Bilingual language acquisition. In P. Fletcher and B. MacWhinney (eds) _The Handbook of Child Language_ (pp. 219–50). Oxford: Blackwell.

Deuchar, M. (1999) Are function words non-language-specific in early bilingual two-word utterances? _Bilingualism: Language and Cognition_ 2, 23–34.

Deuchar, M. and Quay, S. (2000) _Bilingual Acquisition: Theoretical Implications of a Case Study._ Oxford: Oxford University Press.

Döpke, S. (1992) _One Parent, One Language: An Interactional Approach._ Amsterdam: John Benjamins.

Döpke, S. (2000a) Generation of and retraction from cross-linguistically motivated structures in bilingual first language acquisition. In F. Genesee (ed.) _Bilingualism: Language and Cognition_ (pp. 209–26). Cambridge: Cambridge University Press.

Döpke, S. (ed.) (2000b) _Cross-linguistic Structures in Simultaneous Bilingualism._ Amsterdam: John Benjamins.

Fennel, C.T., Polka, L. and Werker, J. (2002) _Bilingual Early Word Learner's Ability to Access Phonetic Detail in Word Forms._ Paper presented at the Fourth International Symposium on Bilingualism, Tempe, Arizona.

Gawlitzek-Maiwald, I. and Tracy, R. (1996) Bilingual bootstrapping. _Linguistics_ 34, 901–26.

Genesee, F. (1989) Early bilingual development: One language or two? _Journal of Child Language_ 16, 161–79.

Genesee, F. (2003a) Bilingualism and language impairment. In R.D. Kent (ed.) _MIT Encyclopedia of Communication Disorders_ (pp. 275–8). Cambridge, MA: MIT Press.

Genesee, F. (2003b) Rethinking bilingual acquisition. In J.M. deWaele (ed.) _Bilingualism: Challenges and Directions for Future Research._ Clevedon, UK: Multilingual Matters.

Genesee, F. and Nicoladis, E. (1995) Language development in bilingual preschool children. In E.E. Garcia and B. McLaughlin (eds) _Meeting the Challenge of Linguistic and Cultural Diversity in Early Childhood Education_ (pp. 18–33). New York: Teachers College Press.

Genesee, F. and Sauve, D. (2000) Grammatical constraints on child bilingual code-mixing. Paper presented at the Annual Conference of the American Association for Applied Linguistics, March 12, Vancouver, Canada.

Genesee, F., Tucker, G.R. and Lambert, W.E. (1975) Communication skills of bilingual children. _Child Development_ 46, 1010–14.

Genesee, F., Nicoladis, E. and Paradis, J. (1995a) Language differentiation in early bilingual development. _Journal of Child Language_ 22, 611–31.

Genesee, F., Paradis, J. and Wolf, L. (1995b) Lexical development in young preschool bilinguals. Unpublished paper. Psychology Department, McGill University.

Genesee, F., Boivin, I. and Nicoladis, E. (1996) Talking with strangers: A study of bilingual children's communicative competence. _Applied Psycholinguistics_ 17, 427–42.

Genesee, F., Paradis, J. and Crago, M. (2004) _Dual Language Development and Disorders._ Baltimore: Brookes.

Goodz, N.S. (1986) _Parental Language to Children in Bilingual Families._ Paper presented at the Third Congress of the World Allied Association of Infant Psychiatry and Related Disciplines, Stockholm.

Goodz, N.S. (1987) Parental language mixing in bilingual families. *Journal of Infant Mental Health* 10, 25–44.

Hulk, A. and Müller, N. (2000) Bilingual first language acquisition at the interface between syntax and pragmatics. *Bilingualism: Language and Cognition* 3, 227–44.

Johnson, C. and Lancaster, P. (1998) The development of more than one phonology: A case study of a Norwegian-English child. *International Journal of Bilingualism* 2/3: 265–300.

Juan-Garau, M. and Pérez-Vidal, C. (2000) Subject realization in the syntactic development of a bilingual child. In F. Genesee (ed.) *Bilingualism: Language and Cognition* 3, 173–92.

Kasuya, H. (1998) Determinants of language choice in bilingual children: The role of input. *International Journal of Bilingualism* 2, 327–46.

Köppe, R. (in press) Is codeswitching acquired? In J. MacSwan (ed.) *Grammatical Theory and Bilingual Codeswitching*. Cambridge, MA: MIT Press.

Lanza, E. (1997) *Language Mixing in Infant Bilingualism: A Sociolinguistic Perspective*. Oxford: Clarendon Press.

Lanza, E. (2001) Bilingual first language acquisition: A discourse perspective on language contact in parent-child interaction. In J. Cenoz and F. Genesee (eds) *Trends in Bilingual Acquisition* (pp. 201–30). Amsterdam: John Benjamins.

Leopold, W.F. (1939) *Speech Development of a Bilingual Child: Volume 1*. New York: AMS Press.

Leopold, W.F. (1949) *Speech Development of a Bilingual Child: Volume 3*. New York: AMS Press.

Leopold, W.F. (1978) A child's learning two languages. In E. Hatch (ed.) *Second Language Acquisition: A Book of Readings* (pp. 23–82). Rowley, MA: Newbury House.

MacSwan, J. (1999) *A Minimalist Approach to Intrasentential Code Switching*. New York: Garland.

Maneva, B. and Genesee, F. (2002) Bilingual babbling: Evidence for language differentiation in dual language acquisition. In B. Skarabela, S. Fish and A. H-J. Do (eds) *The Proceedings of the 26th Boston University Conference on Language Development* (pp. 383–92). Somerville, MA: Cascadilla Press.

McLaughlin, B. (1978) *Second-language Acquisition in Childhood*. Hillsdale, NJ: Lawrence Erlbaum.

Meisel, J.M. (1989) Early differentiation of languages in bilingual children. In K. Hyltenstam and L. Obler (eds) *Bilingualism Across the Lifespan: Aspects of Acquisition, Maturity and Loss* (pp. 13–40). Cambridge: Cambridge University Press.

Meisel, J.M. (1994) Code-switching in young bilingual children: The acquisition of grammatical constraints. *Studies in Second Language Acquisition* 16, 413–41.

Meisel, J.M. (2001) The simultaneous acquisition of two first languages: Early differentiation and subsequent development of grammars. In J. Cenoz and F. Genesee (eds) *Trends in Bilingual Acquisition* (pp. 11–42). Amsterdam: John Benjamins.

Müller, N. and Hulk, A. (2001) Crosslinguistic influence in bilingual language acquisition: Italian and French as recipient languages. *Bilingualism: Language and Cognition* 4, 1–21.

Myers-Scotton, C. (1997) *Duelling Languages: Grammatical Structure in Codeswitching*. Oxford: Clarendon Press.

Nicoladis, E. (1995) Code-mixing in young bilingual children. Unpublished PhD dissertation. Psychology Department, McGill University.

Nicoladis, E. (2002) What's the difference between 'toilet paper' and 'paper toilet'? French–English bilingual children's crosslinguistic transfer in compound nouns. *Journal of Child Language* 29, 843–63.

Nicoladis, E. and Genesee, F. (1998) Parental discourse and code-mixing in bilingual children. *International Journal of Bilingualism* 2, 85–100.

Nicoladis, E. and Secco, G. (2000) The role of a child's productive vocabulary in the language choice of a bilingual family. *First Language* 58, 3–28.

Oller, D.K., Eilers, R.E., Urbano, R. and Cobo-Lewis, A.B. (1997) Development of precursors to speech in infants exposed to two languages. *Journal of Child Language* 24, 407–26.

Paradis, J. (1996) Phonological differentiation in a bilingual child: Hildegard revisited. In A. Stringfellow, D. Cahana-Amitay, E. Hughes and A. Zukowski (eds) *Proceedings of the 20th Annual Boston University Conference on Language Development* (pp. 428–39). Somerville, MA: Cascadilla Press.

Paradis, J. (2001) Do bilingual two-year-olds have separate phonological systems? *International Journal of Bilingualism* 5, 19–38.

Paradis, J., & Genesee, F. (1996) Syntactic acquisition in bilingual children: Autonomous or interdependent? *Studies in Second Language Acquisition* 18, 1–25.

Paradis, J., Nicoladis, E. and Genesee, F. (2000) Early emergence of structural constraints on code-mixing: Evidence from French-English bilingual children. In F. Genesee (ed.) *Bilingualism: Language and Cognition* (pp. 245–61). Cambridge: Cambridge University Press.

Paradis, J., Crago, M. and Genesee, F. (2005) Representational and processing accounts of SLI: Evidence from object pronoun use by bilingual children. Unpublished MS. Department of Linguistics, University of Alberta, Edmonton, Canada.

Paradis, J., Crago, M., Genesee, F. and Rice, M. (2003) Bilingual children with specific language impairment: How do they compare with their monolingual peers? *Journal of Speech, Language and Hearing Research* 46, 113–27.

Pearson, B.Z., Fernández, S.C. and Oller, D.K. (1993) Lexical development in bilingual infants and toddlers: Comparison to monolingual norms. *Language Learning* 43, 93–120.

Pearson, B.Z., Fernández, S. and Oller, D.K. (1995) Cross-language synonyms in the lexicons of bilingual infants: One language or two? *Journal of Child Language* 22, 345–68.

Petersen, J. (1988) Word-internal code-switching constraints in a bilingual child's grammar. *Linguistics* 26, 479–93.

Petitto, L.A., Katerelos, M., Levy, B.G., Gauna, K., Tetreault, K. and Ferraro, V. (2001) Bilingual signed and spoken language acquisition from birth: Implications for the mechanism underlying early bilingual language acquisition. *Journal of Child Language* 28, 453–96.

Polka, L. and Sundara, M. (2003) Word segmentation in monolingual and bilingual infant learners of English and French (pp. 1021–24). *Proceedings of the 15th International Congress of Phonetic Sciences*, Barcelona, Spain.

Poplack, S. (1980) 'Sometimes I start a sentence in English y termino en Espanol': Toward a typology of code-switching. *Linguistics* 18, 581–618.

Poplack, S. (1987) Contrasting patterns of code-switching in two communities. In E. Wande, J. Anward, B. Nordberg, L. Steensland and M. Thelander (eds) *Aspects of Multilingualism* (pp. 51–77). Uppsala: Borgströms, Motala.

Poulin-Dubois, D. and Goodz, N. (2001) Language differentiation in bilingual infants: Evidence from babbling. In J. Cenoz and F. Genesee (eds) _Trends in Bilingual Acquisition_ (pp. 95–106). Amsterdam: John Benjamins.

Ronjat, J. (1913) _Le développement du langage observé chez un enfant bilingue._ Paris: Librairie Ancienne H. Champion.

Sundara, M., Polka, L. and Baum, S. (2004) Production of coronal stops by adult bilingual first language learners of Canadian English and Canadian French: Language-specific and language general constraints. Unpublished MS. Department of Communication Sciences and Disorders, McGill University.

Tucker, G.R. (1998) A global perspective on multilingualism and multilingual education. In. J. Cenoz and F. Genesee (eds) _Beyond Bilingualism: Multilingualism and Multilingual Education_ (pp. 3–15). Clevedon: Multilingual Matters.

Vihman, M.M. (1985) Language differentiation by the bilingual infant. _Journal of Child Language_ 12, 297–324.

Vihman, M. (1998) A developmental perspective on codeswitching: Conversations between a pair of bilingual siblings. _International Journal of Bilingualism_ 2, 45–84.

Volterra, V. and Taeschner, T. (1978) The acquisition and development of language by bilingual children. _Journal of Child Language_ 5, 311–26.

White, L. and Genesee, F. (1996) How native is near-native? The issue of ultimate attainment in adult second language acquisition. _Second Language Research_ 12, 233–65.

Yip, V. and Matthews, S. (2000) Syntactic transfer in a Cantonese-English bilingual child. _Bilingualism: Language and Cognition_ 3, 93–208.

Zentella, A.C. (1999) _Growing up Bilingual._ Malden, MA: Blackwell.

Chapter 5

Social Factors in Bilingual Development: The Miami Experience

REBECCA E. EILERS and BARBARA ZURER PEARSON and
ALAN B. COBO-LEWIS

Generations of immigrants to the US have followed the 'three-generation rule.' Adults typically remain monolingual in their heritage language, but their children become fluently bilingual, and their grandchildren largely monolingual English speakers. Thus, typically within three generations, immigrant families are thoroughly anglicized. This process has been documented in great detail for the Norwegian language in the Midwest (Haugen, 1953), and for an array of other heritage languages in America (Fishman, 1966) and elsewhere (Dorian, 1982; Lambert & Freed, 1982). Analyzing data from a large national database, Veltman (1988, 1990) established that the use and reported proficiency of Spanish in the various Hispanic communities in the US was also declining in accordance with the three-generation rule, and that, in fact, in many Spanish-speaking families, Spanish appeared to be disappearing even faster, i.e. within two generations.

In studies of families of five different ethnicities, Lambert and Taylor (1990, 1996) outline three major factors that contribute to language maintenance or loss: (1) parents' commitment to the heritage language, (2) the size and cohesiveness of the immigrant language group, and (3) the openness of the host community to the arrival of the immigrants and to a multicultural ideal. Others identify perceived 'threat' to a community's identity as the most critical factor in minority language maintenance (Southworth, 1980; Eilers et al., 2002). These authors observe that minority languages do not generally disappear when they are actively suppressed by an authority; rather, they may flourish. Catalan in Spain under Franco is a clear example; ancient Hebrew in the diaspora, another.

In Miami, without an explicit threat to encourage speakers to close ranks against English, there was nonetheless another factor in the Cuban exile that may have created an equivalent linguistic response. That is, when the first large waves of Cuban immigrants arrived in Miami in the early 1960s to flee the revolution of Fidel Castro, they were convinced that Castro would fall quickly and that they would be able to return and pick up their lives in Cuba. Toward that end, they recreated in Miami many of the institutions – schools, banks, trade associations, and even social clubs – that they hoped would be a bridge between their departure and imminent return to Cuba (Resnick, 1988). Those institutions created an Hispanic infrastructure in the community which persists to the present. It creates a strong, though permeable 'ghetto' that serves to bring new immigrants slowly into US society and maintains strong contacts between established members of the community and the newcomers. These factors might make Miami an ideal cultural and linguistic milieu for language maintenance in childhood bilinguals.

Although it is home to primarily Cuban and Central and South Americans who constitute only about 5% of US Hispanics (Boswell, 1998; Pérez, 1998), the structure of the Miami community provides a great range of linguistic options for Hispanic minority language speakers (Boswell, 1998; Boswell & Curtis, 1984). According to sociologists and geographers who study South Florida, the ethnic community there is both cohesive, creating a platform for minority language use, and of high social status, leaving it open to assimilation and access to the majority language from the earliest stages (Boswell, 1998; Boswell & Curtis, 1984). The presence of the Spanish language alongside that of English is very strong in the media, in boardrooms and government offices, and on the street. There is also a large, continuing immigration still in progress. Within the Hispanic community, there is a wide range of SES, home language practices, community language practices, language education alternatives, and language attitudes, to name the most important. It would seem then that a large cohesive minority population that enjoyed high status in its host community might promote greater maintenance of a minority language than would be found elsewhere. Could Miami be an exception to the three-generation rule?

In this paper we examine the efficacy of existing language practices in South Florida for maintaining the heritage language into the third generation. From reports in the literature and in data collected by the University of Miami Bilingualism Study Group (BSG), we seek to identify the factors that contribute to minority language maintenance among the most successful childhood English (majority language) learners of different generational status.

Types of Bilingual Development

Bilingualism can arise in many ways. It can arise in the homes of children while they are in their infancy (early, home or natural bilingualism), or late, upon entry to school in the host country (late sequential or school bilingualism). Commonly, school bilingualism begins at the Kindergarten level, but it may do so at any time during the school years. If children's arrival is late in their formal schooling, e.g. junior high or older, they may be termed 'very late sequential' learners. In addition, the acquisition of the first and second language in bilinguals may interact in important ways. Lambert (1977), characterized the learning of two languages as 'additive' or 'subtractive'. In additive situations, the two languages have sufficient support so that they can both develop without having one language diminish the performance of the other. In subtractive bilingualism, learning supports are withdrawn from the first language and devoted exclusively to the new one, with the result that the second language displaces the first. Finally, bilingual ability is not 'all or none'. In general it exists on a spectrum from limited use of the second language in circumscribed situations to full, interchangeable use of two languages in both public and private spheres. In situations where an individual is most likely to fall on that continuum, Hakuta and D'Andrea found that greater precision than 'generations' was necessary to describe the distinctions they observed. They adopted the concept of 'Immigration Depth' to help reduce sources of confusion based on factors that are tied to age at immigration, such as educational history, language usage in the home, or peer usage. Depths (Hakuta & D'Andrea, 1992: 81) are roughly equivalent to first, second, or third 'generation' but with important subcategories of first generation, as follows:

- Depth 1: children born abroad with age of arrival (AoA) to US > 10 years.
- Depth 2: AoA 6–10 years.
- Depth 3: born abroad, AoA 5 years or younger.
- Depth 4: born in US, both parents born abroad.
- Depth 5: born in US, at least one parent born in US.
- Depth 6: born in US, at least one parent and associated grandparent born in US.

Applied to the terms above, 'early or simultaneous bilinguals' are usually Depth 4 or higher, and sequential bilinguals are usually Depth 1 or 2, although they might be Depth 3 or even 4, depending on parents' depth. Our term 'very late sequential bilingual' (above) appears to be asking for a sub-division of Depth 1, 'born abroad, AoA after age 18'. Even among those with 'AoA after 18' one would need yet another sub-category of Depth 1 according to whether the individual came in time for formal (university) schooling in the new language.

Language alternatives for immigrants

The literature strongly identifies minority language maintenance as the key to effective bilingualism. That is, immigrant children by the end of their schooling, all develop some degree of English fluency – usually quite high – but whether they develop (or maintain) the heritage language is much more variable. At the community level, demographic factors such as those discussed above play deciding roles. At the level of the individual, whether the child will develop two languages involves a complex inter-relationship between language attitudes, language use, and language proficiency.

The bottom line for successful bilingualism is whether one uses two languages consistently, and the bottom line for developing two languages is the presence of long-term consistent exposure to two languages. If one's interlocutors can use only one language, then the language of the interaction is more or less fixed and the only choice is whether to speak with them or not. But if one's interlocutors can converse in either language, then the speakers make an abstract choice based on the value they accord to each language in the particular communicative setting. A key question for us in this investigation is how often and in what circumstances that abstract choice is decided in favor of the minority language.

Previous Studies

Hakuta and D'Andrea (1992) carried out a comprehensive investigation to see which were the most important factors in language choice and, where possible, to discern the direction of influences. Their subjects were 308 Mexican-American teenagers in a central California high school. Key variables studied were the proficiencies in Spanish and English, the various settings in which students used their languages, and student and family attitudes toward the two languages. The authors present a chart (p. 81) of their subjects' English and Spanish proficiency measures by immigration depth that reflects the three-generation rule; at Depth 1, Spanish-proficiency was the rule, while by Depth 6, English proficiency (at the expense of Spanish) was the rule. By Depth 5, the third generation, English ability remained similar to individuals at Depths 3 and 4, but Spanish ability had plummeted. Hakuta and D'Andrea (1992: 96) demonstrated a steep increase in English proficiency for the first 1 to 8 years of residency in the US. By contrast, there was nothing to suggest that children with low Spanish proficiency in American high school environments improved their Spanish without a significant change in their home or educational circumstances. Spanish was not absent from the lives of Depth 5 children, but it was restricted to fewer domains. It even shared the remaining domains with English. Preference for English increased systematically across depth. Maintenance of Spanish proficiency, on the other hand, was primarily tied to the adult language usage of the home. As adults in the family became more proficient in English, inside and outside the home, students' choice and use of language shifted rapidly toward English. The extent of the shift was not related to the students' Spanish fluency, but instead to their attitudes toward the two languages.

Lambert and Taylor (1996) studied junior high students and their families (56 high-SES and 56 low-SES) and extended Hakuta and D'Andrea's results, especially with respect to attitudes. They found attitude differences that were predictive of language choice to be strongly associated with mothers' social class. For working-class mothers, the emphasis was on encouraging their children to learn English in order to succeed in America, especially in school. For these mothers there was little explicit concern that emphasizing English would diminish Spanish use and Spanish identity. They seemed to have implicitly accepted a decline in Spanish to support English, what Lambert (1977) called a subtractive bilingualism and biculturalism. Children's advances in English in those families appeared to be at the expense of Spanish fluency and heritage culture maintenance. In contrast, middle-class mothers' conception of success for themselves and their children was associated more with the encouragement of Spanish competence, along with English. They showed a concern that the heritage language and culture be protected in the process of Americanization. In interviews, they articulated an additive form of bilingualism as a goal. In the working-class families, the mothers' language behavior had no effect on their children's Spanish, but a strong effect on their reported proficiency in English. By contrast in the mid-SES sample, mothers' language choice had little effect on the children's English, but a strong positive effect on their Spanish.

Together these two studies show the importance of the three major variables: generation (or depth), social class, and language attitudes, against a backdrop of minimal institutional support for the minority language. However, each study has tended to focus on a subset of these important variables. Lambert and Taylor (1996) studied largely Depth 4 individuals, limiting the explanatory power of Depth, while Hakuta and D'Andrea (1992) had little discussion of SES.

Spanish Maintenance by Generation: Miami Studies

The studies of the BSG, benefiting from the previous research, attempted to address all three factors – depth, attitudes, and SES. We report here on four studies carried out by the BSG that bear on the question of language maintenance: one each with toddlers, elementary school children, junior high, and college-age students. Three of the four studies have been reported elsewhere (Oller & Eilers, 2002a; Pearson, 1993; Pearson *et al.*, 1993, Pearson & Fernandez, 1994; Pearson & McGee, 1993), but in this chapter we highlight information that was not in focus in previous reports. Our primary question for this analysis is whether we can find evidence of Spanish language maintenance at higher immigration 'depth' than the three-generation rule would imply. In particular, did we note in Miami any mitigation in the sharp drop-off of Spanish use and ability after Depth 4, so clearly described by Hakuta and D'Andrea (1992)? Taking Veltman's findings of accelerated loss into consideration, it was also important to note whether there were signs of Spanish loss before Depth 5. How did the loss of Spanish coincide with gains in English? Did gains in English precede loss of Spanish, as suggested in Hakuta and D'Andrea? Further, we were interested in knowing how attitudes affected the outcomes of use and proficiency. Was greater desire for Spanish maintenance actually associated with more Spanish use and proficiency?

Language attitudes

The Miami studies took place among participants with positive attitudes about their bilingualism, who expected to pass it on to their children. For a longitudinal study of simultaneous bilingual language acquisition from age 3 to 36 months, 24 families were recruited who had firm plans to provide equal exposure to English and Spanish for their newborns through the first three years of life. Through interviews and questionnaires, we determined that the circumstances of their lives appeared to support their plans, in that there were speakers of both languages within their extended families who would be involved in their child's care. As it happened, only one of the 24 families ended up providing equal exposure to both languages throughout the three years of the study. The average exposure was 70:30 in favor of one or the other language. By age 3 (when the study ended), several children had already ceased to speak one or the other language on a regular basis.

Children were audiotaped bi-weekly or monthly in each language and took various tests in both languages. Although all of the children began their language learning in two languages, by study's end, six children would not speak enough Spanish (or in one case enough English) for a language sample or for other assessments in that language. As it happened, those children were spending less than 20% of their time in the environment of that language. They all learned some words and phrases of their non-primary language, but it did not appear to be enough to allow them to function comfortably in that language. Although there was an expressed plan to speak equal amounts of English and Spanish to their babies, five of these bilingual families faced a reality in which their children had insufficient exposure and little competence in Spanish.

A similar desire for bringing Spanish to the next generation was expressed universally by students taking language surveys in our lab. The surveys probed their language background, patterns of usage, and 'comfort level' in each language (Pearson & McGee, 1993), and included as the final question, 'Will you raise your children to speak Spanish?' In a sample of 110 junior high school students over 90% answered 'yes', regardless of whether they used Spanish actively in their own lives. A similar survey, conducted with 75 undergraduates in psychology courses at the University of Miami (Pearson & Andrews de Flores, unpublished manuscript) also yielded an overwhelming majority of students who said 'yes' and thereby portrayed a positive orientation toward Spanish. Only one student (realistically) questioned whether she would be in a situation that would allow her to teach her child Spanish. Thus, there appeared to be little attitudinal impediment to Spanish-language maintenance.

Language use/language choice

The parents of the bilingual infants studied by the BSG realized that their child would not learn Spanish if they, or a significant caregiver did not speak it, but they were unsuccessful in estimating the proportion of each language used by bilingual speakers. They were also not prepared for the difficulty they would encounter in maintaining Spanish as a medium of communication among family members and other caregivers. For example, one late-talking toddler at 17 months successfully switched her monolingual Spanish-speaking grandmother to speaking English, instead of having the grandmother use Spanish with the child as anticipated. There was also an expectation by many parents that two bilingual speakers would each use Spanish half of the time and English the other half. However, judging from the pattern of the children's vocabulary learning and the longitudinal questionnaires, about one-third of the children heard less Spanish (or English) than originally projected (Pearson *et al.*, 1997). Much of the failure to accurately predict language use stemmed from the inability to predict consistently the language that bilingual individuals would use with each other.

Language use between bilinguals

Scholars of minority language retention (and its flip side, attrition) point to the inherent instability of a bilingual environment. At the community level, bilingualism is generally considered a transitional phenomenon (at least where it is not institutionalized, as in Quebec or Switzerland, for example). According to scholars like Fishman (1966), unless two languages can avoid direct competition by establishing distinct domains for each language (as in 'diglossia'), one language gradually takes over and the other recedes. Bilingualism serves a function in a community when there are two monolingual groups who need a bridge of communication between them. In this situation bilingualism is greatly valued. But as more people become bilingual and fewer people remain monolingual, bilingualism outlives its purpose and tends to decline rapidly (Haugen, 1953; Eilers *et al.*, 2002).

Thus, when the majority of a population is bilingual, bilingualism is self-limiting. However, in the face of continuing immigration and a steady influx of monolingual speakers of a minority language, a minority language's community presence may be prolonged beyond its 'natural' life. In particular, if Spanish is institutionalized outside the home, it may have the potential to foster more use of the language in a greater number of contexts. Miami, in particular, has a reputation for significant amounts of Spanish in the public sphere. Former mayor Maurice Ferre has been quoted as saying of Miami 'You can go through life without having to speak English at all' (Morgan, 1983). More recently, it has been claimed that the wide-ranging Hispanization of Miami includes third generation speakers of Spanish (Kilborn, 2000).

Despite public perception to the contrary, we have several indications that young bilingual speakers in Miami and possibly even new immigrants are shifting toward monolingual English when they are speaking together. Extensive evidence of English language choice was provided by Oller and Eilers in *Language and Literacy in Bilingual Children* (henceforth *LLBC*) (2002a, Chapter 3). In this study of almost 1000 elementary school children in Miami, subjects were pro-actively selected to fit the cells of a nested design that crossed bilingualism vs. monolingualism with Language in the Home and with Language of the School (whether English-only in 'English immersion' or Spanish and English equally in '2-way' programs). Only families who stated that Spanish was used in the home at least half of the time were selected into the study. All children in the study were born in the US, and they were attending heavily Hispanic schools with approximately 35% of children being very recent immigrants (Dade County Public Schools, Office of Educational Accountability, 1985–2003).

There were 10 cells at each of three grade levels – Kindergarten, 2nd, and 5th grade (mean ages 5.9, 7.10 and 10.10, respectively). The eight cells for bilinguals presented a four-step gradation of Spanish exposure, from no Spanish in the school coupled with only half-Spanish at home, to half-Spanish at school coupled with all Spanish at home. For each grouping, there was both a high-SES and a low-SES cell. All children at the

Table 1 Table of *LLBC* factorial design, along with summary of highlighted findings among bilinguals, arranged from least Spanish to most Spanish exposure

1. Design										
Linguality	Monolingual		Bilingual							
School Language:			E_S — English Immersion (English only in school)				ES_S – 2-way (Eng & Spanish in school)			
Home Language:			English & Spanish in the home ES_H		Only Spanish in the home S_H		English & Spanish in the home ES_H		Only Spanish in the home S_H	
SES:	High	Low	High	Low	High	Low	High	Low	High	Low
N	141	107	91	77	86	101	85	80	82	102
			E_SES_H		E_SS_H		ES_SES_H		ES_SS_H	
2. Summary of Results										
		least Spanish ——————————————————> most Spanish								
		Number of Average-Range Scores in both English and Spanish summed across 9 subtests								
		2	1	3	3	4	5	5	6	

three grade levels were administered a battery of eight standardized tests in English from the Woodcock Language Proficiency Battery-Revised (1991) plus the PPVT-R (Dunn & Dunn, 1981), and all children in the bilingual cells were also administered Spanish versions of the same standardized tests (Woodcock & Muñoz-Sandoval, 1995; Dunn *et al.*, 1986). In addition, there were three experimental 'probe' studies on syntax, phonology and narrative. (See Oller & Eilers, *LLBC*, 2002a, for details). The full design is summarized in part 1 of Table 1.

The first bilinguals from the left, labeled 'E_SES_H' are those with the least Spanish exposure. They were in English immersion schools (indicated by the subscripted 'S') and reported equal amounts of English and Spanish in the home (as indicated by the subscripted 'H'). Their only exposure to Spanish was the half Spanish in the home and whatever Spanish they heard in the community outside of school. At the far right are those with the most Spanish input: ES_SS_H, half day Spanish in the school and only Spanish at home. We inferred from the parents' language proficiency self-report data (Oller & Eilers, 2002b) that the high-SES bilinguals would have more choices of settings in which English might be spoken and that low-SES children would have fewer choices, with Spanish the only possible choice in their homes. Thus, the group with highest Spanish exposure is the one with children from two-way schools, with only Spanish at home, coupled with low SES (ES$_S$S$_H$ low).

As part of the project, the project included a 'deep description' that confirmed the differences in language use between children experiencing the contrasting instructional methods that constituted a major independent variable. Bilingual observers with clipboards and tape recorders observed students and teachers and followed groups of students in classrooms, in hallways, to the library and the cafeteria, and gathering at bus loading times. Findings indicated that teachers and students complied quite well in classrooms: with minor exceptions they spoke in classrooms in the designated language of instruction.

It has been noted that while 'ethnic enclave' (private) schools in Miami did not offer instruction in the medium of Spanish (except for Spanish subject classes), the life of the schools – from custodians to cafeteria service and exchanges in the school office – took place primarily in Spanish (Garcia & Otheguy, 1988). But further *LLBC* observations uncovered a surprisingly strong move toward *English* throughout all schools: in unregulated peer conversations (private conversations at their desks or in the halls and in other environments less structured than classrooms) children conversed overwhelmingly in English, even in schools with a large instructional component in Spanish, even among students who spoke little or no English. The trend began at Kindergarten, even in heavily Hispanic neighborhood schools.

Perceptions of language use

Data collected by Pearson and McGee (1993) speak to attitude of language use among 110 junior high students (13–15 years old). While most of the children claimed Spanish as their first language, only 15% considered it the language in which they had the most proficiency. By contrast, students reported that their parents' proficiency was greater in Spanish than English, and 40% of the parents were reported to speak English poorly or not at all. Pearson and McGee (1993) found that Spanish was relegated largely to the home and, in the home, used mostly with parents. Even in the home, there was a high frequency of English usage among siblings signaling an erosion of Spanish in the home of even first generation immigrants (Depths 2 and 3).

A similar preference for English in multiple non-academic settings with friends and siblings emerged in the language background surveys of bilingual college students (Pearson, 1993; Pearson & Andrews de Flores, unpublished data). In surveys of college students born in the US or who had immigrated during elementary school (Depth 2, 3, 4, or 5), a strong preference for speaking English with peers was reported, despite the fact

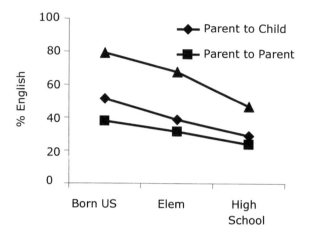

Figure 1 Relative frequency of language use by interlocutor, University of Miami Language Survey (Pearson & Andrews de Flores, unpublished)

that the students were balanced bilinguals by self-report, with verification from their PPVT and TVIP scores. Only students who immigrated later in life, at high school or university-age, reported preferring Spanish and having more than just a very few monolingual Spanish-speaking friends.

Figures 1–2 illustrate that, of the 75 University of Miami bilingual undergraduates surveyed by Pearson and Andrews de Flores, only those who immigrated after elementary school (Depth 1) chose Spanish more than 20–30% of the time when speaking with peers. About half the students reported that they were born in the US and that they remained bilingual and continued to use Spanish at home. Figure 1 illustrates that these students reported using on average nearly as much Spanish as English with parents and in activities that involved parents (e.g. church, dinner table conversation). In activities offering more choice of language use – for example, with media (movies, books, TV) – their choices were similar to those of Hakuta and D'Andrea's high school bilinguals: they chose English. Even the very popular Latin music accounted for only a third of their music listening preferences and activities.

Preference for English was also reflected in the language background of the friends with whom the students reported associating. This differed according to the students' age of arrival in the US. Figure 3 shows the relative number of bilingual, monolingual English, and monolingual Spanish-speaking friends aggregated by Depth cohort. Simultaneous (or

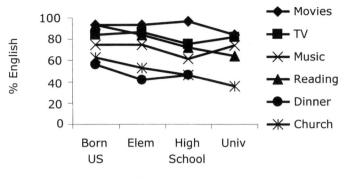

Figure 2 Relative frequency of language use by activity, University of Miami Language Survey (Pearson & Andrews de Flores, unpublished)

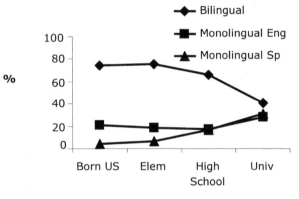

Figure 3 Linguality of friends, University of Miami Language Survey (Pearson & Andrews de Flores, unpublished)

early bilingual) children in the Pearson and Andrews de Flores survey (half of whom grew up in Miami), and those who came to Miami during preschool or elementary school, also reported having mostly bilingual friends, about 80% on average. There appears to be little linguistic pressure for these bilinguals to choose Spanish for their social life.

From a number of data sets, then, a similar picture is painted about language preference and use. English emerges as the preferred language early in the lives of infants and children who are born to first generation households or who immigrate to the US. The question remains whether a functional level of both languages is attained and maintained during assimilation.

Proficiency in two languages

The true measure of a bilingual capacity is the ability to carry on daily discourse in two languages. Therefore, it is important to ask how well young Miamians speak Spanish and English. Can they get along in both? Can they excel in both? The BSG data show that the range of exposure to each language produced a range of capacity in each language, closely related, but not entirely so, to language exposure (Pearson *et al.*, 1997). Gathercole (2002: 253) suggests that in several domains, bilinguals may take longer to gain a 'critical mass' of exposure and thus to reach levels similar to monolinguals in each language. For the 24 infants in Pearson *et al.* (1993), productive vocabulary was generally below monolingual norms in each language, but when total vocabulary in the two languages was summed (even without double-counting words known in both languages), the total conceptual vocabulary of bilinguals equaled monolingual norms. Receptive vocabulary was even more robust. Levels of receptive vocabulary in one language at a time were comparable to monolingual norms. Because of lack of normative guidelines, though, babies can give only a partial answer to questions of relative proficiency.

The college survey and vocabulary testing reported earlier also provide a partial answer to the question of proficiency. In Figure 4 we graph English and Spanish vocabulary scores by Depth. It shows a pattern much like Hakuta and D'Andrea (1992: 81) for Depths 1 to 4. (We add additional data from the older immigrants at Depth 'pre-1', those who came after high school, to extend the comparison.) In the comparison of vocabulary knowledge in English and Spanish, there was a significant interaction of Depth by Language, $F(3, 71) = 9.85$, $p < 0.0001$. English means differed by Depth, $F(3, 71) = 3.31$, $p = 0.024$, while Spanish means, up to Depth 4, showed no significant change $F(3, 71) = 2.12$, $p = 0.11$. *Post hoc* pairwise comparisons (Tukey HSD) showed that students at Depth 4 had better English than those at Depth 1 (mean difference = 10.3, $p = 0.025$). Unlike Hakuta and D'Andrea, English at Depth 2 did not differ significantly from Depth 4 (Mean diff. = 2.286, $p = 0.595$). Spanish vocabulary, as in Hakuta and D'Andrea, did not differ reliably at any depth between Depth 1 and 4.

Aside from mean differences, it is important to note that all of the means for these groups, even at the lower Depths for English and the higher Depths for Spanish, were in the average range or above average. These results suggest that Spanish vocabulary appears to remain at a functional

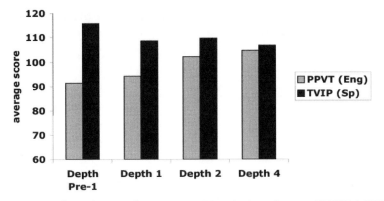

Figure 4 English and Spanish Receptive Vocabulary Scores (PPVT & TVIP, Dunn & Dunn, 1981; Dunn *et al.*, 1986) by Depth (University of Miami Language Survey, Pearson & Andrews de Flores, unpublished)

level as English scores rise across Depth (although there does appear in the graph to be some non-significant trade-off).

This *LLBC* study tested the strength of the effect of three major factors – home language practices, language(s) of instruction in the school, and SES – on an array of outcome measures in both English and Spanish. Children at all three grades took nine standardized tests of oral and written language in English, and all bilingual children also took them in Spanish. (For our discussions here, we look principally at 5th grade outcomes, when the different instructional methods or potential 'additive' or 'subtractive' factors will have had time to take effect.)

The analysis summarized in Table 2 rests on the findings in *LLBC* chapters 4–5 (Cobo-Lewis *et al.*, 2002a,b) but examines the comparison of mean scores in the two languages for the individual cells. For each of the nine standardized tests, Table 2 lists the groups of bilingual 5th[th] graders scoring at least average (mean standard score 85 or higher) in both English and Spanish.

Two findings stand out. (1) Receptive language skills (reading and receptive vocabulary) were more likely to be adequate in both languages than expressive language skills (writing and tests that require a spoken response, as opposed to a recognition response, or an interpretation of what is presented). By 5th grade, all cells were in the average range in English reading scores (Passage Comprehension, Letter-Word, and Word Attack). In Spanish, all children were in the average range in basic reading (Word Attack and Letter-Word) and all cells in two-way schools were also average in Spanish Passage Comprehension. This may reflect an additive

Table 2 Summary of cells scoring in the average range in English and Spanish standardized scores in tests of language and literacy (5th graders)

Test	Number of cells	School Lang/ Home Lang/ SES
Productive Vocabulary	none	–
Proofing	1 cell	ES_S S_H low
Dictation	2 cells	ES_S S_H high ES_S S_H low
Oral Vocabulary	3 cells	E_S S_H low ES_S ES_H low ES_S S_H low
Receptive Vocabulary	4 cells	E_S S_H high ES_S ES_H high ES_S ES_H low ES_S S_H high
Passage Comprehension	4 cells	ES_S ES_H high ES_S ES_H low ES_S S_H high ES_S S_H low
Verbal Analogies	7 cells	E_S ES_H high E_S S_H high E_S S_H low ES_S ES_H high ES_S ES_H low ES_S S_H high ES_S S_H low
Word Attack (same results for Letter word)	8 cells	E_S ES_H high E_S ES_H low E_S S_H high E_S S_H low ES_S ES_H high ES_S ES_H low ES_S S_H high ES_S S_H low

process, an interpretation which is supported by factor analysis (Cobo-Lewis *et al.*, 2002) where literacy skills in both languages loaded on a single factor. Thus, Spanish and English learning seemed to be mutually beneficial resulting in bilingual proficiency in reading. (2) In contrast, expressive language skills (productive vocabulary and writing [dictation and proofreading]) did not show a similar ability in both English and Spanish, and were mastered in both languages by relatively few children. To have adequate expressive proficiency in both languages, it would seem one needs greater amounts of exposure than one would require for receptive skills.

Part 2 of Table 1 shows, for each bilingual cell of the design, the number of the nine sub-tests that fell in the average range in both English and Spanish. We see that the two-way schools have a clear advantage in helping children achieve proficiency in two languages regardless of the language of the home. By 5th grade, the English of children in two-way schools was similar to that of children in English Immersion schools and their Spanish was markedly better.

The two-way (ES_S) groups, those with the most Spanish exposure on a daily basis, were most likely to be adequate in both languages in most domains. As Part 2 of Table 1 shows, English Immersion cells (E_S), the ones with the least Spanish exposure, were least likely to be adequate in both languages. Similarly, when one looks at the non-standardized results in the narrative probe study (Pearson, 2002), E_S children with English and Spanish in the home (E_SES_H-low) were the only group whose mean on language measures in Spanish were nearly a standard deviation lower in 5th grade than in 2nd.

So, which factors matter most for keeping both languages?

From the point of view of maintaining Spanish, it is just those students with no schooling in Spanish and lesser Spanish in the home who appear to lose ground in Spanish from 2nd to 5th grade. Having half-Spanish in the home does not appear sufficient for most children to develop an acceptable level of expressive language nor literacy in Spanish (excepting phonics) without explicit teaching, as in the two-way schools.

From the point of view of promoting English, it seems that in some domains, having half English in the home compensates for having only half English in the school. But having no English at home (S_H) and only half English at school (ES_S) seems to depress English vocabulary scores, even receptive vocabulary. English expressive *and* receptive vocabulary are the two domains in which the low SES children with only Spanish at home in two-way schools (ES_SS_H-low) showed the least proficiency.

Still, there is a case to be made that for expressive capability in both languages; the most effective combination is the two-way school, only Spanish at home, low SES (ES_SS_H-low). The cell with highest scores overall is two-way, English and Spanish at home, high SES (ES_SES_H-high), but it is the ES_SS_H-low children who were most balanced between the languages in more domains. This most-balanced cell is the one with the most Spanish exposure in Table 2, reflecting perhaps that in an English-dominant society, maximal Spanish exposure is needed to maintain the most balanced bilingualism, provided that threshold English exposure is also achieved.

Adding depth

To see whether the same principles hold as depth increases (as the children move from 2nd to 3rd generation), we added a new variable (Depth 4 or Depth 5) to the analysis of the *LLBC* data. The database for the multi-factor study provides information on the birthplace of two parents of study children and the number of years those parents resided in the US for 95% of the bilinguals. Of those children, 75% were Depth 4 (both parents born abroad), and 25% were Depth 5 (at least one parent born in US). (Only 16 children had both parents born in the US.) At Kindergarten, 29% of the bilingual children were Depth 5, at 2nd grade, 26% were Depth 5 and at 5th grade, only 17% were Depth 5.

Figure 5 illustrates that although there are (by design) approximately equal numbers of high and low SES families in the study overall, there are

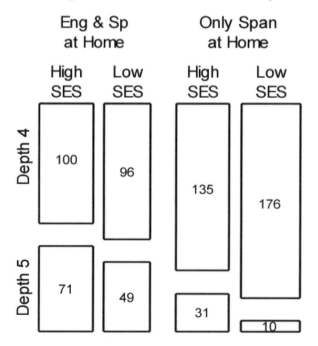

Figure 5 Relationship among Depth, SES, and Language Spoken in the Home in the *LLBC* design (Oller & Eilers, 2002a). In this mosaic plot (Hartigan & Kleiner, 1981) the area of a rectangle is proportional to the number of corresponding children (written in the middle of each rectangle)

associations between Depth and the study design variables. The biggest effects are that Depth 5 is associated with higher SES and that Depth 5 is associated with speaking less Spanish at home. Among the Depth 4 families (both parents born abroad), not surprisingly, there are more homes with only Spanish than with English and Spanish together in both high and low SES cells. Among Depth 5 families, the proportions are reversed, with more English and Spanish than Spanish-only. There is also a three-way association among Depth, SES, and Home Language, $\chi^2(1) =$ 6.06, $p = 0.014$. In the low-SES cells, the ratio of only-Spanish to English-and-Spanish households at Depth 5 is 1 in 5 (10:49), whereas in the high-SES cells the ratio is closer to 1 in 2 (31 vs. 71). This disproportion is in the direction of Lambert and Taylor's (1996) claim that high-SES mothers were more committed to Spanish language maintenance: among families with both parents born in the US, high-SES families may have been more likely to enforce a practice of only Spanish in the home than were their low-SES counterparts. Another way of viewing the three-way association is that the relationship between Home Language and Depth was especially strong for low-SES families – although more English is spoken at home at Depth 5 for both high- and low-SES families, the high-SES families are more apt than the low-SES families to continue speaking only Spanish at home even when both parents are fluent in English.

We re-ran the Anova of the 5th grade scores ($N = 213$). Because Depth was associated with other factors in the *LLBC* design, we statistically controlled for those other factors and their interactions. Results, plotted in Figure 6, mirror the Hakuta and D'Andrea findings for the move from Depth 4 to Depth 5 – Depth had little or no effect on English scores. Depth 5 English scores exceeded Depth 4 English scores on only 4 of 9 sub-tests, consistent with the hypothesis of no overall effect in English. The largest effect among the English scores was only 3 points (Word Attack, $p < 0.05$), and it actually favored Depth 4 over Depth 5. In Spanish, by contrast Depth 4 scores exceeded Depth 5 scores on all 9 sub-tests (sign test rejects hypothesis of no overall effect, $p < 0.004$, and individual t tests are significant [$p < 0.05$] on 5 of 9 sub-tests). Depth had a substantial effect on Spanish Picture Vocabulary and PPVT scores (9–10 points), a smaller but still substantial effect on phonics scores, Word Attack and Letter–Word (6–8 points), and a marginal effect on other Spanish literacy scores (0 to 3 points, $p < 0.05$ for Passage Comprehension).

In the two phonics tests, the effect is greater in Spanish than in English, but surprisingly even the English effect favors Depth 4. This may reflect our speculation in *LLBC* (Cobo-Lewis *et al.*, 2002:130; also Labov, 2004) that there was a beneficial effect on English phonics for those who had also learned the more regular Spanish phonics. The pattern observed here may

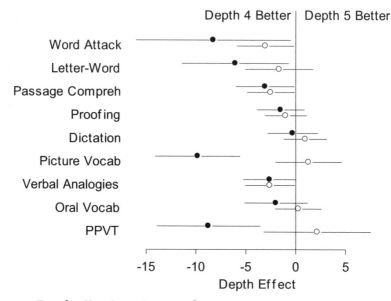

Figure 6 Depth effect by subtest in the *LLBC* data (Oller & Eilers, 2002a). Filled circles are Spanish; open circles are English. Bars indicate non-simultaneous 95% confidence intervals

be a reflection of the lesser benefit to English when Spanish is weaker, as in Depth 5. The picture in the two vocabulary tests appears more straightforward: Depth 5 benefits English by only 1–2 standardized points (a non-significant difference from zero), but Depth 5 loses 9–10 points, two-thirds of a standard deviation in Spanish.

It appears that in this study, Depth has only a small effect, if any, on scores that measure how children perform academic tasks in each language, but has a greater effect when the focus of the measure is the language itself. Pearson *et al.* (1996) and Oller (2003, and in preparation) reanalyzed the *LLBC* data and described what Oller calls a 'profile effect'. That is, otherwise competent bilinguals appear to have disproportionately low levels of vocabulary. Whereas in monolinguals, low levels of vocabulary are associated with poor academic performance, a small vocabulary does not appear to be as much of a handicap for bilinguals, except for scores on specific tests of vocabulary. This phenomenon was also shown in Pearson (1993), but the mechanism behind it is still not known.

Hakuta and D'Andrea (1992: 83) showed adult language choice to shift dramatically from Depth 4 and 5, from 'mostly Spanish' to 'more English than Spanish'. It therefore occurred to us that Depth might be confounded with Home Language. Using Anova with Type III sums of squares, we tested the effect of Depth independently from the other independent variables (Language of the Home, Language of the School, and SES) on a dependent measure combining all Spanish scores. The Depth effect [$F(1, 212) = 10.837, p = 0.001$] and the Home Language effect [$F(1, 212) = 8.416, p = 0.004$] were both significant, and there was no interaction involving Depth and Home Language [$F(1, 212) < 1, p = 0.933$]. The two factors are thus distinct statistically. However, perhaps our Home Language variable, with just two categories (Spanish-only and English and Spanish equally) was incapable of showing an effect of 'more English than Spanish'. Although all families perceived themselves as speaking English and Spanish equally in the home, there may actually have been differences within the groups. There is also, no doubt, more assimilation among Depth 5 families. The Depth variable may capture such differences.

In summary, as Depth increased from 4 to 5, English scores remained stable but Spanish scores decreased. What does this mean for theories that insist Spanish must be lost in order for English to improve? Although an inverse relationship between English and Spanish is sometimes observed in the short run (e.g. Goldenberg *et al.*, 2005), it appears that in studies of language achievement in the long term, English shows marked improvement before Spanish declines. The decline in Spanish in these data (as in Hakuta and D'Andrea's) does not appear to be so directly related to gains in English and vice versa.

Conclusions

Despite Miami's rich cultural diversity and the value it puts on Spanish language and culture, despite the existence of a high-SES community infrastructure with political and financial power, and despite high rates of immigration of Spanish-speaking peoples to Miami, Spanish appears to be losing ground as it is elsewhere in the US. In this climate, two-way schools offer little if any threat to English proficiency. Evidence suggests that by 5th grade, children in two-way schools are as proficient in English as their counterparts in English immersion schools. There is also evidence that English immersion schools do little to support Spanish proficiency, and in those schools there is evidence of weakness in Spanish by 5th grade in most language domains.

It also appears that when Spanish is weakened in the home, there is little prospect for language maintenance, even though there is a cultural desire for it. Even in Miami, the general Spanish ambiance outside the home supports only a minimal level of 'passive' Spanish when its use is progressively weakened, generation by generation, in the home.

Ironically, the greatest threat to the preservation of Spanish in Miami and similar communities elsewhere may be that the language is perceived as unthreatened by American culture and the English language. This perception may act to curb motivation to promote Spanish language fluency with vigor. When parents and grandparents insist that children use the minority language in daily discourse, proficiency improves. Homes that allow English to replace Spanish in a growing number of familial contexts lose Spanish without a notable boost to English. A potent example of the lack of perceived need to promote Spanish is the small number of two-way schools, one of the few resources that may effectively help retain bilingualism for a while yet.

Acknowledgements

This research was supported in part by a grant from the National Institutes of Health (R01 HD 030762) to D. Kimbrough Oller (P.I.) and Rebecca E. Eilers (Co-P.I.). We wish to thank the many members of the Bilingualism Study Group who have assisted with a broad array of research over the years.

References

Boswell, T.D. and Curtis, J.R. (1984) *The Cuban-American Experience: Culture, Images, and Perspectives.* Totawa, NJ: Rowman & Allanheld.

Boswell, Thomas D. (1998) A demographic profile of Cuban Americans. In T. Boswell (ed.) *Cuban Americans* [electronic resource]: NK08. New Haven, CT.: Human Relations Area Files.

Cobo-Lewis, A.B., Eilers, R.E., Pearson, B.Z. and Umbel, V.C. (2002) Chapter 6: Interdependence of Spanish and English knowledge in language and literacy among bilingual children. In D.K. Oller and R.E. Eilers (eds) *Language and Literacy in Bilingual Children* (pp. 118–34). Clevedon, UK: Multilingual Matters.

Cobo-Lewis, A.B., Pearson, B.Z., Eilers, R.E. and Umbel, V.C. (2002a) Chapter 5: Effects of bilingualism and bilingual education on oral and written Spanish skills: A multifactor study of standardized test outcomes. In D.K. Oller and R.E. Eilers (eds) *Language and Literacy in Bilingual Children* (pp. 98–117). Clevedon, UK: Multilingual Matters.

Cobo-Lewis, A.B., Pearson, B.Z., Eilers, R.E. and Umbel, V.C. (2002b) Chapter 4: Effects of bilingualism and bilingual education on oral and written English skills: A multifactor study of standardized test outcomes. In D.K. Oller and R.E. Eilers (eds) *Language and Literacy in Bilingual Children* (pp. 64–97). Clevedon, UK: Multilingual Matters.

Dade County Public Schools, Office of Educational Accountability (1985–2003) Statistical Abstracts/ District and School Profiles.

Dorian, N.C. (1982) Language loss and maintenance in language contact situations. In R.D. Lambert and B.T. Freed (eds) *The Loss of Language Skills.* Rowley, MA: Newbury.

Dunn, L. and Dunn, L. (1981) *Peabody Picture Vocabulary Test-Revised.* Circle Pines, MN: American Guidance Services.

Dunn, L., Padilla, E., Lugo, D. and Dunn, L. (1986) *Test de Vocabulario en Imagenes Peabody –Adaptacion Hispanoamericana [Peabody Picture Vocabulary Test – Latin American Adaptation]*. Circle Pines, MN: American Guidance Services.

Eilers, R.E., Oller, D.K. and Cobo-Lewis, A.B. (2002) Chapter 3. Bilingualism and cultural assimilation in Miami Hispanic children. In D.K. Oller and R.E. Eilers (eds) *Language and Literacy in Bilingual Children* (pp. 43–63). Clevedon, UK: Multilingual Matters.

Fishman, J. (1966) *Language Loyalty in the U.S.* The Hague: Mouton.

Garcia, O. and Otheguy, R. (1988) The language situation of Cuban Americans. In S.L. MacKay and S.C. Wong (eds) *Language Diversity: Problem or Resource?* Rowley, MA: Newbury.

Gathercole, V.C. (2002) Chapter 10: Monolingual and bilingual acquisition: Learning different treatment of *that*-trace phenomena in English and Spanish. In D.K. Oller and R.E. Eilers (eds) *Language and Literacy in Bilingual Children* (pp. 220–54). Clevedon, UK: Multilingual Matters.

Goldenberg, C., Rezaei, A. and Fletcher, J. (2005) *Home Use of English and Spanish and Spanish-Speaking Children's Oral Language and Literacy Achievement.* Paper presented at the annual meeting of the American Educational Research Association, Montreal.

Hakuta, K. and D'Andrea, D. (1992) Some properties of bilingual maintenance and loss in Mexican background high-school students. *Applied Linguistics* 13, 72–99.

Hartigan, J.A. and Kleiner, B. (1981) Mosaics for contingency tables. In W.F. Eddy (ed.) *Computer Science and Statistics: Proceedings of the 13th Symposium on the Interface* (pp. 286–273). New York: Springer-Verlag.

Haugen, E. (1953) *The Norwegian Language in America. Volume I, The Bilingual Community.* Philadelphia: University of Pennsylvania Press.

Kilborn, P.T. (2000, January 16) Custody case is overshadowing shift among Cuban immigrants. *New York Times.*

Labov, W. (2004) *Testing the Effectiveness, Sustainability and Scalability of an Individualized Reading Program for African-American, Latino and Euro-American Inner-City Children.* Paper presented at annual meeting of American Speech-Language-Hearing Association, Philadelphia.

Lambert, W.E. (1977) Effects of bilingualism on the individual: Cognitive and sociocultural consequences. In P.A. Hornby (ed.) *Bilingualism: Psychological, Social, and Educational Implications* (pp. 15–28). New York: Academic Press.

Lambert, R.D. and Freed, B.T. (eds) (1982) *The Loss of Language Skills.* Rowley, MA: Newbury.

Lambert, W.E. and Taylor, D.M. (1990) *Coping with Cultural and Racial Diversity in Urban America.* New York: Praeger.

Lambert, W.E. and Taylor, D.M. (1996) Language in the lives of ethnic minorities: Cuban-American families in Miami. *Applied Linguistics* 17, 477–500.

Morgan, T. (1983) The latinization of America. *Esquire* May 47–56.

Oller, D.K. (2003, May) *The Distributed Characteristic in Bilingual Learning: Effects in Various Realms of Grammar.* Paper presented at the 4th International Symposium on Bilingualism (ISB4). Tempe, Arizona.

Oller, D.K. and Eilers, R.E. (eds) (2002) *Language and Literacy in Bilingual Children.* Clevedon, UK: Multilingual Matters.

Oller, D.K. and Eilers, R.E. (2002b) Chapter 2: An integrated approach to evaluating effects of bilingualism in Miami school children. *Language and Literacy in Bilingual Children.* Clevedon, UK: Multilingual Matters.

Pearson, B.Z. (1993) Predictive validity of the Scholastic Aptitude Test for Hispanic bilingual students. *Hispanic Journal of the Behavioral Sciences* 15, 342–56.

Pearson, B.Z. (2002) Chapter 7: Narrative competence in bilingual school children in Miami. In D.K. Oller and R.E. Eilers (eds) *Language and Literacy in Bilingual Children* (pp. 135–74). Clevedon, UK: Multilingual Matters.

Pearson, B.Z. and McGee, A. (1993) Language choice in Hispanic-background junior high school students in Miami: 1988 update. In A. Roca and J. Lipski (eds) *Studies in Anthropological Linguistics*. Mouton de Gruytere.

Pearson, B.Z. and Fernandez, S. (1994) Patterns of interaction in the lexical development in two languages of bilingual infants. *Language Learning* 44, 617–53.

Pearson, B.Z., Fernandez, S. and Oller, D.K. (1993) Lexical development in bilingual infants and toddlers: Comparison to monolingual norms. *Language Learning* 43, 93–120.

Pearson, B.Z., Fernandez, S., Lewedag, V. and Oller, D.K. (1997) Input factors in lexical learning of bilingual infants (ages 10 to 30 months). *Applied Psycholinguistics* 18, 41–58.

Pearson, B.Z., Oller, D.K., Umbel, V.M. and Fernandez, M.C. (1996, October) *The Relation of Lexical Knowledge to Measures of Literacy and Narrative Discourse in Monolingual and Bilingual Children.* Paper presented at Second Language Research Forum, Tucson, Arizona.

Pérez, L. (1998) Cuban Miami. In T. Boswell (ed.) *Cuban Americans* [electronic resource]: NK08. New Haven, CT.: Human Relations Area Files.

Resnick, M. (1988) Beyond the ethnic community: Spanish language roles and maintenance in Miami. *International Journal of Sociology of Language* 69, 89–104.

Southworth, F.C. (1980) Indian bilingualism: some educational and linguistic implications. In V. Teller and S.J. White (eds) *Studies in Child Language and Multilingualism* (Vol. 345, pp. 121–46). New York: New York Academy of Sciences.

Veltman, C. (1988) Modelling the language shift process of Hispanic immigrants. *International Migration Review* 22 (4), 545–62.

Veltman, C. (1990) The status of the Spanish language in the United States at the beginning of the 21st century. *International Migration Review* 24 (1), 108–23.

Woodcock, R. (1991) *Woodcock Language Proficiency Battery: English Form – Revised.* Chicago: Riverside.

Woodcock, R. and Muñoz-Sandoval (1995) *Bateria Woodcock-Munoz: Pruebas de Aprovechiamiento-revisada [Woodcock Language Proficiency Battery: Spanish Form – Revised].* Chicago: Riverside.

Chapter 6

Developing Literacy in English-language Learners: An Examination of the Impact of English-only Versus Bilingual Instruction

DIANE AUGUST, MARGARITA CALDERÓN, MARÍA CARLO and MICHELLE NUTTALL

It is critical that we have a better understanding of the attributes of programs that contribute to positive literacy outcomes for English-language learners because of their overall low literacy performance. For example, state-by-state data collected by the US Department of Education indicate that only two states of 36 that reported such data – Alabama and Michigan – met their targets for English-language learners' scores on standardized reading/language arts during the 2003–2004 school year. One important attribute of instructional programs for language minority students is the language in which they are educated. This chapter explores literacy outcomes for students instructed in two types of programs – those that use the native language for some period of time for core academics (i.e. transitional bilingual education programs) and those that do not use the native language in any regular or systematic way (i.e. English as a second language [ESL] and its variants, such as structured immersion and content-based ESL, as well as 'submersion programs').

There has been an ongoing debate about which model is most effective (August & Hakuta, 1997). Those that support native language instruction argue that first language proficiency can be promoted in school at no cost to the development of second language proficiency because once developed, the cognitive capacities underlying language skills such as reading and writing can be applied to another language (Cummins, 1978, 1979, 1980,

1984; Lambert, 1987; Toukomaa & Skutnabb-Kangas, 1977). Proponents of programs that do not use the native language in any regular way argue that time on task is important and less time in second language instruction hinders its development (Rossell & Baker, 1996).

There have been a series of reviews over the past 25 years that address this question; they have reached different conclusions about the effectiveness of bilingual instruction with regard to building proficiency in a second language. Most studies examine outcomes in language arts, but some also assess content knowledge, particularly math. In an early review, Baker and de Kanter (1981) conclude: 'The case for the effectiveness of transitional bilingual education is so weak that exclusive reliance on this instruction method is clearly not justified' (p. 1). Working from Baker and de Kanter (1981), as well as Baker and Pelavin (1984) reviews, Rosell and Baker (1996) concluded that most methodologically adequate studies found that transitional bilingual education was not more effective than programs with English only instruction: 'Thus the research evidence does not support transitional bilingual education as a superior form of instruction for limited English proficient children' (p. 7). Willig (1985) conducted a meta-analysis of the studies reviewed by Baker and de Kanter (1981) and concluded that bilingual education does work (better than not having anything in place). Greene (1998) re-analyzed the set of studies cited by Rossell and Baker and found that the evidence favored programs that made significant use of native language instruction (effect size + 0.21).

Differences in study outcomes can be attributed in part to differences in the questions asked, the methodological standards set for study inclusion, and the methods used to synthesize the studies. With regard to the questions asked, for example, the nature of the samples differed depending on the question (e.g. Willig eliminated studies conducted outside the United States whereas Baker and de Kanter did not; Green eliminated studies if students had not been in the bilingual program for at least an academic year before the effects of the programs were measured whereas Rossell and Baker did not). Standards for methodological rigor also differed across the reviews (e.g. Greene eliminated 61 studies that had been included by Rosell and Baker because he required that previous test scores as well as at least some of the individual demographic factors that influence test scores such as family income or parental education be included as covariates in the quasi-experimental studies). Only two of the authors used meta-analytic techniques and as such their syntheses took into account the program effects in each study, even if they were not statistically significant. As Greene points out, 'simply counting positive and negative effect sizes is less precise than a meta-analysis because it does not consider the magnitude or confidence level of effects' (p. 11).

Of note is that study conclusions from the syntheses just reviewed did not actually differ that much. Many of the reviews that have been labeled as anti-bilingual education did not find that use of the native language was worse than English-only instruction, merely that there were no overall differences. The two reviews favorable to bilingual instruction found differences in favor of native language instruction, but the effect sizes were small to moderate. Interesting, Willig's results indicate that the better the technical quality of the study – for example, if a study used random assignment as opposed to creating *post hoc* comparison groups – the larger the effects. These results raise an interesting possibility: that the 'effectiveness' debate may really be a debate carried on at the relatively superficial level of a study's technical quality.

Although the authors of reviews may have disagreed on the effectiveness of bilingual education, they do not disagree about the overall quality of the studies; all had to eliminate large numbers of studies from their reviews: Baker and de Kanter (1981) found only 28 of 300 studies acceptable; Rossell and Baker (1996) eliminated 128 studies; Willig (1985) eliminated 177 studies; Green (1998) eliminated all but 11 studies. A flaw in many of the studies was the failure to equate experimental and control groups on important variables. For example, in some instances students in the control groups were students who had been exited from bilingual programs (Stern, 1975; Danoff *et al.*, 1978); in other instances students in the control groups were students who had not needed bilingual services. Willig found that in instances of the latter, the mean effect size for the bilingual group was one of the lowest in her study and favored the English-only groups. However, when the comparison children did qualify for the program but were eliminated through the process of random assignment, the effect size favored the bilingual group. Language exposure in the neighborhood and school setting also influenced the two groups. In the studies Willig reviewed, regardless of whether the language was English or non-English, effect sizes were positive for the bilingual program groups when both treatment groups had the same neighborhood language. On the other hand, when the neighborhood language of the comparison group was English and the neighborhood language of the experimental groups was Spanish, results showed little or no differences between the two groups. A second important study flaw is that in many cases the program characteristics are not clearly described; there is very little information about fidelity of program implementation or quality or program implementation. In cases where program quality is examined, bilingual programs suffer from instability (1975).

The purpose of the present study is to examine differences in broad reading outcomes (a construct that combines word reading and passage comprehension) for three groups of grade 5 students: Spanish-speaking students instructed in Spanish only, Spanish-speaking students instructed in English; and Spanish-speaking students instructed first in Spanish and then transitioned into English-only instruction in grade 3 or 4. The present study improves on the flaws that characterize previous research by drawing students for the different instructional groups from the same schools and neighborhoods, ensuring that students in each instructional group had been in that group since they began school, and using initial literacy and demographic variables to control for initial group differences. Finally all instructional groups were exposed to the same intervention with parallel versions in English and Spanish, and implementation data were collected across the classrooms and sites to ensure fidelity of implementation.

It was hypothesized that students instructed bilingually or only in Spanish would outperform students instructed only in English on measures of Spanish reading at the end of grade 5; whereas students instructed bilingually or in English would outperform students instructed only in Spanish on measures of broad reading in English at the end of grade 5. It was also hypothesized that there would be no statistically significant differences between students instructed bilingually and those instructed in English on the English reading outcomes at the end of grade 5 and no statistically significant differences between students instructed solely in Spanish and those instructed bilingually on the Spanish reading outcomes at the end of grade 5.

Method

Participants

The 113 children in this study were participants in a larger project designed to assess English and Spanish reading skills from grade 2 to grade 5. This project was a longitudinal study that assessed children at the end of each school year for four years, with an additional assessment time at the beginning of grade 3. A total of 269 children were assessed over these four years. For the purposes of this study we included only children who had been involved in the study since its beginning and remained in the program through grade 5. The language of instruction groups included: English only for four years ($n = 37$), Spanish and English ($n = 30$) and Spanish only for four years ($n = 21$). The sample was 53% female and no child repeated a grade. Table 1 presents the breakdown of highest grade completed for mothers in each group. We use this variable as a proxy for socio-economic status.

Table 1 Mother's level of education

Group	Highest education level completed	N	(%)
All English (*n* = 37)	Grade school High school College	4 26 7	10.81 70.27 18.92
Bilingual (*n* = 30)	Grade school High school College	14 13 3	46.7 43.3 10.0
All Spanish (*n* = 21)	Grade school High school College	7 13 1	33.3 61.9 4.8

English only instructed group

The majority of students in this group spoke only English (23.5) or mostly English (41.2) at home. The majority began formal schooling in the United States while enrolled in pre-k (50%) or kindergarten (35%) and the majority received instruction in English during their kindergarten year (91.2%). One student received some type of special education or special reading services. Whereas, the highest percentage of parents (44%) reported using both English and Spanish at home, approximately 17% of parents reported using only English at home and 14% of parents reported using only Spanish at home. A majority of parents (73.6%) reported reading to their children every day or almost every day.

Spanish instructed group

The majority of students in this group spoke only Spanish (55.6%) or mainly Spanish (22.2%) at home. The majority began formal schooling in the United States while enrolled in a pre-k (55.6%) or kindergarten program (27.8 %). All students received instruction in Spanish during their kindergarten year (76.5%). No students received special education or special reading services. Most parents reported that they used only Spanish (61.1%) or mainly Spanish (27.8%) at home. Most parents reported reading to their children every day (61.1%) or almost every day (22.2%).

Bilingually instructed group

Students in this group spoke only Spanish (48.8%) or mainly Spanish at home (29.3 %). About 40% began formal schooling in the United States in pre-kindergarten or in kindergarten (53.7%). The majority (82.9 %) received instruction in Spanish during their kindergarten year. No children received special education or reading services. A majority of the parents reported that they used only Spanish (58.5%) or mostly Spanish (26.8%) at home. A majority of parents reported reading to their children every day (24.4%) or almost every day (26.8%).

Site selection

The study took place in Success for All (SFA)/Éxito para Todos schools in Boston, El Paso, and Chicago. SFA is a theory-driven, research-based reading program that teaches all component skills of literacy. At the heart of the program is 90 minutes of uninterrupted daily reading instruction that emphasizes a balance between phonics and meaning, using both phonetically regular student text and children's literature. SFA schools were selected because their curriculum is consistent across sites, there are parallel versions in Spanish (Éxito para Todos) and English, and students have an opportunity to fully develop their Spanish skills. We collected data from four to six classrooms at each site, depending on the number of target students available in each classroom.

With regard to the specific sites selected, criteria included fidelity of implementation of the SFA instructional model and relative proximity to the research teams. The Texas Education Agency had labeled the two schools in El Paso (90% Latino students from Mexico) as 'recognized' schools for consistent achievement among all students. They both have bilingual programs from pre-kindergarten through fifth grade. The Chicago school (91% Latino students from different countries of origin) has been recognized as an exemplary bilingual SFA school; it has had SFA for the past 5 years. The Boston school (over 70% Latino), serves students of predominantly Puerto Rican and Dominican origin. It has a bilingual program serving students in kindergarten through grade 6. It was in the fourth year of implementation of the SFA curriculum. Staff from the Center for Applied Linguistics (CAL), in Washington, DC, worked with the Chicago site since no local SFA programs in the Washington area met the other criteria. One of its partners, Harvard University, conducted the study in Boston, while the remaining partner, The Johns Hopkins University, worked with the El Paso schools through its El Paso-based office.

Assessment procedures

Research associates from three sites were trained at the Center for Applied Linguistics to administer the assessments. In April 1999, grade 2 students receiving Spanish SFA instruction and grade 2 students receiving English SFA instruction were individually assessed in a quiet space outside of the classrooms. It was necessary to assess all students in both English and Spanish even though they had not been formally instructed in both languages to determine how they compared with each other at the end of grade 5. The

English assessments were administered first and the Spanish assessments were administered next during separate sessions. In April 2002, students were tested a fifth time, at the end of their grade 5 year. In addition to student assessments, the research associates collected information from school records, parents filled out a demographic questionnaire that was part of the student consent form, and implementation data were obtained from the Success for All administrative offices.

Measures

Measures included the Computer-based Academic Assessment System (CAAS) and two subtests of the Woodcock Language Proficiency Battery (1991), including letter–word identification and passage comprehension. All assessments were administered in English and Spanish.

Woodcock Language Proficiency Battery (WLPB)

In the WLPB Passage Comprehension subtest, the first four items require the student to point to a picture represented by a phrase. The remaining items measure the student's skill in reading a short passage and identifying a missing key word. The task requires the student to state a word that would be appropriate in the context of the passage. The WLPB letter–word identification is used to measure orthographic skills. The first five letter–word identification items measure symbolic learning, or the ability to match a rebus (pictographic representation of a word) with an actual picture of an object. The remaining objects measure the student's reading identification skills with isolated letters and words. The student does not need to know the meaning of any of the words presented, but must be able to respond to letters or words he/she may not have seen before.

Woodcock Language Proficiency Battery Broad Reading scores were used to assess reading performance in English and Spanish. The Broad Reading W Score is obtained by averaging the W scores from two subtests: Letter–Word Identification and Passage Comprehension. This cluster is a broad measure of reading achievement, i.e. it is an aggregate measure of reading identification, comprehension and vocabulary skills. W scores are a special transformation of the Rasch ability scale. It has an equal-interval characteristic. The W scale is centered on a value of 500, which is the average performance of beginning grade 5 students.

CAAS

The success in reading depends not only on being able to recognize letters and words accurately, but also on being able to recognize them quickly and efficiently. Thus, the measure of letter and word recognition consisted of the time it took students to recognize a letter or word accurately. These measurements were obtained using CAAS, which consists of six tasks that measure component reading skills (Sinatra & Royer, 1993). Only two of those tasks were used for this study–letter naming and word naming. Letter naming is measured by having examinees identify single uppercase and lowercase letters that appear in the center of a laptop-computer screen. The examinee is asked to say the letter into a microphone. The pronunciation of the letter name activates a voice key that stops a clock in the computer. The computer records the response time in milliseconds, and the experimenter records the accuracy of the student's response. In the word naming task, examinees are asked to pronounce as quickly and as accurately as possible a word that appears in the center of the computer screen. The administration of the task involves presenting the words on the computer screen and having the examinees say the word into a microphone. The pronunciation of the word activates a voice key that stops the clock in the computer. The computer records the response time, and the experimenter records the accuracy of the student's response. In both Spanish and English versions of the test, there are 30 target words; approximately one-third of these are monosyllabic, one-third bisyllabic, and one-third multisyllabic. The words vary from highly common words, such as *men*, to more uncommon words, such as *effortful*. Within syllables, the words vary with regard to their syllable structure. Data from the CAAS subtests consisted of three measures: Average Accuracy (% correct), Response Time (in seconds) and Reading Efficiency Index (REI).

Reliability of researcher-developed measures

Reliability indices for the CAAS were obtained through Rasch analysis. The reliability indices for the accuracy scores of the English Letter Naming subtests are as follows: Wave 1 = 0.37, Wave 2 = 0.19 and Wave 3 = 0.00. The reliability indices for the accuracy scores of the Spanish Letter Naming subtests are as follows: Wave 1 = 0.79 and Wave 2 = 0.70. The reliability indices for the accuracy scores of the English Word Naming subtests are as follows: Wave 1 = 0.77, Wave 2 = 0.71, and Wave 3 = 0.68.). The reliability indices for the accuracy scores of the Spanish Word Naming subtests are as follows: Wave 1 = 0.90 and Wave 2 = 0.85. The decrease in the reliability indices in Waves 2 and 3 across the subtests is due to the fact that more children are finding these subtests easier than in Wave 1 (i.e. the subtest becomes less powerful in differentiating low from high ability children).

Demographic survey and school records

To collect family background information, a parent questionnaire was developed in Spanish and English. The background information collected included time of arrival in the United States to enable comparisons between students who had arrived recently and those who had lived most of their lives in the United States. Family factors of likely relevance were noted: maternal education, home literacy practices, and home language use. School records were examined for students' instructional history, including the number of years in SFA and the language of instruction outside of SFA literacy instruction.

Fidelity of implementation

SFA schools are monitored throughout the year for fidelity of implementation for all program components. Each teacher is observed in the classroom three times a year by SFA Foundation trainers. Systematic observation instruments are used by all trainers across the nation. From these observations, plus interviews and follow-up feedback sessions with teachers, administrators, and parents, 30-page reports are prepared and provided to the school, highlighting accomplishments and areas for improvement. Every component (assessment and regrouping, staff development, early learning/aprendizaje inicial, reading roots/lee conmigo, reading wings/alas para leer, tutoring, and family support services) at every grade level is rated for level of implementation. Schools are able to review their previous performance compared with current performance every three to four months.

Results

Fidelity of implementation

Ratings for School A that correspond to data collection during the study (2000–2001) indicated the program was in place and refined (extremely well implemented) in almost all its components. Ratings for School B indicated that program components were mostly in place, and some components were refined. Ratings for School C indicated the program was mostly in place, and some components were refined.

Performance of students at the end of grade 5

English Broad Reading

Two univariate ANCOVAs were performed separately on English Broad Reading grade 5 scores. The independent variable for both ANCOVA's was language of instruction (All English, All Spanish, and Bilingual). The first model included two covariates: prior level of ability by including the child's score on similar tasks in grade 2 and socio-economic status (SES). Prior level of ability was a sum of the child's scores in grade 2 on the English tests of CAAS word and CAAS letter reading efficiency

Table 2 Fifth grade reading outcomes by language of instruction (adjusting for initial performance and mother's level of education)

Group	N	Variable	Mean	SD	Grade level equivalent*	Adjusted means with covariates	Standard score	Percentile rank
All Spanish	18	Broad Reading English	90.61	15.88	4.3	93.68	89	22
	18	Broad Reading Spanish	121.06	12.92	6.9	113.91	109	73
Bilingual	26	Broad Reading English	106.00	10.90	6.7	108.15	108	70
	30	Broad Reading Spanish	112.97	12.85	6.4	108.72	105	62
All English	31	Broad Reading English	101.84	8.81	5.2	98.25	96	40
	13	Broad Reading Spanish	78.00	17.35	4.9	97.69	93	33

* Grade level equivalents were calculated using the adjusted means which included both covariates: Mother's level of education and composite score of CAAS word and letter reading, and Woodcock Johnson Passage Comprehension in grade 2.

index and Woodcock Johnson Passage Comprehension. Mother's level of education was used as a proxy for SES. The overall model was significant F $(4,70) = 15.88$, $p < 0.001$. After adjustment by the covariates, there were significant group differences on the outcome, $F (2, 70) = 13.02$, $p < 0.001$. The strength of the relationship between language of instruction and grade 5 English reading outcome was moderate: partial $\eta^2 = 0.271$. The covariate of grade 2 performance on a composite of the skills in Broad Reading was significantly associated with grade 5 Broad Reading scores, $F (1, 70) = 37.26$, $p < 0.001$. However, the SES covariate was not significantly associated with grade 5 outcomes in this model, $F (1, 70) = 0.23$, $p > 0.05$. Post hoc pairwise comparisons were computed using Tukey's correction. These comparisons revealed significant mean differences between the group that was instructed only in Spanish and the remaining two groups (English instructed and bilingual instructed), Tukey's critical value $(1, 70) = 3.39$, $p < 0.05$. However, the comparison between the English only instruction group and the Bilingual instruction group was not significant indicating that the means on grade 5 outcomes were not significantly different. See Table 2.

The second ANCOVA was performed using the same dependent variable of grade 5 English Broad Reading scores; however, this model controlled only for mother's level of education as a proxy for SES. The overall model was significant $F (3, 82) = 5.56$, $p < 0.01$. After controlling for mother's education, there were significant group differences on the outcome, $F (2, 82) = 8.2$, $p < 0.01$; The test of the covariate, mother's level of education, was not significant. Follow up analyses using Tukey's pairwise comparisons again demonstrated significant differences between the Spanish only instructed group and both the English only instructed group and Bilingual instructed groups. Again, the English only instruction group and the Bilingual instruction group grade 5 outcomes means were not significantly different, in the _post hoc_ comparison. See Table 3.

Spanish Broad Reading
To examine group differences on Spanish outcomes, two separate ANCOVAs were performed using grade 5 Spanish Broad Reading scores as dependent variables. The first model controlled for both prior level of ability by using the sum score of grade 2 Spanish scores on the CAAS letter and word reading measures and Spanish Woodcock-Munoz Passage Comprehension and SES by using mother's level of education. Again the overall model was significant, $F (4, 56) = 39.38$, $p < 0.001$. After controlling for prior level of ability, there were group differences on grade 5 reading outcomes, $F (2, 56) = 3.55$, $p < 0.05$. The covariate of prior level of ability, $F (1, 56) = 140.41$, $p < 0.001$ was significantly associated with Spanish grade 5 reading outcomes. The remaining covariate, mother's level of education, did

Table 3 Fifth grade reading outcomes by language of instruction (adjusting for mother's level of education)

Group	N	Variable	Mean	SD	Grade level equivalent*	Adjusted means with covariates	Standard score	Percentile rank
All Spanish	20	Broad Reading English	89.15	15.68	3.7	89.26	83	22
	20	Broad Reading Spanish	119.55	13.08	8.6	119.50	122	73
Bilingual	29	Broad Reading English	103.59	13.38	5.8	103.85	100	70
	30	Broad Reading Spanish	112.97	12.85	7.2	112.81	112	62
All English	37	Broad Reading English	100.92	10.20	5.6	100.65	98	40
	27	Broad Reading Spanish	70.44	19.14	2.1	70.65	59	33

* Grade level equivalents were calculated using the adjusted means which included mother's level of education.

provide a reliable unique adjustment, $F = (1, 56) = 10.02$, $p < 0.01$. *Post hoc* pairwise comparisons were computed using Tukey's correction. These comparisons revealed significant mean differences between all three groups, Tukey's critical value $(1, 56) = 3.40$, $p < 0.05$. See Table 3.

The second ANCOVA only controlled for SES as measured by the mother's level of education in examining the effect of language of instruction on Spanish reading outcomes. Again the overall model was significant $F (3, 73) = 50.36$, $p < 0.001$. After controlling for SES using mother's education as a proxy, language of instruction was significantly associated with Spanish fifth grade reading outcomes, $F (2, 73) = 69.37$, $p < 0.001$, partial Mother's education level was a significant covariate, $F (1, 73) = 12.33$, $p < 0.001$. *Post hoc* pairwise comparisons revealed differences between the English only instructed group and both the Spanish only instructed and Bilingual instructed groups Tukey's critical value $(1, 73) = 3.38$, $p < 0.05$. The comparison between the Spanish instructed and Bilingual instructed groups were not significant indicating that there were no mean differences on Spanish grade 5 reading outcomes between these two groups. See Table 4.

Table 4 Correlations of reading measures

Variable	1	2	3
1. Grade 5 WJ BR – English			
2. Grade 5 WJ BR – Spanish	0.22		
3. Grade 2 Reading – English	0.52	–0.15	
4. Grade 2 Reading – Spanish	0.15	0.83	–0.04

Discussion

The study improves on study design issues that made previous research difficult to interpret (August & Hakuta, 1997). A first design issue relates to the intervention itself–how clearly specified it is and whether there is information about program implementation that can be used to interpret study results. The authors selected a program – Success for All – that was based on both a theory of second-language learning and its relationship to student achievement as well as on successful educational practice. The program had clearly specified goals, and curriculum and professional development aligned with the goals to ensure that the model was well implemented. For example, as part of the program, site coordinators collected program implementation data that helped them determine whether each of the instructional components had been implemented; program implementation data also served as the basis for ongoing professional development. A second design issue relates to how similar the sample of students in each group is. Because of legislative, judicial, and administrative constraints random assignment is often not feasible and other ways must be found to ensure that the groups are similar. As recommended by Meyer and Fienberg (1992), the control group students were selected from the same schools so that there was a greater likelihood of equivalence. Although ideally there should be little or no difference at baseline, this is often not the case so statistical analyses were used to make groups more similar. A third design issue relates to student assessment. The study employed researcher-developed assessments that had been validated as well as standardized measures. All assessments had counterparts in Spanish. In addition, all students received the same assessments. This was not often the case in previous program evaluations. Finally, unlike many previous evaluations, all students had been in the SFA program since kindergarten. Students were assessed at the end of grade 5, after the program had been completed.

The goal of the study was to examine the effect of language of instruction on Broad Reading outcomes for three groups of Spanish-speaking students: those instructed only in English, those instructed bilingually, and those instructed only in Spanish. With regard to English Broad Reading scores, the data indicate that Spanish-speaking students, controlling for both SES and initial literacy performance in the outcome of interest (English Broad Reading) in one model, and controlling for SES in a second model, achieved significantly different reading outcomes depending on the language of instruction. Spanish-speaking children instructed bilingually (initially in Spanish and then in English) did not fare any worse on Broad Reading outcomes than students instructed only in English. However, the data also indicated that Spanish-speaking students needed some instruction in English, as the Spanish-only group fared significantly worse than the other two groups. With regard to Spanish outcomes, the findings favor Spanish-speaking children who had received some instruction in Spanish. More specifically, controlling for SES, Spanish-speaking students instructed bilingually did not fare any worse than students instructed only in Spanish. And both these groups performed significantly better than students instructed only in English. Of note, is that when initial differences in Spanish reading at the end of grade 2 were taken into account, there are no differences among the three groups of students.

In summary, the findings indicate that sound instruction in Spanish followed by sound instruction in English benefits Spanish-speaking children. They perform as well in Spanish as students instructed only in Spanish and as well in English as students instructed only in English. However, this is not the case for students instructed in one language or the other. Without Spanish instruction, English-instructed students do not perform as well as the other two groups. Without English instruction, Spanish instructed students do not compare as well as the other two groups. Thus in contexts where there are sufficient numbers of speakers of the same first language and teachers qualified to teach in student's first language, bilingual instruction is beneficial in that students acquire bilingual literacy skills, but are not disadvantaged in the acquisition of literacy in the societal language. It is also important to point out that the students instructed bilingually were achieving at grade level norms in both Spanish and English on measures of Broad Reading.

The research contributes to our understanding of childhood bilingualism in that it elucidates the important role that instructional context plays in the development of literacy in second language learners. We also hypothesize that not only is language of instruction an important component of the instructional context, but so is the quality of the instructional program itself.

Future research needs to examine the manner in which native language and English instruction is sequenced across the curriculum. In this case, students were taught entirely in Spanish through grade 2 (except for English as a second language) and then transitioned into English. But there are many other models of how English and Spanish can be distributed within and across school years. For example, in some programs it is in vogue to teach the same subjects in Spanish one day and in English the next; in other programs, instruction alternates between English and Spanish on a weekly or monthly basis. Other programs pair English and Spanish instruction from the beginning but some subjects are taught in English and others in Spanish.

Notes

1. The REI score was calculated as follows: The student's accuracy score was transformed into an inaccuracy score for each task by subtracting the accuracy score from 100. Each student's mean response time and mean inaccuracy was divided by their task standard deviation for the sample. The response time and inaccuracy scores were squared, added, and the square root was obtained
2. Ensuring equivalence by matching individual scores at the pretest only appears to create equivalence (Campbell & Stanley, 1963).

References

August, D. and Hakuta, K. (1997) _Improving Schooling for Language Minority Children: A Research Agenda_. Washington, DC: National Academy Press.

Baker, K.A. and de Kanter, A.A. (1981) _Effectiveness of Bilingual Education: A Review of the Literature_. Washington, DC: US Department of Education.

Baker, K.A. and Pelavin, S. (1984) *Problems in Bilingual Education*. Paper presented at the annual meeting of American Education Research Association, New Orleans, LA: American Institutes for Research, Washington, DC.

Campbell, D.T. and Stanley, J.C. (1963) Experimental and quasi-experimental designs for research on teaching. In N.L. Gage (ed.) *Handbook of Research on Teaching* (pp. 171–246). Chicago: Rand McNally.

Cummins, J. (1978) Educational implications of mother tongue maintenance in minority-language groups. *The Canadian Modern Language Review* 35, 395–416.

Cummins, J. (1979) Linguistic interdependence and the educational development of bilingual children. *Review of Educational Research* 49 (2), 221–51.

Cummins, J. (1980) The cross-lingual dimensions of language proficiency: Implications for bilingual education and the optimal age issue. *TESOL Quarterly* 142 (2), 175–87.

Cummins, J. (1984) *Bilingual Education and Special Education: Issues in Assessment and Pedagogy* San Diego, CA: College Hill.

Danoff, C., Coles, G.J., McLaughlin, D.H. and Reynolds, D.J. (1978) *Evaluation of the Impact of ESEA Title VII Spanish/English Bilingual Education Programs, Vol. III: Year Two Impact Designs*. Palo Alto, CA: American Institutes for Research.

Green, J.P. (1998) *A Meta-analysis of the Effectiveness of Bilingual Education*. Caremont, CA: The Thomas Rivera Policy Institute.

Lambert, W.E. (1987). The effects of bilingual education and bicultural experiences on children's attitudes and social perspectives. In P. Homel, M. Palij and D. Aaronson (eds) *ChildhoodBbilingualism: Aspects of Linguistic, Cognitive, and Social Development* (pp. 197–221). Hillsdale, NJ; Lawrence Erlbaum.

Meyer, M.M. and Fienberg, S.E. (eds) (1992) *Assessing Evaluation Studies: The Case of Bilingual Education Strategies.* Panel to Review Evaluation Studies of Bilingual Education, Committee on National Statistics, National Research Council. Washington, DC: National Academy Press.

Rossell, C.H. and Baker, K. (1996) The educational effectiveness of bilingual education. *Research in the Teaching of English* 30 (1), 7–74.

Sinatra, G.M. and Royer, J.M. (1993) The development of cognitive component processing skills that support skilled reading. *Journal of Educational Psychology* 85, 509–19.

Stern, C. (1975) *Final Report of the Compton Unified School District's Title VII Bilingual-Bicultural Project: September 1969 through June 1975*. Compton City, CA: Compton City Schools.

Toukomaa, P. and Skutnabb-Kangas, T. (1977) *The Intensive Teaching of the Mother Tongue to Migrant Children of Preschool Ages and Children in the Lower Level of Comprehensive School*. Helsinki: Finnish National Commission for UNESCO.

United States Department of Education (2005) *Biennial Evaluation Report to Congress on the Implementation of State Formula Grant Program*, Washington, DC.

Willig, A.C. (1985) A meta-analysis of selected studies on the effectiveness of bilingual education. *Review of Educational Research* 55 (3), 269–317.

Woodcock, R.W. (1991) *Woodcock Language Proficiency Battery-revised, English and Spanish Forms: Examiner's Manual*. Itasca, IL: Riverside.

Chapter 7

Bilingualism at School: Effect on the Acquisition of Literacy

ELLEN BIALYSTOK

Of the potential educational consequences of being bilingual, one of the most significant is the possibility that bilingualism influences the manner or efficiency with which children become literate. In our society, literacy admits children to educational opportunities that shape their futures, a future that enters the genetic code because it moulds the expectancies and outcomes of subsequent generations. The social sectors that enjoy greatest success are those who are most educated, and those who are most educated are most literate. If bilingualism mediates success in becoming literate, then it is important to understand its role.

There are two questions addressed in this paper. The first is whether the process of acquiring literacy skills is different for bilingual children than for monolinguals specifically because they are bilingual. Put another way, is there a systematic effect on literacy acquisition that comes from having two linguistic systems at the time children are beginning to learn to read? Such differences may be either enhancing or distracting, but in either case, they would need to be traced to specific effects of bilingualism on the acquisition process rather than some other factor, such as social or educational circumstances, that may correlate with bilingualism. The second question is to determine the relation between progress in the acquisition of literacy in each of the two languages for bilingual children. Answers to this question may reveal aspects of the way that literacy is related to other cognitive or linguistic skills by identifying patterns of commonality across languages.

Figure 1 provides a means of conceptualizing the relation between bilingualism and reading that frames both questions. The first layer of boxes indicates three skills that have been documented to be significant in determining the acquisition of literacy for monolingual children in their first language. The second layer represents the counterpart for each of these

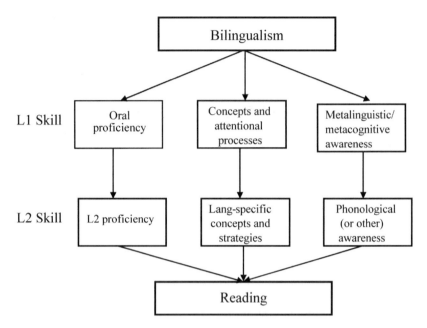

Figure 1 Diagram of relation between bilingualism and reading

skills when reading is learned (either successively or simultaneously) in another language. The important feature of this framework is the set of arrows connecting the top box, bilingualism, to the layers beneath it. This is because bilingualism has been shown to influence the acquisition of each of these component skills for first language literacy, so bilingualism itself may logically be responsible for altering the course of that development for children who control more than one linguistic system. Evidence for this influence would bear on the first question regarding the role of bilingualism in learning to read. However, the manner in which bilingualism influences each of these three skills is different, sometimes providing facilitation and sometimes not, so no arithmetic prediction can be made by summing the weights of these relations. The arrows connecting the L1 skills to the L2 skills indicate the relation between skills developed in one language and the same skills instantiated in the other. Again, however, the arrows reveal nothing about the strength or direction of those relations. Understanding the correspondences between the development of these skills in the two languages will contribute to the second question regarding the commonality in reading skill in the bilingual child's two languages. This model is discussed in more detail elsewhere (Bialystok, 2002).

The first factor identified in the model is oral language proficiency. The importance of this factor in the acquisition of literacy has been consistently demonstrated (Adams, 1990). There is also reasonable evidence that the relation is causal, in that vocabulary competence both precedes and predicts reading level. In a meta-analysis conducted by Stahl and Fairbanks (1986), instructional methods aimed at improving vocabulary reliably increased reading ability as well. Just as clearly, however, it has been frequently demonstrated that vocabulary acquisition is slower for bilingual children than for comparable monolinguals (Ben-Zeev, 1977; Bialystok, 1988; Merriman & Kutlesic, 1993; Oller & Eilers, 2002; Rosenblum & Pinker, 1983; Umbel et al., 1992). On this factor, therefore, the framework predicts a bilingual disadvantage for learning to read in either language. This disadvantage is a direct result of being bilingual, a situation that depresses skill in an established prerequisite for literacy.

The second factor is the development of print concepts relevant to literacy. These include the basic notions of how reading works, what the notations mean, and how the notations encode meaning, all of which have been shown to be significant in children's acquisition of literacy (Ferreiro, 1984; Snow & Ninio, 1986; Tolchinsky-Landsmann & Karmiloff-Smith, 1992). These developments are also affected by bilingualism, but more felicitously than was the case for oral vocabulary. In studies with 4-year-old pre-readers, bilingual children consistently outperform mono-lingual children in a test assessing the extent to which they understand the symbolic concepts that underlie print (Kin Tong & Astington, 2004; Bialystok, 1997; Bialystok et al., 2000). The test examines children's under-standing of the way that print refers to meanings, for instance, that the relation is based on the letters (or other notations for different writing systems), that the meaning encoded in these symbols is invariant, and that the letters have a predictable relation to the sounds of the word. Clearly, these are crucial insights to reading, so if bilingual children develop them earlier than monolinguals, it could lead to an advantage in developing the literacy skills required for independent reading.

The third factor is awareness of the metalinguistic concepts required for reading. In many ways, reading is metalinguistic by nature – the meanings of language must be extracted through a set of conscious processes that require explicit knowledge of language and the structure of the writing system. However, the metalinguistic concept most closely related to reading, particularly in alphabetic writing systems, is phonological awareness. Evidence for a strong relation between phonological awareness and the acquisition of alphabetic literacy is massive (e.g. Bryant &

Goswami, 1987; Liberman *et al.*, 1977; Morais, 1987; Perfetti *et al.*, 1988; Wagner *et al.*, 1994) and has been shown as well in some respects for acquisition of literacy in character languages (Hanley *et al.*, 1999; Ho & Bryant, 1997; Shu *et al.*, 2000). Because of the significance of phonological awareness for reading, evidence for a bilingual influence in this development would be striking, but such a relation has not been clearly demonstrated. Some studies have reported modest advantages for young bilinguals, but the differences between groups usually disappear in first grade when children are learning to read (Bruck & Genesee, 1995; Campbell & Sais, 1995; Yelland *et al.*, 1993). Research in my lab has also produced mixed results: modest bilingual advantages were found in some tasks for Spanish–English bilinguals, but no advantages at all for French–English bilinguals or Chinese–English bilinguals (Bialystok *et al.*, 2003).

Each of the three background factors indicated in the model for the acquisition of literacy makes a different prediction for the role the role of bilingualism in learning to read. Bilinguals have a deficit in oral vocabulary, so that should hinder literacy acquisition; bilinguals have an advantage in the development of relevant symbolic concepts, so that should facilitate literacy acquisition; and bilinguals may have a benefit in some circumstances but no difference in others in regard to phonological awareness, so that should have little effect on literacy acquisition. Therefore, the relation between bilingualism and learning to read will depend on a number of specific factors. More detailed analyses of the properties of the languages and the writing systems are needed to determine the relative weight that each of these factors exerts on literacy acquisition for specific bilinguals. Consequently, evidence comparing monolinguals and bilinguals learning to read in different languages, with different levels of skill development, and under different circumstances, is needed to establish the patterns that emerge from the interaction of these three factors. Three studies will be described, each of which explores a different set of variables that contribute to those relations. The first study focuses on the role of the concepts underlying reading by comparing bilinguals whose two languages differ in the conceptual and metalinguistic insights required for literacy; the second examines the role of cognitive variables and their effect on reading and phonological awareness; and the third considers the child's level of bilingualism by examining children with different degrees of proficiency in each of the languages.

Languages, Writing Systems and Scripts

Part of the reason that learning to read is so difficult is that determining the principles by which spoken language is translated into writing requires an analysis of both systems to establish the correct correspondences. These correspondences can be based on different linguistic units, such as sounds (alphabetic languages) or morphemes (character languages), endowing the written forms of different writing systems with different representational functions. Coulmas (1989) has organized these possibilities into categories that make the differences among them precise. These differences in writing systems are deeply implicated in how reading takes place, so any effect on learning to read that comes from children's experience with other languages and other literacies most likely depends on the relation between the writing systems used in the child's two languages. In terms of the framework described above, writing systems exploit different symbolic connections between oral and written language, making the concepts of print and writing needed for reading in each to be somewhat different. Therefore, bilingual children learning to read in writing systems that differ in this way may enjoy no particular advantage over monolingual children attempting to master just one. In fact, bilingual children learning to read in two different systems may be disadvantaged relative to monolinguals, especially at the early stages, as the principles governing each system may be confused.

We investigated this possibility by examining the ability of four groups of first grade children, all of whom were being educated in English, to decode a set of nonsense words that were strongly based on English orthography (Bialystok *et al.*, in press). The first group consisted of 40 monolingual speakers of English (mean age = 81.1 months) recruited from two schools in similar middle-class neighborhoods. School literacy instruction used a variety of approaches but was largely phonics-based. The second group consisted of 29 Cantonese–English bilingual children (mean age = 78.7 months). These children attended public elementary schools where instruction was in English and also participated in weekly Chinese classes that concentrated on instruction in speaking and reading. The instructional method for the Chinese classes was 'look and say'; the teacher would present a new character, indicate the pronunciation, and explain the vocabulary item in an example sentence. The third group consisted of 30 Hebrew–English bilingual children (mean age = 80.8 months) who attended a private day school in which Hebrew was the language of instruction for some subjects and English was used for others. Children received daily literacy instruction in both Hebrew and English primarily using a phonics-based approach. Hebrew was introduced in the dotted script that includes vowel sounds, making the written language an alphabetic system with a shallow orthography. The fourth group consisted of 33 Spanish-English bilingual children (mean age = 82.7 months) who attended elementary schools in English and were additionally enrolled in an after-school Spanish program. Like the Cantonese classes, the program included instruction in spoken and written Spanish.

The children in all four groups lived in similar neighborhoods and were learning to read English in similar instructional programs in the same public school system. The children in the three bilingual groups were fluent bilinguals who spoke one language at home and another language (i.e. English) in the community and at school. All the bilingual children were learning to read in both languages. For each of the three groups, however, the relation between the two languages and two writing systems is different. For Spanish–English bilinguals, the languages are similar (Indo-European) and both are written alphabetically in a Roman script; for Hebrew–English bilinguals, the languages are different (Indo-European vs. Semitic) and both are written alphabetically (because they are learning the vowelled form of Hebrew) but use different scripts; for Chinese–English bilinguals, the languages and the writing systems share no resemblance. These similarity relations are expected to influence the degree to which bilingualism affects children's progress in learning to read in English.

The children were administered a battery of tests, and the bilingual children completed all the tests in both their languages. The background measures were the PPVT-R (Dunn & Dunn, 1981) test of receptive vocabulary, forward and backward digit span derived from the WISC-R (Wechsler, 1974) to assess short-term verbal memory, and a phoneme-counting task (Bialystok *et al.*, 2003) to assess knowledge of phonetic units and segmentation ability. The experimental task was a decoding test consisting of 20 English-like non-words adapted from the list used by Treiman *et al.* (1990) to determine children's progress with the correspondence principles of English reading in the early stages of literacy.

The children in the four groups differed in their performance on the background tests. Replicating results often found, the bilingual children in two of the groups displayed weaker command of English vocabulary than did the monolingual English children, although the Hebrew–English bilinguals performed as well as the monolinguals. There was also a difference in the digit span tasks in which the Spanish–English bilinguals and the monolinguals scored higher than the Hebrew–English bilinguals and the Chinese–English bilinguals. This ordering mirrors a difference among the groups in mean age, so age might bear the actual responsibility for the differences in digit span performance. Finally, the groups also diverged in their ability to solve the phoneme counting task. In this case, Hebrew–English and Spanish–English bilinguals outperformed the Chinese–English bilinguals and the English monolinguals. This pattern replicates earlier research with this task (Bialystok *et al.*, 2003). In that study, Spanish–English bilinguals outperformed monolinguals and Chinese–English bilinguals, and the explanation was that the advantage found for the Spanish–English bilinguals was because they were learning to read in two alphabetic languages. In the present study, a group of Hebrew–English bilinguals who were also learning to read in two alphabetic languages similarly outperformed both monolinguals and Chinese–English bilinguals and scored as well as a group of Spanish–English bilinguals. This replication supports the interpretation for the difference offered in the original study.

The purpose of the study was to isolate the role of bilingualism in children's ability to establish literacy skills by determining the role of language and script differences that intervene in this relation. Furthermore, the framework described to organize this research indicates that literacy develops as a function of many factors, some of which have opposing influences: the reduced vocabulary (lower PPVT scores for two of the groups) is a disadvantage for literacy but the increased phonological awareness (for two of the groups) should enhance literacy acquisition. Because children differed in several of these variables, the scores for the English decoding task were examined by an ANCOVA that used age, phoneme counting, forward digit span, and PPVT-R scores as covariates to isolate bilingualism from these variables and determine its impact on early progress in reading English. This procedure statistically equates the groups on these variables to determine if there is any remaining difference attributable to some other aspect of the difference between the three groups. If found, this difference is presumably the experience of bilingualism.

The analysis produced the following LS Means (and standard error) out of a maximum of 20 for each group: Monolingual, 10.63 (SE = 0.77), Chinese–English, 13.13 (SE = 0.86), Hebrew–English, 15.86 (SE = 0.89), and Spanish-English, 16.00 (SE = 0.86). The difference between language groups was significant, $F(3, 124) = 7.64$, $p < 0.01$, and conservative comparisons using Bonferroni adjustments revealed that the monolingual group was lower than each of the Hebrew and Spanish groups. The Chinese group was between these two clusters, but none of the differences between any of the bilingual groups was significant.

The results were also examined in terms of the correlation between reading level across languages. Pearson correlations comparing reading scores in English and the other language showed that there was no cross-language correlation in reading skill for the Chinese children, $r(29) = -0.09$, n.s., but strong positive correlations for the Hebrew, $r(30) = 0.57$, $p < 0.01$, and Spanish children, $r(33) = 0.72$, $p < 0.01$. These results reinforce the importance of considering the relation between the two writing systems in evaluating literacy acquisition of bilingual children and demonstrate again that the Chinese group who is dealing with two different systems profits less from learning to read in two languages than do children whose two languages offer the opportunity to generalize their emerging skill and insights.

These results lead to two main conclusions. The first is that bilingual children whose two languages were based on alphabetic writing systems were making better progress than monolinguals or non-alphabetic bilinguals on a difficult test of phonological segmentation. The second is that progress in early decoding skills, once levels of background ability especially for phonological awareness had been controlled, favored the bilinguals. However, the extent of the advantage depended on the relation between the two writing systems in which their languages were encoded. For children who were learning to read in two alphabetic systems, progress in early reading was more advanced than that for the children in the other groups. The Chinese–English bilingual group was in transition between the monolinguals and the two alphabetic bilinguals, not significantly different from either. However, the ability of the Chinese–English bilinguals to do even as well as the English monolinguals is impressive, given the challenge they face: learning to read in writing systems based on different correspondence principles in which the symbolic function of the notations in each system is entirely different. For their level of mastery of the under-lying skills, their decoding ability was slightly, but not significantly better than the monolinguals, but neither was it significantly worse than the bilingual children whose two languages supported each other through their common symbolic base. In these terms, their progress is impressive, and it is possible that the challenges brought as a consequence of bilingual-ism and the need to learn to read in two systems are responsible for their success.

Phonological Awareness and Reading: The Cognitive Link

The evidence showing the importance of phonological awareness for reading in alphabetic languages is uncontroversial, but its role in reading in a non-alphabetic language is more complex. In this case, syllabic awareness is more relevant, since characters segment speech into syllables (because each character is one syllable) making this metalinguistic concept more of a premium for character reading. In a study by McBride-Chang *et al.* (in press), a group of children beginning reading instruction in Hong Kong performed better than a comparable group of children in Canada on a syllable awareness task but worse than the Canadians on a phoneme deletion task. The interpretation is that children are establishing the skills most relevant to the language they will be reading. Although bilingualism has been shown to influence the development of metalinguistic skills, clear evidence for advantages in phonological awareness have not been consistently found. It is possible that bilingualism can enhance the development of phonological awareness without accelerating reading acquisition if reading is based on different systems and dependent on different metalinguistic concepts. In this case, the effect of bilingualism would be confined to the cognitive aspects of language knowledge without affecting literacy *per se*. The second study addressed these issues by examining the relation between phonological awareness and reading for bilingual children learning to read in an alphabetic language and a character language.

The participants were 57 first-grade children who were just beginning to receive formal instruction in reading. All the children were Chinese–English bilinguals, and like those in the last study, used Cantonese at home with their families and in their communities and English at school and with friends. The children attended the neighborhood schools where English was the language of instruction and communication and were also receiving formal instruction in Cantonese and learning to read in weekend Chinese classes.

The purpose of the study was to determine how reading and phonological awareness developed for these bilingual children whose two languages were based on different systems and to discover the connection between reading and phonological awareness in each of their languages. In alphabetic reading, the relation between phonological awareness and reading is so intertwined that it is practically impossible to establish whether one directly influences the other, or whether the connection reflects their individual generation from a common cognitive process. The difference is important: if phonological awareness and alphabetic reading are directly related through specific language competencies, then bilingual children who are learning a character language should have no particular advantage relative to monolinguals (and possibly a disadvantage) in developing both of these skills. The bilingual experience in two languages that do not share a phonologically based writing system would not contribute to a precocious development of these abilities. In contrast, if phonological awareness and reading each emanate from independent cognitive abilities, then the pattern of development for Chinese–English bilingual children may show dissociation between them that is different from the strong correlation found in monolingual children and in bilingual children learning two alphabetic languages. For these children, phonological awareness would develop through cognitive activities and not through specifically linguistic representations.

In order to discover the underlying structure represented by the superficial correlations between literacy and phonological awareness, it was necessary to evaluate the results of a large test battery that included a range of phonological awareness tasks and a number of cognitive measures. These, in conjunction with reading tasks, were administered in both languages to all the children. As before, there was a test of receptive vocabulary, the PPVT-III (Dunn & Dunn, 1997) and a translation of the test into Cantonese. The Raven's Colored Progressive Matrices (Raven, 1998) was included as a measure of non-verbal (fluid) intelligence and a version of the sequencing span task as a measure of short-term verbal memory. The task is based on a measure developed by Craik (1986) in which participants hold in mind increasingly long strings of items and reassemble them. In the present task, children listened to strings of single digits in random order and repeated back the numbers in the proper ascending sequence. The span length was calculated on the basis of the largest string that could be reproduced in the correct order. This was the only task that was administered only in English. There were three phonological awareness tasks. In the syllable deletion task, 10 three-syllable nonsense words were presented with an instruction to delete one of the syllables, with the position of the deleted syllable counterbalanced. In the phoneme onset deletion task, 10 nonsense words were presented with the instruction to delete the first sound. These two tasks were administered in parallel versions in English and Chinese, but the third pair of phonological tasks was different for the two languages. In English, the task was phoneme counting. The concept of counting phonemes is difficult to convey in Chinese, and a set of adult Cantonese speakers had great difficulty in understanding the instructions in a pilot study, so it was not pursued in Chinese with the children in this study. For the English phoneme counting task, children were given a set of 10 words whose phonological structure ranged from having two to five phonemes. The children were carefully taught an explicit strategy to segment the word into phonemes and then count the segments. The Cantonese substitute for this task was tonal awareness, a concept that has no counterpart in English but is crucial to understanding Chinese. To determine whether children attended to tone as a significant feature, participants were given 10 pairs of characters that had the same combinations of phonemes but in half the cases had different tones. Children needed to determine whether or not the two items were the same word. In addition to these tasks, there were measures of reading in each language. For English, the task was the Woodcock Reading Mastery Tests-R's word identification subtest (Woodcock, 1998) and for Chinese it was a test adapted from Ho and Bryant (1997) that consisted of 25 single character items.

The main analyses were a principal components analysis to identify the structure of the phonological awareness variables and regression analyses to determine the relation between these components and reading scores in each language. For the principal components analysis, the six phonological awareness tasks (irrespective of language) were entered into the analysis and revealed only a single factor accounting for the variance in all these tasks. None of the variance was attributable to the specific language. The loadings for the six tasks onto this single factor were: English phoneme deletion, 0.83, Chinese phoneme deletion, 0.77, Chinese syllable deletion, 0.76, English phoneme counting, 0.71, English syllable deletion, 0.63, Chinese tone awareness, 0.45. The weakest, but still significant loading was for Chinese tone awareness, but this task was also most dissimilar to the others. This pattern shows that the ability to demonstrate phonological awareness is common across a variety of tasks and similar regardless of the languages in which they are administered. Phonological awareness, therefore, may be a general cognitive skill that enables children to treat language analytically.

The common factor representing phonological awareness was entered into a regression analysis to determine the extent to which it accounted for variance in reading in each of the languages. One would expect a strong role in explaining the variance in English reading because of the consistency with which a relation between phonological awareness and alphabetic reading has been reported, but the relation to Chinese reading is less easy to predict, especially since the common factor is based on performance in both languages. Although some studies have reported a relation between pho-nological awareness and character reading, the results are usually weaker and less consistent than those between phonological awareness and alpha-betic reading. The regression analyses were structured by entering the cognitive variables, namely Raven's matrices and sequencing span memory scores, in the first two steps, and then entering the phonological awareness factor. The results showed a clear divide between the languages. For English, the phonological awareness factor continued to explain variance in reading scores after the cognitive variables had been entered and accounted for 54% of the variance in reading, $t(1) = 5.78$, $p < 0.0001$, $R^2 = 0.54$. In contrast, the phonological awareness factor contributed nothing to explaining reading performance in Chinese once the cognitive variables had been entered, $t(1) = 1.13$, n.s., $R^2 = 0.09$. Supporting this pattern, corre-lation analyses showed a strong relation between phonological awareness tasks in the two languages, as expected from the principal components analysis, but no significant correlation between reading scores in English and Chinese. This absence of a correlation between children's early reading scores in English and Chinese replicates those found by Bialystok *et al.* (in press) described above.

Previous research investigating the relation between phonological awareness and reading across languages has usually reported a positive correlation (e.g. Geva & Siegel, 2000; Gholamain & Geva, 1999; Wade-Woolley & Geva, 2000). But those studies have typically been conducted on bilingual children whose two languages used the same writing system. The present results differ from those in several respects. First, there was no correlation between reading scores in the two languages but a strong correlation between phonological awareness scores that showed all six tasks loading onto the same factor. In this sense, phonological awareness is more rooted in general cognitive abilities and reading is more dependent on language specific variables that may not be shared if reading takes place in different systems. This result can help to explain the pattern obtained in the previous experiment. There was greater benefit to English reading for bilingual children whose two languages shared a writing system than for the Chinese children who dealt with different systems. Therefore, bilingual children learning to read two languages in the same system profit as well from the transfer of skill across languages. All bilingual children, however, can apply their emerging facility with phonological awareness to any language they speak, but this ability to analyze linguistic sounds may not help them master reading if the language is not written alphabetically. These results again point to the importance of characteristics of the languages and writing systems in mediating the effect of bilingualism on the acquisition of literacy. The results also replicate those found in previous research in which it has been asserted that phonological awareness is a general cognitive ability whereas reading is a more specific skill (Lindsey *et al.*, 2003; Swanson *et al.*, 2004).

How Bilingual is Enough?

The studies described so far have shown that bilingualism influences the development of both phonological awareness and reading and that these effects are mediated by the relation between the languages and the writing systems. In these studies, the children were carefully selected to assure that their bilingualism was reasonably balanced and that their language skills were developing similarly in both languages. In most cases, this meant that children spoke one language at home and another (i.e. English) at school. But would the acquisition of literacy also be affected for children who were second-language learners, that is, children learning a language at school that they did not speak with the same facility as their first language?

To examine this question, we tested 6-year-olds who were monolingual English ($N = 64$), bilingual English–Chinese ($N = 70$), or Chinese-speaking children beginning to learn English at school ($N = 70$) (Bialystok *et al.*, submitted). Children in the first two groups lived in Canada where English is the language of the community and schooling, but the bilingual group was being raised in homes where Cantonese was the first language. Children in the third group lived in Hong Kong, a predominantly Cantonese-speaking environment where schooling was conducted in Cantonese. These children, however, were receiving formal instruction in English language and literacy in school, and the imbalance of their abilities across these two languages qualifies them as second-language learners of English.

As in the previous studies, the bilingual children were tested in parallel versions of all instruments (with one exception) in both languages. The tasks included the PPVT-III test of receptive vocabulary, syllable deletion task in which the syllable to be deleted occurred in various positions, phoneme onset deletion task, phoneme counting in English only (for reasons described above), and non-word decoding tasks in each of English and Cantonese.

The English vocabulary competence of each of the three groups was different, with the monolingual English children scoring the highest and the children in Hong Kong scoring the lowest. The difference between the two groups in Canada replicates the usual finding that bilingual children at this age score lower on vocabulary scores than comparable monolingual children in that language (e.g. Oller & Eilers, 2002) and the difference between the bilingual children in Canada and those in Hong Kong reflects differences in their exposure to English and their fluency in the language. The results were opposite for the Cantonese vocabulary test, where the Hong Kong children outperformed those in Canada. Furthermore, the relation between English and Cantonese vocabulary was different for the two bilingual groups: for the children in Canada there was no difference between scores on the English and Chinese vocabulary tests, $t < 1$, but the Hong Kong group scored higher on the Chinese test than on the English test, $t (68) = 29.9$, $p < 0.0001$. These results confirm the classification of the Canadian and Hong Kong groups as bilingual and second language learners, respectively.

The results of the test battery were entered into regression models to determine the factors that predict progress in reading for each of the three groups and for each of the languages. The three groups, monolinguals, bilinguals, and second-language learners, produced models that accounted for decreasing proportions of the variance in reading in English. For the monolinguals, the model accounted for 70% of the variance and was driven largely by phoneme onset deletion; for the bilinguals, the model accounted for 58% of the variance and included important contributions from phoneme onset deletion and syllable deletion; for the second-language learners, the model, although still significant, accounted for only 32% of the variance, the largest component being phoneme counting. These results indicate that the children in the three groups were approaching English literacy differently in terms of the skills that were most relevant for their progress, although the importance of phonological awareness in English remained relevant for all the groups. For progress in Chinese reading, in contrast, the regression model for the bilingual children accounted for none of the variance, and that for the second-language learners (who were learning to read in Chinese, their first language) accounted for a modest 15% of the variance. The majority of this effect was provided by the role of the syllable deletion task in explaining skill in Chinese reading. Since the characters indicate syllabic units, this relation is not surprising. In general, however, progress in learning to read Chinese was not determined by progress in the linguistic and metalinguistic variables measured in this battery.

The different constellation of factors that contribute to explaining variance in English reading and Chinese reading and the differences between the three groups in the English reading analyses indicate that reading in English and in Chinese is built on different skills. Moreover, children at different levels of language proficiency in each of these languages approach these tasks differently, drawing on these background skills in different measure. In the two studies described previously, all the children were fully bilingual. In those studies, there were strong correlations between reading in the two languages when both languages were written in an alphabetic script (Bialystok *et al.*, in press) and strong correlations between phonological awareness tasks in both languages regardless of the specific languages (Luk, 2003). However, in neither of these studies was there a correlation between reading scores in Chinese and reading scores in English. This was surprising because most previous research has reported a relation between these two measures. For the Canadian bilingual children in the present study, all these patterns were replicated. There were positive correlations across English and Chinese for phonological awareness (syllable deletion, $r = 0.70$; phoneme onset deletion, $r = 0.72$) and no cross-language correlation for reading ($r = -0.10$). For the Hong Kong second-language learners, the pattern was different: the phonological awareness scores remained correlated as in the previous studies (syllable deletion, $r = 0.73$; phoneme onset deletion, $r = 0.67$), but this time there was a significant correlation between reading scores across the two languages ($r = 0.60$).

The primary difference between the children in Hong Kong and those in Canada was their relative proficiency in the two languages. The children in Hong Kong had very weak English skills and were learning to read in English in the same way that they learned to read Chinese, namely, by memorizing visual patterns and associated the whole sequence with a meaning. They had poor phonological analysis skills in both languages, and demonstrated essentially no relation between their phonological awareness and reading progress, unlike children who were more proficient Chinese–English bilinguals or children who were bilingual in two alphabetic languages. Thus, the cognitive skills that the Hong Kong children brought to the task of reading were likely more heavily rooted in such things as pattern analysis and memorization, applied equally to both languages, and resulting in parallel progress (in relative terms) in learning to read in each. In contrast, the bilingual children in Canada approached reading in English primarily through their skill with phonological analysis, an ability that was not very useful in learning to read in Chinese. Therefore, their progress in each language was separate, based on the development of the individual skills needed to read in that language. This interpretation follows from the regression model that points to different types of factors that are most relevant for mastering literacy in each of the languages and the different extent to which each group recruits those language-relevant skills in learning to read.

Bilingualism and Learning to Read

In each of the three studies described above, competence with another language and the experience of learning to read in another language, sometimes in another writing system, influenced the manner or efficiency with which children were acquiring literacy skills in English. In the first study, all the bilingual children demonstrated some benefit of learning to read in two languages, but children learning to read in two alphabetic systems profited particularly. In the second study, bilingual children learning to read in English and in Chinese revealed a common basis for phonological awareness across languages as a developmental achievement and the uniqueness of literacy acquisition in each language when the writing systems were not the same. In the third study, children similar to those investigated in Study 2 but having only limited competence with both oral and written English confined some of the results of Study 2 (and by extension, other research in the literature) to those children whose language skills in the two languages are more balanced.

The main conclusion from the combination of these three studies is that there is no simple answer to the question of whether or not bilingualism affects children's acquisition of literacy. The most general answer is that it does, but the nature of that effect changes with the circumstances. The apparently contradictory results in the literature, demonstrating different types of bilingual advantage or disadvantage, are likely all correct, but each applies to a more limited set of circumstances than perhaps was previously expected. Consider the model in Figure 1. In that rather simplistic diagram, the route from bilingualism to literacy indicates at least three possible outcomes depending on which set of skills is taken to be most central. In conjunction with the empirical results of the studies described here, it is clear that some of the specificity that determines outcomes arises from the relation between the two languages and nature and similarity of the two writing systems, as well as from children's degree of bilingualism. But surely there are other factors as well. Research aimed at understanding the impact of children's language competence, and especially children's bilingual competence, on the most crucial of all school skills, learning to read, will need to consider all these factors and uncover others that help us understand these complex relations.

Acknowledgement

The research reported in this paper was funded by Grant A2559 from the Natural Sciences and Engineering Research Council of Canada (NSERC).

References

Adams, M.J. (1990) *Beginning to Read: Thinking and Learning about Print*. Cambridge, MA: MIT Press.

Ben-Zeev, S. (1977) The influence of bilingualism on cognitive strategy and cognitive development. *Child Development* 48, 1009–18.

Bialystok, E. (2002) Acquisition of literacy in bilingual children: A framework for research. *Language Learning* 52, 159–99.

Bialystok, E. (1988) Levels of bilingualism and levels of linguistic awareness. *Developmental Psychology* 24, 560–7.

Bialystok, E. (1997) Effects of bilingualism and biliteracy on children's emerging concepts of print. *Developmental Psychology* 33, 429–40.

Bialystok, E., Luk, G. and Kwan, E. (in press) Bilingualism, biliteracy, and learning to read: Interactions among languages and writing systems. *Scientific Studies of Reading*.

Bialystok, E., Majumder, S. and Martin, M.M. (2003) Developing phonological awareness: Is there a bilingual advantage? *Applied Psycholinguistics* 24, 27–44.

Bialystok, E., McBride-Chang, C. and Luk, G. (submitted) *Bilingualism, Language Proficiency, and Learning to Read in Two Writing Systems*.

Bialystok, E., Shenfield, T. and Codd, J. (2000) Languages, scripts, and the environment: Factors in developing concepts of print. *Developmental Psychology* 36, 66–76.

Bruck, M. and Genesee, F. (1995) Phonological awareness in young second language learners. *Journal of Child Language* (22), 307–24.

Bryant, P., and Goswami, U. (1987) Beyond grapheme-phoneme correspondence. *Current Psychology of Cognition* 7, 439–43.

Campbell, R. and Sais, E. (1995) Accelerated metalinguistic (phonological) awareness in bilingual children. *British Journal of Developmental Psychology* 13, 61–8.

Coulmas, F. (1989) *The Writing Systems of the World*. Oxford: Blackwell.

Craik, F.I.M. (1986) A functional account of age differences in memory. In F. Klix and H. Hagendorf (eds) *Human Memory and Cognitive Capabilities, Mechanisms, and Performance*. Amsterdam: North Holland.

Dunn, L.M. and Dunn, L.M. (1981) *Peabody Picture Vocabulary Test-Revised*. Toronto, Canada: Psycan.

Dunn, L.M. and Dunn, L.M. (1997) *Peabody Picture Vocabulary Test – III*. Circle Pines, MN: American Guidance Service.

Ferreiro, E. (1984) The underlying logic of literacy development. In H. Goelman, A. Oberg and F. Smith (eds) *Awakening to Literacy* (pp. 154–73). Exeter, NH: Heinemann Educational Books.

Geva, E. and Siegel, L.S. (2000) Orthographic and cognitive factors in the concurrent development of basic reading skills in two languages. *Reading and Writing: An Interdisciplinary Journal* 12, 1–30.

Gholamain, M. and Geva, E. (1999) Orthographic and cognitive factors in the concurrent development of basic reading skills in English and Persian. *Language Learning* 49, 183–217.

Hanley, J.R., Tzeng, O. and Huang, H-S. (1999) Learning to read Chinese. In M. Harris and G. Hatano (eds), *Learning to Read and Write: A Cross-Linguistic Perspective* (pp. 173–95). Cambridge: Cambridge University Press.

Ho, C-H. and Bryant, P. (1997) Learning to read Chinese beyond the logographic phase. *Reading Research Quarterly* 32, 276–89.

Kin Tong, C. and Astington, J.W. (2004) *Is There a Bilingual Advantage in Theory-of-Mind Development?* Paper presented in symposium, 'Why language matters for theory of mind' at the meeting of the ISSBD, Ghent, Belgium, 11–15 July.

Liberman, I.Y., Shankweiler, D., Liberman, A.M., Fowler, C. and Fischer, F.W. (1977) Phonetic segmentation and recoding in the beginning reader. In A.S. Reber and D. Scarborough (eds) *Toward a Psychology of Reading: The Proceedings of the CUNY Conference* (pp. 207–25). Hillsdale: NJ: Lawrence Erlbaum.

Lindsey, K.A., Manis, F.R. and Bailey, C.E. (2003) Prediction of first-grade reading in Spanish-speaking English-language learners. *Journal of Educational Psychology* 95, 482–94.

Luk, G. (2003) Exploring the latent factors behind inter-language correlations in reading and phonological awareness. Unpublished Master's thesis, York University, Toronto, Ontario, Canada.

McBride-Chang, C., Bialystok, E., Chong, K.K.Y. and Li, Y. (in press) Levels of phonological awareness in three cultures. *Journal of Experimental Child Psychology*.

Merriman, W.E. and Kutlesic, V. (1993) Bilingual and monolingual children's use of two lexical acquisition heuristics. *Applied Psycholinguistics* 14, 229–49.

Morais, J. (1987) Phonetic awareness and reading acquisition. *Psychological Research* 49, 147–52.

Oller, D.K. and Eilers, R.E. (eds) (2002) *Language and Literacy in Bilingual Children*. Clevedon, UK: Multilingual Matters.

Perfetti, C.A., Beck, I., Bell, L.C. and Hughes, C. (1988) Phonemic knowledge and learning to read are reciprocal: A longitudinal study of first grade children. In K.E. Stanovich (ed.) *Children's Reading and the Development of Phonological Awareness* (pp. 39–75). Detroit: Wayne State University Press.

Raven, J.C. (1998) *Raven's Coloured Progressive Matrices*. San Antonio, TX: Psychological Corporation.

Rosenblum, T. and Pinker, S.A. (1983) Word magic revisited: Monolingual and bilingual children's understanding of the word-object relationship. *Child Development* 54, 773–80.

Shu, H., Anderson, R.C. and Wu, N. (2000) Phonetic awareness: Knowledge of orthography-phonology relationships in the character acquisition of Chinese children. *Journal of Educational Psycholog,* 92, 56–62.

Snow, C.E. and Ninio, A. (1986) The contracts of literacy: What children learn from learning to read books. In W.H. Teale and E. Sulzby (eds) *Emergent Literacy: Understanding Reading and Writing* (pp.116–38). Norwood, NJ: Ablex.

Stahl, S.A. and Fairbanks, M.M. (1986) The effects of vocabulary instruction: A model-based meta-analysis. *Review of Educational Research* 56, 72–110.

Swanson, H.L., Saez, L., Gerber, M. and Leafstedt, J. (2004) Literacy and cognitive functioning in bilingual and nonbilingual children at or not at risk for reading disabilities. *Journal of Educational Psychology* 96, 3–18.

Tolchinsky-Landsmann, L. and Karmiloff-Smith, A. (1992) Children's understanding of notations as domains of knowledge versus referential-communicative tools. *Cognitive Development* 7, 287–300.

Treiman, R., Goswami, U. and Bruck, M. (1990) Not all nonwords are alike: Implications for reading development and theory. *Memory and Cognition* 18, 559–67.

Umbel, V.M., Pearson, B.Z., Fernandez, M.C. and Oller, D.K. (1992) Measuring bilingual children's receptive vocabularies. *Child Development* 63, 1012–20.

Wade-Woolley, L. and Geva, E. (2000) Processing novel phonemic contrasts in the acquisition of L2 word reading. *Scientific Studies of Reading* 4, 295–311.

Wagner, R.K., Torgesen, J.K. and Rashotte, C.A. (1994) Development of reading-related phonological processing ability: New evidence of bidirectional causality from a latent variable longitudinal study. *Developmental Psychology* 30, 73–87.

Wechsler, D. (1974) *Wechsler Intelligence Scale for Children – Revised.* New York, NY: Psychological Corporation.

Woodcock, R.W. (1998) *Woodcock Reading Mastery Tests – Revised.* Circle Pines, MN: American Guidance Service.

Yelland, G.W., Pollard, J. and Mercuri, A. (1993) The metalinguistic benefits of limited contact with a second language. *Applied Psycholinguistics* 14, 423–44.

Chapter 8

Adult Bilingualism and Bilingual Development

JUDITH F. KROLL

Introduction

Second language (L2) acquisition for individuals past the earliest years of childhood is typically considered to be a difficult task, leaving learners with indelible traces of an accent from the first language (L1) and less than complete grammatical abilities (e.g. Johnson & Newport, 1989; Piske *et al.*, 2001). In part for that reason, psycholinguistic investigations of language and cognitive processing in adult second language learners have been viewed as addressing a set of questions distinct from those that define the study of childhood bilingualism. Traditionally, those questions have been considered interesting with respect to cognitive processes but not informative with respect to language acquisition.

In the past two decades this situation has changed. Alternative accounts of early language learning have challenged traditional ideas about innate constraints present in early acquisition (e.g. MacWhinney, 1999). At the same time, recent studies investigating adult second language performance have shown that even among the most proficient bilinguals, there is simultaneous activity of both languages even when only a single language is required. The observed activity of both languages and the interactions between them, even once bilinguals achieve a high level of skill in the L2, suggests that second language acquisition is not a matter of developing an encapsulated representation for the L2 that becomes functionally automatic and independent of the L1. Instead, there appears to be a restructuring that renders the bilingual distinct in some respects from his or her monolingual counterparts (e.g. Grosjean, 1989). The focus of much of the current research on adult bilinguals and second language learners is to understand how bilinguals negotiate the parallel activity and interactions of their two languages, the cognitive consequences that result in response to the need to resolve potential competition across the grammar and lexicon of the two languages, and the constraints that remain as a function of the context in which the L2 was acquired and in which it is used. Each of these topics is reviewed briefly in the sections that follow and the implications for childhood bilingualism are discussed.

Major Themes in Research on Adult Bilingualism

Parallel activation of the bilingual's two languages

When relatively proficient adult second language learners and bilinguals listen to, read, and speak words and sentences in each of their two languages, there is evidence suggesting that the other language is also active and influences performance (see Kroll *et al.*, 2005, and Kroll & Dussias, 2004, for recent reviews). Although learners who are less proficient in their L2 than in their L1 may also rely on the L1 translation equivalent to mediate access to meaning for the L2 (e.g. Kroll & Stewart, 1994), even among the most proficient bilinguals performing language tasks in their L1 alone, the evidence suggests that L2 affects lexical access (e.g. Van Hell & Dijkstra, 2002) and sentence processing (e.g. Dussias, 2003).

At the lexical level, parallel activation of both languages has been found in visual word recognition (e.g. Dijkstra, 2005; Dijkstra & Van Heuven, 2002), in spoken word recognition (e.g. Marian & Spivey, 2003), and in spoken word production (e.g. Costa *et al.*, 1999). A range of methods has been used to reveal the fundamental nonselectivity of language processing. A complete review is beyond the scope of the present paper but a few examples will suffice to illustrate the approach. In languages that share the same script, there are words that resemble one another in part or completely. For example, in languages such as Dutch and English, there are translation equivalents that have identical or similar orthography (*cognates*), words that have identical or similar orthography but different meanings (*interlingual homographs* or *false friends*), and words that overlap to some degree in their spelling (*lexical neighbors*).

If bilinguals are able to maintain separation across their two languages at a lexical level, then performance in tasks that require access to words in one language alone should not be affected by the presence of cross-language relatives. Bilinguals should perform in a manner that is functionally indistinguishable from the performance of monolinguals. However, in what is now a compelling body of evidence (see Dijkstra, 2005), there is overwhelming support for the view that lexical access is nonselective and that lexical information associated with both of the bilingual's languages is activated in parallel even when processing words in one language only. Performance on a range of word recognition tasks is sometimes facilitated and sometimes inhibited by the activation of information in the nontarget language. Furthermore, the evidence to date in the visual domain suggests that bilinguals have little control over this process. In reading words, the bottom-up mechanisms that govern initial perceptual processing appear to be immune to the reader's intention, to deliberate instruction, and to individual differences in cognitive capacity (e.g. Michael *et al.*, in preparation; Dijkstra *et al.*, 2000). More recent word recognition studies have extended the evidence for nonselectivity to the domain of cross-language phonology, demonstrating that in both visual and spoken word recognition, bilinguals are sensitive to form relatives that are phonologically similar to the target word (e.g. Jared & Kroll, 2001; Marian & Spivey, 2003).

In spoken production, the conceptual nature of the event that initiates the planning of an utterance might seem to provide a vehicle for controlling unwanted intrusion from the unintended language. However, even in a task as apparently simple as speaking the name of a common object, there is evidence that candidates in the language not to be spoken are also activated (e.g. Costa & Caramazza, 1999) and that under some circumstances that activation may reach all the way to the phonological encoding of the nontarget alternatives (e.g. Colomé, 2001). Indeed, research on tip-of-the-tongue states (TOTs) have shown that bilinguals have more TOTs than monolingual speakers (e.g. Gollan & Acenas, 2004). However, unlike word recognition, in which word form relatives are activated, in spoken production, the relevant candidates are semantically related to the target word and its translation.

Fewer studies have investigated these issues at the sentence level, but a number of recent experiments also suggest a surprising level of structural permeability across the bilingual's two languages. Dussias (2003) exploited the presence of different parsing preferences in Spanish and English to examine the effects of bilingualism on sentence processing. Cross-linguistic studies have shown that monolingual Spanish and English speakers use different parsing strategies to interpret temporarily ambiguous sentences. If the bilingual maintains the preferences associated with each language, then different outcomes should be observed depending on the language of processing. Dussias found that native Spanish speakers who were highly proficient in English parsed sentences in Spanish as if they were English. Although many previous studies have demonstrated transfer from L1 grammar to the L2 (e.g. MacWhinney, 1997), Dussias' findings suggest that the structural interpretation of sentences in the native language is influenced by exposure to and skill in the L2. Using a different approach, Hartsuiker *et al.* (2004) asked whether syntactic priming could be observed across a bilingual's two languages. Syntactic priming in sentence production occurs when the structure of a preceding prime sentence influences the form of production of a subsequent target sentence. Like syntactic priming that has been observed within language (e.g. Bock, 1986), Hartsuiker *et al.* (2004) demonstrated that it was possible to observe syntactic priming across languages. The picture of language processing that emerges from these studies is one that suggests a high degree of permeability across language boundaries, consistent with actual bilingual performance outside of the laboratory where code-switching with other bilingual speakers is a common phenomenon. (See also Bullock & Toribio, 2004, for a recent issue of *Bilingualism: Language and Cognition* devoted to the issue of convergence across the bilingual's two languages, and Malt & Sloman, 2003, for evidence of convergence in the effects of bilingualism on the labeling of familiar objects.)

The consequences of cross-language activation

A recent focus of research has concerned the consequences of cross-language activation. What mechanisms are available to the bilingual to resolve cross-language competition? If the two languages are always active, then bilinguals must have a means of resolving the competition to allow accurate language use. The observed interactions across the bilingual's two languages have been taken by some cognitive psychologists to suggest that bilinguals possess an exquisitely developed mechanism of executive control. How do bilinguals negotiate the parallel activity of the two languages and yet manage to speak in a single language when that is required by the context but just as easily code-switch with other bilinguals? A number of solutions have been proposed but at some level they all require adjustments to cognitive and attentional mechanisms. Grosjean (2001) proposed the notion of a language mode, whereby bilingual speakers find themselves on a continuum between bilingual mode, in which both languages can be expected to be used actively, and monolingual mode, in which only a single language is dominant. The evidence reviewed above suggests that even in a strongly monolingual mode there is significant evidence of parallel activation of both languages, so that the attenuation of one language to achieve complete monolingual mode in the other language may be quite difficult. But even if an extreme monolingual mode is not possible, there are suggestions in recent studies that the relative activity of the two languages can be modulated (e.g. Jared & Kroll, 2001). A complete account of bilingual control will have to provide details about the circumstances that influence these changes, whether they be in the nature of the linguistic context or in the cues present within the environment in which language processing occurs.

A number of recent papers have proposed solutions to the cross-language competition problem for comprehension (e.g. Dijkstra & Van Heuven, 2002) and for production (e.g. Green, 1998). In general, these solutions appeal to the contribution of task schemas that fall outside the representation of linguistic information but that act on the output of language processing to meet the goals of the task. For example, Green's inhibitory control model proposes a mechanism of reactive inhibition that serves to suppress the activation of the more dominant language when the task requires that the less dominant language be spoken. Support for an inhibitory mechanism of this sort comes from language switching experiments (e.g. Meuter & Allport, 1999). Meuter and Allport asked bilinguals to name numbers in a cued sequence such that some numbers were named in sequence in the same language and others required a switch of language. They found that the processing cost for switch trials was greater when switching into the more dominant L1 than into the less dominant L2. If speaking the number name in L2 requires suppression of the more dominant L1, then if a number must be named in L1 on the next trial, there will be a cost reflecting the suppression of L1 on the preceding trial.

An interesting implication of the language switching evidence is that the results suggest that among the skills acquired by L2 learners, there are attentional processing skills beyond the acquisition of the L2 lexicon and grammar. If so, we might then expect that proficient bilingualism would be associated with enhanced attentional control. Indeed, Bialystok and her colleagues (e.g. Bialystok, 2005, and this issue), have shown that young bilingual children and elderly bilingual adults provide evidence for superior executive control relative to their monolingual counterparts. For children, these enhancements are evident in their performance on tasks that require that they ignore irrelevant information. For elderly bilinguals, there appear to be similar advantages on tasks that reflect the cognitive declines associated with normal aging. Perhaps most significant is that these cognitive consequences of bilingualism appear to similarly affect cognitive control in both young children and older adults and extend into cognitive and perceptual tasks that are nonlinguistic (e.g. see Bialystok *et al.*, 2004 for evidence on the Simon task, a purely cognitive-perceptual domain in which these bilingual advantages have been observed). The implication is that the mental juggling required by the frequent use of two languages has profound consequences for the development of cognitive control.

Constraints on bilingual language performance

The picture of adult bilinguals presented by our brief review of the current literature suggests an open language system in which interactions and influences can be observed bidirectionally and at many different levels of language representation and processing. However, it is misleading to suggest that these interactions are unconstrained. The recent literature suggests a number of factors that may ultimately provide structural constraints or cues that can functionally limit the activation of one language or allow language selection to take place at an early point in processing. One source of evidence comes from studies of bilingual phonology. As noted earlier (Piske *et al.*, 2001), there is a great deal of support for the idea that late L2 learners speak an accented version of L2. But even for bilinguals who acquired both languages in early childhood, there is a suggestion that subtle phonetic contrasts may be tuned during infancy and that a child who is exposed to the second language ever so slightly later than the first may not be able to perceive those contrasts as a fully proficient adult bilingual (e.g. Pallier *et al.*, 2001). Similarly, there appear to be semantic constraints that are affected by the timing and context of acquisition of the L2 (e.g. Silverberg & Samuel, 2004).

At a functional level, there is also evidence that subtle phonetic differences across the bilingual's two languages may serve as a cue to limit the degree of parallel activation, at least in the spoken modality (e.g. Ju & Luce, 2004). In the visual modality, a number of studies (e.g. Schwartz, 2003; Van Hell, 1998) have begun to ask about the fate of the activity of nontarget lexical candidates when words appear in sentence context. Although the issue is far from resolved, the first results from these in-context studies suggest a mixed pattern; some effects of nonselectivity remain even in rich sentence context but other effects are eliminated. What is clear is that the language status of the sentence context does not, in and of itself, function to eliminate activation of candidates in the other language.

A recent study has made the provocative claim that early exposure has virtually no effect on later adult language performance (Pallier *et al.*, 2003). Pallier and his colleagues tested a group of adults in France who had been adopted as children from Korea and had no contact with Korean following their adoption. Using behavioral and neuroimaging methods, they demonstrated that these Korean adoptees were no better at discriminating Korean from other languages than native French speakers. Although additional research will have to evaluate the reliability and scope of these results, they suggest that at least under some special circumstances, an L2 can completely replace the L1.

Implications for Childhood Bilingualism

Perhaps the most critical implication of the evidence reviewed here for research on childhood bilingualism is that models of adult bilingualism are as dynamic and developmental as those typically associated with early childhood. Far from suggesting that once the L1 is acquired, there is a fixed sequence by which L2 can be acquired, the available data suggest that the two languages interact with one another and are less constrained by early experience than one might have expected.

Research on adult L2 acquisition has been cautious in drawing parallels with L2 acquisition in childhood because children and adults differ from one another in a number of critical respects. One crucial difference is that adults already have a well-formed lexicon and relatively stable grammar and conceptual system when L2 learning begins, whereas children exposed to an L2 in childhood are developing all of this information in the two languages in parallel. Furthermore, although the data on age of acquisition are open to multiple interpretations (e.g. Birdsong, 1999), that there are age of acquisition effects is not disputed. However, recent neuroimaging studies (e.g. Perani *et al.*, 2003) suggest that age of acquisition alone is not sufficient to account for the brain activation associated with each language. Even when all participants are exposed to both languages in very early childhood, there are significant effects of proficiency associated with the nature and context of language use. In addition, recent studies contrasting cognitive performance in early childhood and adulthood suggest that adults and children are not as different as we might think. Diamond and Kirkham (2005) have shown that when sufficiently sensitive methods are used, adults appear to be influenced by many of the same factors that characterize the cognitive control and executive function performance of young children, such as switching between tasks. This type of evidence suggests that although the basic mechanisms that underlie cognitive performance become increasingly skilled with development, they seem to be qualitatively similar in children and adults. To the extent that this claim can be generalized, we might argue that the interface between language and cognition may be open to similar influences, regardless of the age of the learner.

There is a curious gap in the research on the cognitive basis of bilingualism. Among the youngest bilinguals, there has been a serious research effort focused on the acquisition of phonology in bilingual learning babies and on the acquisition of grammar in bilingual toddlers. This work has profound consequences for theories of neural plasticity and brain development that may partly account for its increasing presence in the literature (e.g. see Werker, Weikum & Yoshida, Chapter 1 this volume, for a review of the recent studies on speech perception). Among adult bilinguals, there is the research reviewed here that concerns itself with late adult acquisition and language processing in relatively proficient bilinguals who have used the two languages since early childhood or for a significant portion of their lives. A number of prominent topics are noticeably absent. One missing topic in the literature concerns school-aged bilingual children who may vary in the age and context in which they have acquired the two languages. The implications of achieving and maintaining proficiency in both languages may be significant for their success in developing literacy and other academic skills. Despite the attempt to argue that child and adults are more cognitively similar than different, there are differences that are clearly critical and whose consequences for language learning have not been fully explored. For example, there may be important differences in the degree to which the structuring of the semantic network changes with development and affects how well differences in the nuances of meaning across languages are appreciated. Children past the earliest years of childhood are also likely to be literate to some degree and how that experience influences the acquisition of a second language is not yet well understood. A clear priority in the next phrase of research on bilingualism will be to better relate research on childhood and adult bilingualism. In this paper I hope to have suggested that there are reasons to be optimistic about developing these connections.

Acknowledgments

The writing of this paper was supported in part by NSF Grant BCS0418071 and NIH Grant MH62479 to Judith F. Kroll. I thank Ton Dijkstra for helpful comments on an earlier version of the paper.

References

Bialystok, E. (2005) Consequences of bilingualism for cognitive development. In J. F. Kroll and A. M.B. De Groot (eds) *Handbook of Bilingualism: Psycholinguistic Approaches* (pp. 417–32). New York: Oxford University Press.
Bialystok, E., Craik, F.I.M., Klein, R. and Viswanathan, M. (2004) Bilingualism, aging, and cognitive control: Evidence from the Simon task. *Psychology and Aging* 19, 2, 290–303.
Birdsong, D. (1999) Introduction: Whys and why nots of the Critical Period Hypothesis. In D. Birdsong (ed.) *Second Language Acquisition and the Critical Period Hypothesis* (pp. 1–22). Mahwah, NJ: Lawrence Erlbaum.
Bock, J.K. (1986) Syntactic persistence in language production. *Cognitive Psychology* 18, 355–87.
Bullock, B.E. and Toribio, A.J. (2004) Introduction: Convergence as an emergent property in bilingual speech. *Bilingualism: Language and Cognition* 7, 91–3.
Colomé, À. (2001) Lexical activation in bilinguals' speech production: Language-specific or language independent? *Journal of Memory and Language* 45, 721–36.
Costa, A. and Caramazza, A. (1999) Is lexical selection language specific? Further evidence from Spanish-English bilinguals. *Bilingualism: Language and Cognition* 2, 231–44.
Costa, A., Miozzo, M. and Caramazza, A. (1999) Lexical selection in bilinguals: Do words in the bilingual's two lexicons complete for selection? *Journal of Memory and Language* 41, 365–97.

Diamond, A. and Kirkham, N. (2005) Not quite as grown-up as we like to think. *Psychological Science* 16, 291–97.

Dijkstra, A. (2005) Bilingual visual word recognition and lexical access. In J.F. Kroll and A.M.B. De Groot (eds) *Handbook of Bilingualism: Psycholinguistic Approaches* (pp. 179–201). Oxford, UK: Oxford University Press.

Dijkstra, A. and Van Heuven, W.J.B. (2002) The architecture of the bilingual word recognition system: From identification to decision. *Bilingualism: Language and Cognition* 5, 175–97.

Dijkstra, A., De Bruijn, E., Schriefers, H. and Ten Brinke, S. (2000) More on interlingual homograph recognition: Language intermixing versus explicitness of instruction. *Bilingualism: Language and Cognition*. 3, 69–78.

Dussias, P.E. (2003) Syntactic ambiguity resolution in L2 learners: Some effects of binguality on L1 and L2 processing strategies. *Studies in Second Language Acquisition* 25, 529–57.

Gollan, T.H. and Acenas, L.A. (2004) What is a TOT?: Cognate and translation effects on tip-of-the-tongue states in Spanish-English and Tagalog-English bilinguals. *Journal of Experimental Psychology: Learning, Memory, & Cognition* 30, 246–69.

Green, D.W. (1998) Mental control of the bilingual lexico-semantic system. *Bilingualism: Language and Cognition* 1, 67–81.

Grosjean, F. (1989) Neurolinguists, beware! The bilingual is not two monolinguals in one person. *Brain and Language* 36, 3–15.

Grosjean, F. (2001) The bilingual's language modes. In J. Nicol (ed.) *One Mind, Two Languages: Bilingual Language Processing* (pp. 1–22). Oxford: Blackwell.

Hartsuiker, R.J., Pickering, M.J. and Veltkamp, E. (2004) Is syntax separate or shared between languages? Cross-linguistic syntactic priming in Spanish/English bilinguals. *Psychological Science* 15, 409–14.

Jared, D. and Kroll, J.F. (2001) Do bilinguals activate phonological representations in one or both of their languages when naming words? *Journal of Memory and Language* 44, 2–31.

Johnson, J.S. and Newport, E. (1989) Critical period effects in second language learning: The influence of maturational state on the acquisition of English as a second language. *Cognitive Psychology* 21, 60–99.

Ju, M. and Luce, P.A. (2004) Falling on sensitive ears: Constraints on bilingual lexical activation. *Psychological Science* 15, 314–18.

Kroll, J.F. and Dussias, P. (2004) The comprehension of words and sentences in two languages. In T. Bhatia and W. Ritchie (eds) *Handbook of Bilingualism* (pp. 169–200). Cambridge, MA: Blackwell Publishers.

Kroll, J.F. and Stewart, E. (1994) Category interference in translation and picture naming: Evidence for asymmetric connections between bilingual memory representations. *Journal of Memory and Language* 33, 149–74.

Kroll, J.F., Sumutka, B.M. and Schwartz, A.I. (2005) A cognitive view of the bilingual lexicon: Reading and speaking words in two languages. *International Journal of Bilingualism* 9, 27–48.

MacWhinney, B. (1997) Second language acquisition and the competition model. In A.M.B. De Groot and J.F. Kroll (eds) *Tutorials in Bilingualism: Psycholinguistic Perspectives* (pp. 113–42). Mahwah, NJ: Lawrence Erlbaum.

MacWhinney, B. (1999) The emergence of language from embodiment. In B. MacWhinney (ed.) *The Emergence of Language* (pp. 213–56). Mahwah, NJ: Lawrence Erlbaum.

Malt, B.C. and Sloman, S.A. (2003) Linguistic diversity and object naming by non-native speakers of English. *Bilingualism: Language and Cognition* 6, 47–67.

Marian, V. and Spivey, M.J. (2003) Competing activation in bilingual language processing: Within- and between-language competition. *Bilingualism: Language and Cognition* 6, 97–115.

Meuter, R.F.I. and Allport, A. (1999) Bilingual language switching in naming: Asymmetrical costs of language selection. *Journal of Memory and Language* 40, 25–40.

Michael, E., Dijkstra, A. and Kroll, J.F. (in preparation) Cross-language activation is not modulated by memory resources: New evidence for language nonselectivity in bilingual word recognition.

Pallier, C., Colomé, A. and Sebastián-Gallés, N. (2001) The influence of native-language phonology on lexical access. *Psychological Science* 12, 445–9.

Pallier, C., Dehaene, S., Poline, J. B., LeBihan, D., Argenti, A. M., Dupoux, E. and Mehler, J. (2003) Brain imaging of language plasticity in adopted adults: Can a second language replace the first? *Cerebral Cortex* 13, 155–61.

Perani, D., Abutalebi, J., Paulesu, E., Brambati, S., Scifo, P., Cappa, S. F. and Fazio, F. (2003) The role of age of acquisition and language usage in early, high-proficient bilinguals: An fMRI study during verbal fluency. *Human Brain Mapping* 19, 170–82.

Piske, T., MacKay I.R.A. and J.E. Flege (2001) Factors affecting degree of perceived foreign accent in an L2: A review. *Journal of Phonetics* 29, 191–215.

Schwartz, A. (2003) Word and sentence-based processes in second language reading. Unpublished doctoral dissertation, The Pennsylvania State University, University Park, PA.

Silverberg, S. and Samuel, A.G. (2004) The effect of age of second language acquisition on the representation and processing of second language words. *Journal of Memory and Language* 51, 381–98.

Van Hell, J.G. (1998) Cross-language processing and bilingual memory organization. Unpublished doctoral dissertation, University of Amsterdam, Amsterdam, The Netherlands.

Van Hell, J. and Dijkstra, T. (2002) Foreign language knowledge can influence native language performance: Evidence from trilinguals. *Psychonomic Bulletin and Review* 9, 780–9.

Chapter 9

Finding the Points of Contact: Language Acquisition in Children Raised in Monolingual, Bilingual and Multilingual Environments

SANDRA WAXMAN

The rapidly increasing number of children being raised in bilingual and multilingual homes and communities raises important questions and serious challenges for researchers, educators, and policy-makers alike. Yet research in cognitive science and developmental psychology has been slow to accommodate this fact in its research agendas, and contact between researchers examining acquisition from monolingual vs multilingual perspectives has been minimal. However, the time has come to consider carefully the course of language and conceptual development in children raised in monolingual, bilingual, and multilingual environments.

In this paper, I first describe a series of fundamental findings that have emerged from basic psychological research on early word learning and conceptual organization in infants and young children acquiring a single language. I then use these findings as a springboard to identify several points of contact for research addressing issues of acquisition from monolingual, bilingual and multilingual perspectives.

Word Learning and Conceptual Organization

Fundamental developmental issues

In my research laboratory I have adopted a cross-linguistic developmental approach to studying early word learning and its relation to conceptual organization, and I have focused exclusively on acquisition in infants and young children who are in the process of acquiring a single language. Although on the face of it, word learning would appear to be a rather straightforward task, a more careful examination reveals several layers of complexity. To be successful word learners, infants must (1) parse the relevant word from the continuous speech stream, (2) identify the relevant concept in the world, and (3) establish a mapping between them. See (Waxman & Lidz, in press) for a full discussion. More difficult still, there are many different words – indeed many different kinds of words – that can all be correctly applied to the very same scene or event in the world, and each kind of word directs attention to a different aspect of that experience. Consider for example a flamingo that is running behind a bluff. As speakers of English, we know that a count noun ('It's a flamingo') will refer to an individual object and can be extended to other members of the same object category (e.g. other flamingos), but that a proper noun ('That is Frieda') will refer to an individual but cannot be extended further. In contrast to these words that can refer to the individual *qua* individual, adjectives ('She's so graceful (or pink)') do not refer to the individual itself, but rather to a property of an individual (or category), and adjectives are extended to other entities sharing that property, independent of the category membership (e.g. 'pink' can be used to describe a flamingo, a coffee cup and a T-shirt).

By two-years of age, monolingual children are quite sensitive to many of the links between kinds of words (e.g. nouns, adjectives, verbs) and kinds of meaning (e.g. roughly speaking, the object categories, object properties, actions). In essence, they have discovered the relevant linguistic units (words and grammatical categories) as well as the relevant conceptual units (individual objects, categories of objects, properties of objects, and actions or relations among objects). More to the point, the evidence suggests that children as young as two years of age have also gathered some rather precise expectations about the mappings between these linguistic and conceptual units. As a result, they can use the grammatical form of a novel word as a clue to discovering its meaning (Hall & Lavin, 2004; Markman & Jaswal, 2004; Waxman & Lidz, in press).

Cross-linguistic investigations offer some important perspective on how these links between linguistic and conceptual units might be acquired (Gathercole & Min, 1997; Waxman, 2004). These investigations reveal that languages differ not only in the words that they use (*chien* vs. *dog*), but also in the grammatical forms that are represented in the language and the way these forms are recruited to convey meaning. For example, although the grammatical distinction between count nouns (e.g. This is a dog) and proper nouns (e.g. This is Magic) is quite clear in English, this is not the case in Japanese, where the grammatical distinction between these two forms is scant, at best (Imai & Haryu, 2004). Nonetheless, speakers of both languages – indeed speakers of any human language – can use the resources of their language to distinguish between categories of objects and individual objects. As another example, there are differences in the kinds of meaning that are permissible for adjectives in English and French, on the one hand, as compared to Spanish and Italian on the other (Waxman & Guasti, under review; Waxman *et al.*, 1997). Therefore, the links between kinds of words and their associated kinds of meaning must be shaped by the structure of the particular language under acquisition.

With a clear view of these fundamental issues, the developmental question becomes: How do infants discover which grammatical forms are represented in their language, and how do they learn to map these linguistic forms to meaning?

Word-learning and conceptual organization: The evidence from a developmental cross-linguistic (though monolingual) perspective

In my program of research, I have focused on these issues, asking which links, if any, are available early enough to guide the process of acquisition at the start, and how are these shaped by the language under acquisition. Any links that are available early in acquisition will be good candidates for universality; these may guide the initial stages of acquisition in all languages, and then become fine-tuned as the infant discovers the particular properties in the language being acquired. We have addressed these questions primarily with monolingual infants acquiring either English, Spanish, French, or Italian (Hall *et al.*, 2003; Waxman & Guasti, under review; Waxman *et al.*, 1997). Our strategy has been to select particular links (e.g. the link between nouns and object categories, or between adjectives and object properties) and ask (1) when this link becomes available, (2) how each link is supported or shaped by the structure of the native language being acquired, and (3) how these various links unfold over the course of development. (See Waxman & Lidz, in press for a review of the theoretical perspective and the empirical evidence supporting it.)

A broad initial expectation links word-learning and conceptual organization from the start . . . and sets the stage for more precise links

We have argued that infants cross the threshold into word learning equipped with a powerful, but very general, expectation that links words and concepts. We have suggested that this broad initial link is universal, that it gets the process of word learning off the ground, and that it sets the stage for subsequent developments in the lexicon and in the grammar (Fulkerson & Haaf, 2003; Waxman & Markow, 1995). Of course, infants move beyond this initially broad link, and the evidence suggests that as they do, they first tease out the grammatical category *noun* from among the other grammatical forms, and map nouns specifically to individual objects and to categories of objects (Waxman, 1999).

The early emergence of a noun-to-category link serves as the foundation that enables infants to discover the other grammatical forms that are present in their language (e.g. adjectives, verbs) and map these grammatical forms to their respective meanings. The patterns of acquisition for these latter forms appear to differ importantly from the acquisition of nouns, and appear to depend upon the prior acquisition of (at least some) nouns. This 'cascading' developmental picture, with nouns emerging early followed by the other grammatical forms, may well be universal, and may follow directly from the distinct informational requirements and conceptual entailments of each of these grammatical forms (Fisher & Gleitman, 2002; Waxman & Lidz, in press).

We can take English as a case in point. Dana Markow and I (Waxman & Markow, 1995) used a novelty-preference design to discover whether infants harbor any links between linguistic and conceptual organization at 12–14 months of age. This is the point at which most infants are just beginning to produce words on their own. During a *familiarization phase*, an experimenter offered the infant four different toys from a given object category (e.g. four animals), one at a time, in random order. This phase was immediately followed by a *test phase*, in which the experimenter simultaneously presented both (1) a new member of the now-familiar category (e.g. another animal) and (2) an object from a novel category (e.g. a fruit). Infants manipulated the toys freely throughout the task. We used the infants' total accumulated manipulation time as the dependent measure. Each infant completed this task four times, with four different sets of objects.

To identify any influence of novel words, infants were randomly assigned to one of three conditions that differed only during the familiarization phase of the experiment. Infants in the Noun condition heard, for example, 'See the *fauna*?'; those in the Adjective condition heard, for example, 'See the *faun-ish* one?'; those in a No Word control condition heard 'See here?'. At test, infants in all conditions heard precisely the same phrase ('See what I have?'). The experimenters presented novel words, rather than familiar ones, because their goal was to discover what links, if any, infants hold when it comes to mapping a new word to its meaning. If they had used familiar words (e.g. *dog*), performance would have been influenced by their understanding of that particular word, and could not speak to the more fundamental issue of the links between words and meaning.

The predictions were as follows: If infants noticed the category-based commonality among the four familiarization objects, then they should reveal a preference for the novel object at test. If infants detected the presence of the novel words, and if these words directed their attention toward the commonalities among the objects presented during familiarization, then infants hearing novel words should be more likely than those in the No Word control condition to reveal a novelty preference. Finally, if the initial link between words and concepts is general at the start, then infants in both the Noun and Adjective conditions should be more likely than those in the No Word condition to form categories.

These predictions were borne out. Infants in the No Word control condition revealed no novelty preference, suggesting that they had not detected the category-based commonalities among the familiarization objects. In contrast, infants in both the Noun and Adjective conditions revealed reliable novelty preferences, indicating that they had successfully formed object categories.

This result provides clear evidence for an early, foundational link between word-learning and conceptual organization. In essence, words served as *invitations* to form categories (Brown, 1958). Providing infants with a common name (at this developmental point, either a noun or an adjective) for a set of distinct objects highlighted the commonalities among them and promoted the formation of object categories. More recent work has revealed that this invitation does more than 'simply' highlight concepts that infants may already represent; it also supports the discovery of entirely novel concepts, composed of entirely novel objects (Booth & Waxman, 2002; Fulkerson & Haaf, 2003; Gopnik *et al.*, 2001; Maratsos, 2001; Nazzi & Gopnik, 2001). Moreover, this invitation has considerable conceptual force: Although novel words were presented only during the familiarization phase, their influence extended beyond the named objects, directing infants' attention to the new – and unnamed – objects present at test.

The evolution of a more specific expectation: Identifying the nouns and mapping them to object categories

The first evidence that infants have begun to establish a more precise link between kinds of words and kinds of meaning comes from infants at roughly 14 months of age. Retaining the logic of the novelty-preference task described earlier, Waxman and Booth (Waxman & Booth, 2001, 2003) shifted the focus to include objects (e.g. purple animals) that shared *both* category-based commonalities (e.g. *animal*) and property-based commonalities (e.g. color: *purple things*). This design feature permitted them to ask (1) whether infants could construe the very *same* set of objects (e.g. four purple animals) flexibly, either as members of an *object category* (e.g. animals) or as embodying an *object property* (e.g. color: purple), and (2) whether infants' construals were influenced systematically by novel words.[1]

At 14 months, infants hearing novel nouns performed differently than those hearing novel adjectives. They mapped nouns specifically to object categories, but not to object properties (e.g. color, texture). However, at this age, infants' expectation for adjectives was less well-defined. Although they sometimes mapped novel adjectives to properties of the objects, in most cases they mapped adjectives broadly to either object categories or object properties.

Taken together, this research suggests that by 13–14 months, infants are sensitive to (at least some of) the relevant cues that distinguish among the grammatical forms, and they recruit these distinctions actively. At this developmental moment, they map nouns rather specifically to object categories, but their expectations for adjectives and verbs remain underspecified. The more specific expectations regarding adjectives and verbs is a subsequent developmental achievement, occurring at roughly 21–24 months of age (Waxman & Braun, in preparation; Waxman & Markow, 1998).

Subsequent evolutions: Linking additional grammatical forms to meaning

The evidence suggests that the mappings between adjectives and object properties emerges later than the mappings for nouns. This fits well when considered from a developmental, cross-linguistic perspective. All languages have a grammatical form *noun*, and across all languages, a core function of nouns is to refer to objects and object categories. In contrast to nouns, there is substantially more developmental and cross-linguistic variation associated with the form *adjective*. Although many languages (like English) have a richly-developed adjective system to refer to properties of objects, in others (like Bantu and other African languages) the adjective system is sparse, including as few as 10 words for denoting property terms. In such languages, the types of meaning typically conveyed with adjectives in one language are expressed with a different grammatical form in another (Choi & Bowerman, 1991; Dixon, 1982; Talmy, 1985; Wierzbicka, 1986). With regard to acquisition, adjectives tend to be acquired later than nouns (Fenson *et al.*, 1994; Gentner, 1982; Maratsos, 1991; Waxman, 1999), and we have seen that infants' specific expectations for adjectives emerges later than their expectations for nouns (Booth & Waxman, 2003; Waxman, 1999). Moreover, because adjectives are semantically, morphologically, and syntactically dependent upon the nouns they modify (Booth & Waxman, 2003; Klibanoff & Waxman, 2000; Mintz & Gleitman, 2002; Waxman & Markow, 1998), it stands to reason that their acquisition would follow that of the nouns.

Taken together, these cross-linguistic and developmental observations suggest (1) that the link between nouns and object categories, which emerges early in infants, may be a universal phenomenon (Gathercole & Min, 1997; Gentner, 1982; Gleitman, 1990; Maratsos, 1991; Waxman & Markow, 1995), and (2) that the specific link between adjectives and their associated meaning, which emerge later in development, may vary systematically as a function of the structure of the language under acquisition (Dixon, 1982; Waxman & Markow, 1995; Wierzbicka, 1986). Recent evidence from children acquiring English, French, Spanish and Italian provides support for the view (Waxman & Guasti, under review; Waxman *et al.*, 1997) that across languages, children extend novel nouns to object categories, but that their extension of novel adjectives varies systematically as a function of the native language under acquisition.

Identifying points of contact: From basic research in monolingual environments to a multilingual agenda

This program of basic research focused primarily on the origin and evolution of links between linguistic and conceptual organization. There are, of course, many other programs of basic research that have taken different foci. Taken together, programs of basic research in monolingual environments offer rich and detailed evidence regarding early acquisition and can therefore provide a strong foundation for considering the process of acquisition in bilingual or multilingual environments.

To be sure, there is also considerable evidence from the bilingual multilingual research communities that may be brought to bear. A recent review by Patterson and Pearson (2004) serves as an example. Unfortunately, however, because evidence on acquisition in bilingual or multilingual environments tends to be scattered across multiple disciplines and because sample sizes tend to be relatively small, this literature is not widely known to the basic science research community. This is unfortunate, because the information should, in principle, inform current and future efforts. It would therefore be advantageous to cull this information together and bring it to the table as the current multilingual, multidisciplinary research agenda is being set.

Using basic research as a strong descriptive, theoretical and methodological base

Basic research offers an excellent descriptive base, which sets the foundation upon which we can consider whether, and in what ways, learners who are acquiring more than one language may differ from those acquiring only a single language. It also provides a broad range of research tools, from experimental methods (e.g. novelty-preference tasks, categorization tasks, grammaticality judgment tasks) to observational tools for analyzing adult input and children's language production (MacWhinney & Snow, 1990). These tools and methods can be tailored to meet the demands of researchers focusing on acquisition in bilingual and multilingual environments. As we move into the arena of acquisition in bilingual and multilingual environments, several other insights from the monolingual research enterprise become relevant.

Identifying structure: In the linguistic input and in the learner

One of the most fundamental insights gained from cross-linguistic developmental research with monolingual populations concerns the role of structure in acquisition. The evidence reveals that learners are exquisitely sensitive to the linguistic input that they receive and at the same time, that there is structure within the learner that guides acquisition. As the field moves forward to consider acquisition in bilingual and multilingual populations, it will be important to be as precise as possible about the balance between these sources (structure in the input and in the mind of the learner) and about the interplay between these sources as development unfolds.

In the case of word-learning, described above, this interplay between the expectations or structure inherent in the learner and the shaping role of the environment is essential (Bloom, 2000; Chomsky, 1980; Gleitman, 1990; Gleitman *et al.*, in press; Goodman, 1955; Jusczyk, 1997; Waxman & Lidz, in press) (Quine, 1960). Certainly, infants gather information from the environment, for they learn precisely the words and the grammatical forms of the language that surrounds them, and precisely the concepts to which they are exposed (e.g. gameboys and groundhogs in the US; scythes and peccaries in rural Mexico). But just as certainly, infants are guided by powerful internal expectations that guide the process, and that themselves evolve over the course of acquisition. This is especially important because, as noted earlier, human languages differ not only in their cadences and their individual words, but also in the ways in which kinds of words (e.g. nouns, adjectives, verbs) are recruited to express fundamental aspects of meaning. A viable theory of word-learning must be sufficiently constrained to account for what appear to be universal patterns of acquisition in the face of this cross-linguistic variation, and also sufficiently flexible to accommodate the systematic variations that occur across languages and across developmental time.

Posing precise questions

If this new generation of research is to yield fruit, the questions that we pose must be precise. Broad questions (e.g., 'Are bilingual learners slower/faster than monolingual learners?') are likely to provide only murky answers. More precise questions ('How does the onset and rate of early word learning in bilingual learners compare to that of monolingual learners?' or 'How does the bilingual infant's discovery of a particular grammatical form or a particular kind of grammatical rule in one language compare with that of monolingual learners in that language?') are more likely to yield information that will be relevant to the larger scientific and educational goals.

Recognizing that all words are not 'created equal'

Another lesson from research in monolingual acquisition is that all words are not 'created equal'. Across languages, infants distinguish the nouns first (before the other grammatical forms) and map them specifically to categories of objects. This early acquisition of the noun-category link then serves as the gateway into the discovery of the other grammatical forms (e.g. adjectives, verbs) and their links to meaning. It will be important to examine more specifically and in greater depth how these developmental processes unfold in monolingual learners acquiring various native languages and in those acquiring multiple languages. We can ask, for example, whether an appreciation of a linkage (e.g. between nouns and object categories) in an infant's native language is recruited in the acquisition of a second language. The answer to this question may vary with the linkage in question, particularly since some linkages appear to be universal and others appear to depend primarily on the structure of the input from the native language. In developing a multilingual research agenda, it will also be important to compare the acquisition of a target language (say, for example, Spanish) in children raised in monolingual and bilingual (e.g. Spanish/English) environments. Comparing the developmental trajectory of one language in monolingual and multilingual milieu will move us closer to understanding the role of the input as well as the challenges faced by learners.

Specifying the relation between L1 and L2

This discussion raises a larger question, one concerned with the structural properties of the particular languages under acquisition and the relations among them. At this point, our knowledge of whether, when and how the structural features of L1 influence the acquisition of L2. At a most general level, we can ask whether a given L2 is more readily acquired if it is structurally quite similar to L1. For example, what are the consequences on acquisition, if any, when L1 and L2 differ in the grammatical forms that they represent and their mappings to meaning? For example, do native speakers of English have more difficulty mastering the verb system in their L2 if the L2 happens to be a language like Spanish (in which the verbs tend to encode different features than in English) than if the L2 happens to be a language like French (in which the verbs tend to encode the same features as in English)?

As another example, consider grammatical gender. Do learners have more trouble mastering grammatical gender in L2 (e.g. French) if their L1 marks grammatical gender (e.g. Spanish) than if it does not (e.g. English)? Going one step further, we can ask, what are the consequences of moving from a binary system of grammatical gender (e.g. Spanish, French) to a three-way system of grammatical gender (e.g. German) and vice versa?

The examples that we have just considered (verb systems, grammatical gender) are tied closely to syntax. But similar issues of 'translation' can also be seen in the semantic system. For example, consider the spatial predicates (Bowerman, 1996; Choi *et al.*, 1999). Some languages, like Korean, make a semantic distinction between tight- and loose-fit, naming loose-fitting spatial relations with one word and tight-fitting spatial relations with a different one. English speakers carve up the semantics of space quite differently, naming all relations having to do with containment with on term (in) and those having to do with contact with another term (on). Infants acquiring either language as L1 master its spatial semantics with apparent ease. But what are the consequences of having a language like English as L1 when it comes to acquiring a language like Korean as L2? Is it more difficult to 're-draw' semantic space after having 'drawn' it in a very different way in the first place? Are new distinctions more easily acquired than distinctions that cut across those already established?

At the most general level, then, it is clear that L1-L2 mismatches may occur in the semantic system, the morphological system, the syntactic system or in the mappings between these systems. Each genre of mismatch is an important topic in its own right.

Elucidating sensitive periods and other effects of age on acquisition

Another important avenue for research concerns age effects in relation to the acquisition of L2. A signature of first language acquisition is that there are sensitive periods, or windows for optimal acquisition (Lenneberg, 1993). Another key finding is that it is better to learn a second language early than to (try to) learn it late (Johnson & Newport, 1989). But we must be more precise about these issues in our examinations of acquisition of a second or later language. For example, what are the consequences of introducing L2 at various developmental points? Are these consequences seen primarily in the mastery of syntactic, prosodic, or semantic components of L2? And does the acquisition of L2 feed back on L1, influencing the learner's performance or processing of L1? What are the consequences, if any, of being raised bilingual from the start and being introduced to a second language after the acquisition of the first language is underway?

Looking to the Future

At this point we have accumulated considerable evidence concerning early linguistic and conceptual development in monolingual (especially English-speaking) children. And the evidence concerning acquisition in monolingual children acquiring languages other than English is currently accumulating. Armed with this evidence, the research community is poised to take a bold step, to launch a full and integrated research agenda to focus squarely on language acquisition in bilingual and multilingual children. A primary goal in this enterprise will be to explore more fully and in greater depth the linguistic and conceptual consequences of acquiring more than a single language.

We suspect that multilingualism will offer the learner significant advantages as well as some challenges. These advantages and challenges will best be viewed from a truly developmental and multidisciplinary perspective. With regard to development, it will be crucial to pinpoint the age effects by weaving this into the very core of our experimental designs. It will also be crucial to consider whether, how, and in what contexts (e.g., classroom, playground, home) the various languages are reinforced. Another key factor will be to consider seriously whether and how the semantic, syntactic, morphologic and pragmatic differences between two languages influences the acquisition of each. In setting the current research agenda, it will be advantageous to foster collaborations between researchers and clinicians studying acquisition in monolingual, bilingual and multilingual environments. This could insure that researchers use one another's findings to inform research design and to guide the interpretation of evidence.

The time has come to consider carefully and to compare the course of language and conceptual development in children raised in monolingual, bilingual, and multilingual environments. Building a truly developmental program of research will enrich our theories of acquisition even as it advances our educational and social goals.

Notes

1. For a discussion of the psychological distinction between category- vs. property-based commonalities, see Waxman (1999), Waxman & Booth (2001) and Gelman & Kalish (1993).

References

Bloom, P. (2000) *How Children Learn the Meanings of Words.* Cambridge, MA: MIT Press.

Booth, A.E. and Waxman, S.R. (2002) Object names and object functions serve as cues to categories for infants. *Developmental Psychology* 38 (6), 948–57.

Booth, A.E. and Waxman, S.R. (2003) Mapping words to the world in infancy: On the evolution of expectations for count nouns and adjectives. *Journal of Cognition & Development* 4 (3), 357–81.

Bowerman, M. (1996) The origins of children's spatial semantic categories: Cognitive versus linguistic determinants. In J.J. Gumperz and S.C. Levinson (eds) *Rethinking Linguistic Relativity. Studies in the Social and Cultural Foundations of Language,* No. 17 (pp. 145–76). Cambridge, UK: Cambridge University Press.

Brown, R. (1958) *Words and Things.* Glencoe, IL: Free Press.

Choi, S. and Bowerman, M. (1991) Learning to express motion events in English and Korean: The influence of language-specific lexicalization patterns. *Cognition* 41 (1–3), 83–121.

Choi, S., McDonough, L., Bowerman, M. and Mandler, J. (1999) Comprehension of spatial terms in English and Korean. *Cognitive Development* 14, 241–68.

Chomsky, N. (1980) *Rules and Representations.* London: Basil Blackwell.

Dixon, R.M.W. (1982) *Where Have All the Adjectives Gone?* Berlin: Mouton Publishers.

Fenson, L., Dale, P.S., Reznick, J.S., Bates, E., Thal, D.J. and Pethick, S.J. (1994) Variability in early communicative development. *Monographs of the Society for Research in Child Development,* 59 (5), v–173.

Fisher, C. and Gleitman, L.R. (2002) Language Acquisition. In H. Pashler and R. Gallistel (eds) *Steven's Handbook of Experimental Psychology* (3rd edn, Vol. 3: *Learning, Motivation, and Emotion,* pp. 445–96) New York: John Wiley.

Fulkerson, A.L. and Haaf, R.A. (2003) The influence of labels, non-labeling sounds, and source of auditory input on 9- and 15-month olds' object categorization. *Infancy* (4), 349–69.

Gathercole, V.C.M. and Min, H. (1997) Word meaning biases or language-specific effects? Evidence from English, Spanish, and Korean. *First Language* 17 (49), 31–56.

Gelman, S.A. and Kalish, C.W. (1993) Categories and causality. In M.L.H.R. Pasnak (ed.) *Emerging Themes in Cognitive Development* (Vol. 2, pp. 3–32). New York: Springer-Verlag.

Gentner, D. (1982) Why nouns are learned before verbs: Linguistic relativity versus natural partitioning. In S. Kuczaj (ed.) *Language Development: Language, Thought, and Culture* (Vol. 2, pp. 301–34). Hillsdale, NJ: Lawrence Erlbaum.

Gleitman, L. (1990) The structural sources of verb meanings. *Language Acquisition: A Journal of Developmental Linguistics* 1 (1), 3–55.

Gleitman, L.R., Cassidy, K., Nappa, R., Papafragou, A. and Trueswell, J.C. (in press). Hard words. *Language Learning and Development* 1.

Goodman, N. (1955) *Fact, Fiction, & Forecast.* Cambridge, MA: Harvard University Press.

Gopnik, A., Sobel, D.M., Schulz, L.E. and Glymour, C. (2001) Causal learning mechanisms in very young children: Two-, three-, and four-year-olds infer causal relations from patterns of variation and covariation. *Developmental Psychology,* 37 (5), 620–9.

Hall, D.G. and Lavin, T.A. (2004) Preschoolers' use and misuse of part-of-speech information in word learning: Implications for lexical development. In D.G. Hall and S.R. Waxman (eds) *Weaving a Lexicon*. Cambridge: MIT Press.

Hall, D.G., Waxman, S.R., Bredart, S. and Nicolay, A.-C. (2003) Preschoolers' use of form class cues to learn descriptive proper names. *Child Development* 74 (5), 1547–60.

Imai, M. and Haryu, E. (2004) The nature of word-learning biases and their roles for lexical development: From a cross-linguistic perspective. In D.G. Hall and S.R. Waxman (eds) *Weaving a Lexicon*. Cambridge: MIT Press.

Johnson, J.S. and Newport, E.L. (1989) Critical period effects in second language learning: The influence of maturational state on the acquisition of English as a second language. *Cognitive Psychology* 21, 60–99.

Jusczyk, P. (1997) *The Discovery of Spoken Language*. Cambridge: MIT Press.

Klibanoff, R.S. and Waxman, S.R. (2000) Basic level object categories support the acquisition of novel adjectives: Evidence from preschool-aged children. *Child Development* 71 (3), 649–59.

Lenneberg, E.H. (1993) Toward a biological theory of language development. In M.H. Johnson (ed.) *Brain Development and Cognition: A Reader* (pp. 39–46). Malden, MA: Blackwell.

MacWhinney, B. and Snow, C. (1990) The Child Language Data Exchange System: An update. *Journal of Child Language* 17, 457–72.

Maratsos, M. (2001) How fast does a child learn a word? *Behavioral and Brain Sciences* (24), 1111–12.

Maratsos, M.P. (1991) How the acquisition of nouns may be different from that of verbs. In N.A. Krasnegor, D.M. Rumbaugh *et al.* (eds) *Biological and Behavioral Determinants of Language Development* (pp. 67–88) Hillsdale, NJ: Lawrence Erlbaum.

Markman, E.M. and Jaswal, V.K. (2004) Acquiring and using a grammatical form class: Lessons from the proper-count distinction. In D.G. Hall and S.R. Waxman (eds) *Weaving a Lexicon*. Cambridge: MIT Press.

Mintz, T.H. and Gleitman, L.R. (2002) Adjectives really do modify nouns: The incremental and restricted nature of early adjective acquisition. *Cognition*, 84 (3), 267–93.

Nazzi, T. and Gopnik, A. (2001) Linguistic and cognitive abilities in infancy: When does language become a tool for categorization? *Cognition* 80 (3), B11–B20.

Patterson, J. and Pearson, B.Z. (2004) Bilingual lexical development: Influences, contexts, and processes. In G. Goldstein (ed.) *Bilingual Language Development and Disorders in Spanish-English Speakers* (pp. 77–104). Baltimore, MD: Paul Brookes.

Quine, W.V.O. (1960) *Word and Object: An Inquiry into the Linguistic Mechanisms of Objective Reference*. New York: John Wiley.

Talmy, L. (1985) Lexicalization patterns: Semantic structure in lexical forms. In T. Shopen (ed.) *Language Typology and Syntactic Description* (Vol. 3, pp. 249–291). San Diego: Academic Press.

Waxman, S.R. (1999) Specifying the scope of 13-month-olds' expectations for novel words. *Cognition* 70 (3), B35–B50.

Waxman, S.R. (2004) Everything had a name, and each name gave birth to a new thought: Links between early word-learning and conceptual organization. In D.G. Hall and S.R. Waxman (eds) *Weaving a Lexicon*. Cambridge: MIT Press.

Waxman, S.R. and Markow, D.B. (1995) Words as invitations to form categories: Evidence from 12- to 13-month-old infants. *Cognitive Psychology* 29(3), 257–302.

Waxman, S.R. and Markow, D.B. (1998) Object properties and object kind: Twenty-one-month-old infants' extension of novel adjectives. *Child Development* 69 (5), 1313–29.

Waxman, S.R. and Booth, A.E. (2001) Seeing pink elephants: Fourteen-month-olds' interpretations of novel nouns and adjectives. *Cognitive Psychology* 43, 217–42.

Waxman, S.R. and Booth, A.E. (2003) The origins and evolution of links between word learning and conceptual organization: New evidence from 11-month-olds. *Developmental Science* 6 (2), 130–7.

Waxman, S.R. and Braun, I.E. (in preparation) Acquisition of adjectives: Semantic boundaries.

Waxman, S.R. and Guasti, M.T. (under review) Linking nouns and adjectives to meaning: New evidence from Italian-speaking children.

Waxman, S.R. and Lidz, J. (in press) Early word learning. In D. Kuhn and R. Siegler (eds) *Handbook of Child Psychology* (6th edn, Vol. 2).

Waxman, S.R., Senghas, A. and Benveniste, S. (1997) A cross-linguistic examination of the noun-category bias: Its existence and specificity in French- and Spanish-speaking preschool-aged children. *Cognitive Psychology* 32 (3), 183–218.

Wierzbicka, A. (1986) Does language reflect culture? Evidence from Australian English. *Language in Society* 15 (3), 349–73.

Chapter 10

Multiple Perspectives on Research on Childhood Bilingualism

MARTHA CRAGO

This chapter addresses the multiple perspectives that emerged in the discussions of a group of researchers brought together, first in a workshop and then in this book, to share their findings on childhood bilingualism. Different perspectives in the world at large have been known to create divisions. Among them are the profound divisions that sometimes separate speakers of different languages, people of different social classes, of different cultures, of different races and of different nationalities. Then there are those relatively unimportant, but professionally absorbing, divisions that separate people such as language acquisition researchers into theoretical camps, methodological advocates, and national clusters. This volume, like the workshop that preceded it, can be construed as an encounter with the other across the lines, both virtual and real, that exist between various perspectives. It brings together the work of researchers from Canada and the United States, highlighting the differences in the dual language context of their two countries. It presents research spanning an array of theoretical and methodological possibilities, stemming from studies of both monolingual and bilingual children. It attempts to find links between basic research findings and theories and the urgent need for practical solutions. This volume and the meeting from which it stems have been attempts to create permeability across boundaries so that ideas from multiple perspectives, addressing various populations and critical concerns, can influence one another and become mutually informing. The aim is to avoid balkanization of thought by bringing ideas together that create transfer from one mindset and set of theories and practices to other ones. In some small way, this work in the borderlands of research mirrors the task that bilingual children confront when they encounter other languages and cultures in their homes, schools and communities. When considering bilingualism, politicians often mention its cost. The ideas assembled here exhort the reader to consider the cost of monolingualism and of research isolationism. In doing so, this chapter addresses issues of bilingual research that cut across a number of domains, ranging from national context to methodological variation, to the age and stage of speakers and the nature of the components of language themselves. This examination of multiple perspectives is done in an attempt to capture the essence of the exchange that occurred among the assembled researchers and that is, in turn, reflected in the chapters of this book.

National Policies and Contexts for Bilingualism

There are fundamental differences that exist between Canada and the United States that have ramifications for bilingual research. These differences in national perspectives highlight the importance of considering national policies and contexts in research on bilingualism. In Canada, at the present time, there are official legal policies such as the Official Languages Act,[1] the Canadian Multiculturalism Act,[2] and the Canadian Charter of Rights and Freedoms[3] that provide a formal recognition of the rights and the status given to speakers of Canada's two official languages and to citizens and immigrants of various cultural backgrounds. Unlike the United States where the rights of the individual are defined exclusively in terms of the state, in Canada, the individual's rights are defined not only with regard to the state but also with regard to 'the other', namely the other official language and its speakers.[4] In line with this, the federal and provincial governments must provide certain services in the two official languages. This fundamental Canadian belief in linguistic duality and cultural plurality has, over time, led to the creation and flourishing of various educational programs that encourage bilingualism and second language learning.

A special situation exists in the province of Quebec. In 1976, the 'Charter of the French Language' commonly known as Bill 101 was passed by the Quebec legislature.[5] This law decreed, among other things, that any child whose parents were from Quebec and were not educated in English or who immigrated to Quebec after 1976 must attend French-language public schools. Despite the mandatory nature of its legal imperatives, Bill 101 has allowed the French-speaking population of Quebec to maintain and strengthen its language to the point where, now, in cities like Montreal there are two majority languages. Both French and English are spoken equally fluently in the same city and often by the same person or in the same home.

Of course, there was a time, not so long ago, in Canada when the recognition and learning of two languages was devalued and under supported. As late as the 1970s, French-speaking teachers in the province of Alberta, for instance, had to teach the French language in secret as no French language instruction was allowed in many schools.[6] There was an even darker past when Canadian Native children had their language and culture mercilessly stripped away from them in residential schools. Today, official laws and policies have curbed the dominance of the English language in Canada.

Recently, it appears as if the United States may be moving in the opposite direction from Canada. Rather than building bilingualism it could be seen as a country that is transiting out of it. In 1998 bilingual educational programs in California were curtailed. By 2002, the Office of Bilingual Education and Minority Language Affairs was renamed the Office of English Language Acquisition, Language Enhancement, and Academic Achievement. Despite the fact that these legislative changes have provided grants to states in such a way that they cover a greater percentage of limited English proficient children,[7] they, nevertheless, leave one to wonder if Catherine Snow's term 'serial monolingualism',[8] is not an apt descriptor for the language education situation in the United States today.

The contrasting legal policies and political realities of these two countries are examples of how various nations create very different social contexts for research on bilingualism and even a difference in vocabulary. As Genesee pointed out in his chapter, in Canada a clear distinction is made between a 'bilingual' person who is exposed to two languages from birth and a 'second language' speaker who has learned another language after three years of age. This distinction is less clear in the United States where the term 'bilingual' often implies either type of person with no distinction made between them. Such different national and social contexts underline the importance of studying childhood bilingualism in various sociopolitical contexts. In Canada, for instance, the existence of two majority languages provides an ideal environment for testing the cognitive capacity of the mind to learn two languages. Canadian educational programs provide opportunities for research into bilingual schooling and various forms of second language educational programs. In contrast, the United States provides a rich setting for research into how various social variables such as class, parental education levels, and poverty influence the teaching and learning of a second language. Such complementarities provide an interesting combination of contexts that need to be explored collaboratively by researchers from the two countries using a variety of methodological and theoretical approaches.

Methodological Array

The research presented in this volume mirrors, to a large extent, the array of methodological approaches that have been and can be used to study bilingualism. The preceding chapters demonstrate the use and usefulness of various different methodologies in the study of bilingual and second language learning. There are research designs that span the range from experimental cross-sectional studies of various types and ages of learners to longitudinal small number studies that trace the time course of language acquisition across the early years of childhood. In addition, there is a wide variety of procedures that can be used to study bilingualism from survey questionnaires of parents, teachers and learners themselves to head-turn, reaction time, evoked potential, magnetic resonance imaging and eye tracking procedures. There are also various measures of productive language that include transcribed data in addition to communication inventories and standardized tests. Not included in the work of the researchers represented in this volume, but nevertheless important to the understanding of the social realities of dual language learning at home, in classrooms and in the workplace, are the studies that employ ethnographic methodologies in which micro- and macro-observations of language use and language learning are combined to form rich qualitative descriptions.

Despite the numerous approaches in use at the present time, there is, nevertheless, a striking need for standardized measures and experimental tasks that are specific to bilingual and second language learning populations. Without the construction of such measurement tools, research on bilingualism will continue to be limited by its reliance on procedures and measures that have been standardized and developed for monolingual populations.

Populations for study need to be expanded to include people from across the age span. The recent work of Bialystok *et al.* (2004) has indicated the importance and interest in expanding the study of the dual language capacity to include speakers who are aging. My own work with Johanne Paradis and others (Paradis *et al.*, 2003) on grammatical acquisition by French- and English- bilingual children with specific language impairment is a further extension of dual language research that provides an understanding of the strength of the language faculty for bilingualism even under impairment. Continued work with a wider variety of language-impaired populations will strengthen our grasp on both the nature of impairment and on the full capacity of the mind for dual language learning.

The study of dual language learning, by definition, involves a large number of variables. There are various populations of dual language learners learning in a variety of ways. This includes simultaneous bilinguals as well as a range of individuals who learn a second language at varied ages and in varied circumstances that involve economic, racial, cultural, class, identity and educational variables. As a result, a more dimensional understanding of bilingualism will require population samples from a wider range of learners and speakers as well as improved characterizations of contexts before meaningful generalizations can be made.

Theoretical Constructs and Disciplinary Contributions

This volume is an excellent example of an encounter between various theoretical and disciplinary constructs that are relevant to research in bilingual and second language learning. However, the disciplinary spectrum and variety of theoretical approaches useful to the study of bilingualism are more numerous than those included in this volume. In addition to the theoretical and disciplinary perspectives of the research carried out by the psychologists and educational researchers represented here, there are pertinent theories from linguistics, ethnographic language socialization research and research in communication sciences and disorders. Research on childhood bilingualism needs to span and knit together the long-standing, deep divide between the 'nature' and the 'nurture' explanations of language acquisition. Working across the borders of generativist grammarians, language socialization researchers, cognitive psychologists, social psychologists and educational researchers can only improve our understanding of the mental abilities and social realities of dual language speakers. For they are, after all, people whose native endowment for language learning has been stretched and shaped in various ways by the circumstances in which they learn and use more than one language. An enhanced range of disciplines and theories that address bilingualism will provide more information on both the capacity of the mind and the variety of contexts for learning two and more languages. Limiting research and thinking to one school of thought is unlikely to expose the full dimensions of dual language learning in much the same way that limiting children to one language is unlikely to release the full capacity of their minds and the richness of possible social worlds.

Language Behaviors and Capabilities

As evidenced in this volume, there are also a number of language-related behaviors and capabilities that call for investigation, including speech perception, oral and signed proficiency, language comprehension and processing, reading and writing skills, language use, interaction and input. In addition to these, there are physiological phenomena such as brain functioning and its relationship to dual language capabilities that are important to study. The investigation of these various language related behaviors needs to be augmented by accounting for how dual language learning takes place in different ways at different maturational stages. Furthermore, the learning of more and different combinations of languages, including signed languages, by bilinguals needs to be explored in order to understand how various language typologies and modalities impact on the acquisition process and on each other during acquisition. In addition, the ways in which dual language learning takes place across various types of learners are also informative to understanding both typical and less typical patterns of development. In fact, determining how dual language development can be encouraged across various learners, by various methods and at various life stages is a central concern to education and clinical intervention with dual language learners. Finally, the social consequences of speaking more than one language need to be explored in terms of language maintenance, academic achievement, employment, aging, and social interaction with peers and family members.

Crafting Connections and Conclusions

The exercise of this volume, of the workshop that preceded it and of this chapter is to craft connections, find links and widen well trod pathways in the interest of bringing new theories, new methods and new interdisciplinary linkages to the study of dual language learners, their capacities and their social contexts. It is an exercise in crossing boundaries and encountering other ideas. What then are some of the most basic links that need to be forged?

Links need to be created between basic research and its application to practice. Basic researchers need to transfer their knowledge to practitioners and educational researchers. Educational researchers, for their part, need to read basic research and investigate its meaning for everyday life in the schools.

Links between various theories, methodologies and disciplines need to be strengthened. This will involve forming interdisciplinary research teams, the very formation of which has a set of consequences for research funding agencies. The appropriate adjudication of research grants to support such teams will, for instance, require multidisciplinary review panels. Furthermore, the sensible funding of interdisciplinary teams is likely to require cross-agency, cross-institutional funding. As pointed out earlier, different national contexts present different and complementary settings for bilingual research. Hence funding agencies will also need to develop cross-national funding mechanisms. They also need to permit creative spending. Anne Fernald, whose work is reported in this volume, carries out her research in a house located in a particular neighborhood in California. The flexibility that her funding agency demonstrated in permitting her to procure this house has greatly facilitated her research and its integration back into the community. Finally, governments and research agencies need to consider the enormous social and psychological implications of research into dual language learners in today's world and provide ample funding to support it with special allocations of money.

The training of future generations of researchers needs to expose them to the links between various theoretical, methodological and disciplinary perspectives. This will mean crafting new interdisciplinary and even inter-institutional graduate studies programs. It will mean providing graduate students and postdoctoral scholars with funds so that they can devote time to their studies and have mobility between different research settings. It may also mean developing multi-institutional and cross-border training grants with provisions for cross-institutional summer institutes, video- and teleconferences as well as distance courses delivered electronically to an interlinked set of universities. Imagine the rich learning experience of an electronic course team-taught by the authors of this volume beamed in to students on Canadian and American university campuses from California to Newfoundland.

The opportunity and the necessity to forge research links across disciplinary and national boundaries as well as across theoretical and methodological ones are essential for understanding dual language learning. Research about bilingualism has become increasingly important in today's world, not only because it elucidates our understanding of the potential of the human mind, but because it elucidates our understanding of the possibilities for productive societal encounters across languages and cultures. An understanding of how to educate children, the full range of children, to become citizens not only of their own linguistic and cultural groups and countries but of the world at large has now become a global imperative. Bilingualism builds an awareness of others as well as an enriched set of abilities with which to encounter others. This awareness and these abilities are precious to our well-being as members of a world-wide community whose cultures and languages are so richly varied that they, unfortunately, can threaten to divide us in perilous ways.

Notes

1. Official Languages Act, R.S.c., 1985, c. 31 (4th Supp.), online: Department of Justice <http://laws.justice.gc.ca/en/O-3.01/>
2. Canadian Multiculturalism Act R.S.c., 1985, c. 24 (4th Supp.), online: Department of Justice, < http://laws.justice.gc.ca/en/C-18.7/>
3. Canadian Charter of Rights and Freedoms, Part I of the Constitution Act, 1982, being Schedule B of the Canada Act, 1982 (U.K.), 1982, c. 11., online: Department of Justice, < http://laws.justice.gc.ca/en/charter/>

4. Rosalie Abella, Justice, Supreme Court of Canada, personal communication, 29 April 2004.
5. Charter of the French Language, R.S.Q., c. C-11, online: Publications Quebec, <http://www2.publicationsduquebec.gouv.qc.ca/home.php#>
6. Ministere d 'Alberta Learning (2001). Affirmer l'education en francais langue premiere: fondements et orientations. <http://www.learning.gov.ab.ca>
7. Kathleen Leos, personal communication, 2005.
8. Catherine Snow, personal communication, 2005.

References

Bialystok, E., Craik, F., Klein, R. and Visawanathan, M. (2004) Bilingualism, aging, and cognitive control: Evidence from the Simon task. *Psychology and Aging* 19 (2), 290–303.
Paradis, J., Crago, M., Genesee, F. and Rice, M. (2003) French-English bilingual children with specific language impairment: How do they compare with their monolingual peers. *Journal of Speech, Language and Hearing Research* 36, 113–27.

Chapter 11

An Agenda for Research on Childhood Bilingualism

PEGGY McCARDLE and ERIKA HOFF[1]

Many children in the US, and indeed throughout the world, grow up exposed to more than one language. To date there has been insufficient research to enable us to fully delineate and understand the developmental trajectories of children acquiring more than one language, either simultaneously or in sequence across childhood, adolescence and adulthood. In this volume, we have presented a sampling of some high quality research that is being or has recently been conducted on language and literacy development in bilingual children, and thoughts on how work on adult bilingualism and cross-linguistic studies of monolingual language development might inform research approaches in childhood bilingualism. As all of the papers seem to make clear, much remains to be done in this increasingly important area. A broad approach is needed in which bilingualism is fully explored as one aspect of the ecology of human development with potential consequences for oral language development, literacy, academic achievement, and social adaptation. Research is needed to document the forms that environmental bilingualism takes, the relations between parameters of environmental bilingualism and child outcomes, and the processes by which bilingualism shapes children's development. Such research will depend on reliable and valid means to assess children's environments and their language development, thus the development of measures will also be crucial. The papers in this volume represent a beginning step in this direction.

The original papers presented and the discussions held at the meeting, *Childhood Bilingualism: Current Status and Future Directions*, described in the introductory chapter of this volume, served as the foundation for the development of a research agenda. The meeting was designed to capitalize on the increasing convergence of interest in the theoretical underpinnings of language development and the translation of research findings for the practical benefit of children. The workshop organizers sought to initiate an open and ongoing discussion among key members of the research community, across disciplines and research approaches, in order to re-energize research and promote the development of novel approaches or the application of approaches not traditionally applied to the area of bilingual development, and to develop a research agenda outlining the major gaps and research needs in bilingual development. Participants were charged with developing major research questions that must be addressed to move the field forward. Much of the research agenda outlined below is drawn from the discussions and recommendations from that meeting (Childhood Bilingualism, 2004).

There were also other sources that contributed to this research agenda. Prior to the meeting on Childhood Bilingualism, a major symposium was held addressing learning disabilities in English language learners (ELLs) (National Symposium on Learning Disabilities in English Language Learners: Symposium Summary, 2003). Among the topics raised, specific recommendations for the development of new measures and the adaptation of extant measures were made at that meeting, and there was a call for classification research in the area of learning disabilities (LD) in ELLs. In addition to a summary document, that symposium also resulted in a thematic journal issue (McCardle *et al.*, 2005b).

To accomplish the goals outlined below, there is a need to draw from what we already know in many areas. Diary studies and case studies of bilingual children raise questions that can be addressed in larger scale, longitudinal studies, and in laboratory work similar to that being conducted with monolingual infants. For example, laboratory studies of infant perception are already being applied to bilingual infants, as noted in the papers by Werker and Vihman, and in the work by Kuhl and colleagues (e.g. Iverson *et al.*, 2003; Kuhl *et al.*, 2001) as well as others. Cross-linguistic studies, such as those conducted by Waxman and colleagues (e.g. Waxman & Booth, 2001; Hall *et al.*, 2003), can raise interesting questions that should be addressed in studies of bilingual language development. Greater collaboration among those studying cross-linguistic development, those investigating infant perception, and those whose primary focus is bilingual language development could result in the sharing of methods and approaches and the development of innovative approaches.

The preceding papers in this issue clearly highlight the need for additional research on bilingual or multilingual development, and directions that such research might take. Workshop participants identified many common themes and offered some specific suggestions for research, which are summarized below together with information drawn from the research agenda presented in McCardle *et al.* (2005a).

Descriptive and Experimental Research on Bilingualism

Descriptive work on bilingualism is needed, to address both the social, cultural, and linguistic contexts of bilingual development, and the cognitive and linguistic processes and outcomes of bilingual development. It will be important to carefully characterize infants and children as they are learning multiple languages, in order to clearly describe and understand the range of variability in bilingual development. Identifying where bilinguals' language and learning profiles differ from those of monolinguals may be beneficial in addressing the needs of bilingual children as they grow to become successful learners and as they develop literacy in both languages.

A systematic understanding of the heterogeneity of bilingualism will be important; such research should consider the variety of situations in which bilingualism or multilingualism develops, such as simultaneous learning of two languages, monolingual early development with the later introduction of a second or additional languages, and the variation introduced by the relatedness (or lack thereof) of the languages in question (similarity in grammatical structure, sound system, writing system). Research at the intersection of bilingualism and special populations (including but not limited to those with learning disabilities or language impairments) must also be encouraged. These issues could all benefit from more large-sample, longitudinal studies beginning in the early preschool years.

From descriptive studies of bilingual development, specific research questions will emerge that can be examined empirically through experimental and quasi-experimental studies. Such experimental work is crucial if we are to determine the most effective methods of formal language and literacy instruction for bilingual and ELL students. It is important to hold in mind that many children who enter US schools as ELLs are not bilingual but may be monolingual in a language other than English, and the situation of a monolingual or bilingual child who enters school unable to speak the language of majority instruction is increasingly occurring in other nations. Instruction or intervention methods that are effective with a child who has learned and is roughly equally proficient in two languages since early in the preschool period will not necessarily be effective or even appropriate for such students. This serves to emphasize the need for careful documentation of the contexts in which students are learning more than one language as well as their history of exposure and their proficiency in the languages to which they have been exposed. It will be crucial that all researchers clearly operationalize labels such as bilingual, sequential bilingual, ELL, second language learner, etc. in their research, in order that the research be replicable and provide the clearest information possible.

Change Across the Life Span

Research on bilingual language development should not be restricted to early childhood or school age children. Additional languages can and are learned by individuals of all ages. There is a need to more fully understand how language-learning ability changes over time, both in those who acquire multiple languages early in life and those who learn additional languages later. It will be important to examine not simply outcomes of language learning but the process itself, including bi-directional influences of the languages, the interface of language and cognitive processes, and how these may change or maintain over time.

Large-scale, longitudinal research on language development in middle school and high school years (including those who arrive in a new language community in high school) is greatly needed, as there is extremely little research on these age groups. In particular, there is a need to include links between oral language development and academic achievement, especially the types of language skills being developed and the match with the language skills needed to succeed academically.

Parent–child and peer interactions and their influence on literacy are also important yet under-researched topics, as is how these interactions are themselves impacted by language and literacy. A fresh perspective on these questions might include consideration of African American adolescents who use Black English; dialect variation can be viewed as another form of bilingualism.

Measurement

There are a number of opportunities for the improved measurement of language abilities in bilingual individuals. The development of formal, standardized assessment tools with good technical qualities is a high priority, and such measures are needed for both L1 and L2, regardless of what those languages are. While there are many extant measures of English, assessments of English as L2 are needed; it should not be assumed that extant measures for native speakers are always appropriate for that language as L2.

In addition to overall language measures, better assessment instruments for the major components of oral language production and comprehension are needed. Because many measures are initially developed for use in particular research studies, mechanisms for sharing instruments across laboratories should be developed. Normative data should be gathered for researcher-developed measures where possible, to give the measures broader applicability.

Measures or approaches are needed to enable researchers to follow research participants over time, across age periods. While using overlapping measures at upper and lower age limits of various measures is possible and often the approach taken, it must be clear that the measures used actually assess the same constructs. Measurement work will therefore need to be integrated with the development of innovative research design and methodology.

Technology should be employed in assessment and ongoing monitoring of language abilities. Electronic administration of assessments can carry with it more accurate and efficient data collection procedures, can enable more rapid data analyses, and can ultimately be used to provide timely analyses of student performance that can guide teachers in adapting instruction or intervention for individual students.

In addition, new technologies that can elucidate brain-behavior links are being used to study the brains of bilinguals. Neuroimaging research has revealed a characteristic neural 'signature' in reading and reading disability (e.g. Fletcher *et al.*, 1994; Pugh *et al.*, 2000), and neuroimaging studies of monolingual language processing have been done (e.g. Holland *et al.*, 2001; Keller, Carpenter & Just, 2001). However, little is known about the neurobiological correlates of language development, reading, or reading disability in bilingual children. Research on the neurobiology of bilingualism is still in the early stages. Simos *et al.* (in press) outlines key issues in using neuroimaging to study the brain function associated with language performance in bilinguals and reviews some studies of Indo-European and Oriental languages. Functional neuroimaging technology holds great promise for new insights about bilingual children with normal and disordered language and reading abilities (Simos *et al.*, in press; Pugh *et al.*, 2005).

In a research agenda on the identification of learning disabilities in English language learners, (McCardle *et al.*, 2005a) neuroimagers' recommendations for work with bilingual and second language learner populations are presented. These include the development of normative data on spatial-temporal brain activation for various language tasks, in both the first language and additional languages in bilinguals; gathering data on bilingual individuals who developed both/all languages in early childhood and those who acquired additional languages later, to examine possible effects based on age of onset of acquisition; and the development of profiles of relative language and cognitive abilities in bilinguals with and without learning disabilities. It was also recommended that researchers consider not only using functional magnetic resonance imaging and magnetoencephalograpy but also newer technologies such as diffusion tensor imaging and combinations of available methods (e.g. Klingberg *et al.*, 2000). Cross-discipline collaborations should be developed so that detailed behavioral information on language behaviors can be linked to neurobiological studies. The National Institutes of Health currently funds the development of a large normative database of anatomical brain development (Pediatric MRI Study of Normal Brain Development; http://www.brain-child.org) for children from birth to age 18 years. In order to map the physiological operations of language acquisition, a parallel database of functional imaging modalities applied to typical language development will be needed. Any such resource should include typical developmental trajectories for the development of bilingualisms at various age ranges. Linking of behavioral studies with brain imaging technologies will be important in the study of bilingual language acquisition, and ultimately may be useful in the identification of aberrations in language and language related abilities.

Environments that Enhance Development

We must better understand the role of environment and culture in language and literacy development, and how issues of identity, classroom environment, and home environment affect children's chances for success. We need to better understand what constitute the optimal language environments for children, and how these might vary with children's specific characteristics – which environments are most facilitative for which children, under what circumstances. Such information will enable us to better address issues of parental concern when language development in bilingual children appears to lag developmentally, to better identify and intervene with those children with delayed or disordered language, and to better predict which children may be at risk for learning difficulties. The importance of early intervention is undisputed; we must be better able to predict which bilingual children may benefit from early intervention for potential learning difficulties and to structure learning environments in ways that benefit and do not limit bilingual learning opportunities for children.

Developing interventions that enhance the development of language and literacy will require research on instruction. In particular, given that almost all education in the US is conducted in English, studies of teaching strategies that enhance not only bilingual language development, but also academic achievement in English and transitions from bilingual to English educational programs should be conducted.

Studies are also needed that would identify the optimal approaches to language maintenance, including in-depth descriptions of student characteristics. Research on successful bilingualism and successful teaching strategies could make strategies explicit that apply across languages. Such studies should also provide the basis for developing strategies for remediating less successful students, and should examine the specific student, teacher, and contextual features that characterize the environments of successful bilingual students.

The multilingual classroom poses very specific challenges to instructors. The multilingual classroom is one in which the language of instruction is not the native language of the majority of students, and the students represent multiple different first languages. Few if any studies address effective instructional interventions under such circumstances, although this is an increasingly common situation for many schools in many nations.

Finally, within American culture in general and in specific communities, there is also a need to consider the perceived threat posed by people speaking another language in a predominantly monolingual community. Attitudes and stigmatization contribute to the community context of bilinguals in our midst, and should be studied and better understood.

Summary and Conclusions

In summary, there is a need for focused research that can address the major issues of measurement, growth, optimal instruction, identification of difficulties, and intervention in language and literacy development in bilingual and multilingual individuals. Such research must examine all aspects of language (vocabulary, syntax, semantics, memory and processing speed), and the neurobiological aspects of language ability, including use of the various methods of neuroimaging, which can link brain function and behavior. Bilingualism research must address change over time (as language is a lifespan learning activity), and the variation introduced by the timing of the introduction of additional languages. The adaptation and development of measures is needed; use of extant measures developed for assessment of abilities in a monolingual speaker of a language should not be automatically assumed to be appropriate for bilingual individuals without the development of norms, and generally some adaptations may be required. There is a need for more in-depth measures in many areas of language generally, and this is no less true for the measurement of bilingual or multilingual abilities. In order to fully understand language learning and to develop effective instructional approaches for language minority students, there is a need for longitudinal research, for large-sample studies, and for studies that examine instructional methods, settings, and teacher preparation. Experimental work on effectiveness of instruction and intervention is needed. Negative attitudes toward bilingualism and the stigmatization of specific languages should also be examined so that the phenomenon can be more fully understood and eliminated if possible.

Greater collaboration among those performing language development studies – cross-linguistic, monolingual language development, bilingualism, infant perception, studies of second language learning – as well as those in related disciplines is needed if we are to move beyond traditional approaches. As the demographic picture in the US and other nations changes, so the attention to research on the role of languages in development, education, employment and social and political interaction must also change. Without such change, we will not be able to build the foundational information than can guide us in providing optimal beginnings and ongoing educational support for all.

Note
1. The assertions and opinions contained herein represent those of the authors and should not be taken as representing official policies of the NICHD, NIH, or the US Department of Health & Human Services.

References

Childhood Bilingualism (2004) National Institute of Child Health and Human Development, U.S. Department of Health and Human Services; Office of English Language Acquisition and Office of Special Education and Rehabilitation Services, U.S. Department of Education. Workshop summary. Available at http://www.nichd.nih.gov/crmc/cdb/cdb.htm

Fletcher, J.M. Shaywitz, S.E., Shankweiler, D.P., Katz, L., Liberman, I.Y., Stuebing, K.K. *et al.* (1994). Cognitive profiles of reading disability: Comparisons of discrepancy and low achievement definitions. *Journal of Educational Psychology* 86, 6–23.

Hall, D.G., Waxman, S.R., Bre´dart, S. & Nicolay, A. (2003) Preschoolers' use of form class cues to learn descriptive proper names. *Child Development* 74, 5, 1547–60.

Holland, S.K., Plante, E., Weber Byars, A., Strawburg, R.H., Schmithorst, V.J. and Ball, W.S. Jr (2001) Normal fMRI brain activation patterns in children performing a verb generation task. *Neuroimage* 14, 837–43.

Keller, T.A., Carpenter, P.A. and Just, M.A. (2001) The neural bases of sentence comprehension: A fMRI examination of syntactic and lexical processing. *Cerebral Cortex* 11, 223–37.

Iverson, P., Kuhl, P.K., Akahane-Yamada, R., Diesch, E., Tohkura, Y., Kettermann, A. and Siebert, C. (2003 A perceptual interference account of acquisition difficulties for non-native phonemes. *Cognition* 87, B47–B57.

Klingberg, T., Hedehus, M., Temple, E., Salz, T., Gabrieli, J.D., Moseley, M.E. and Poldrack, R.A. (2000) Microstructure of temporo-parietal white matter as a basis for reading ability: evidence from diffusion tensor magnetic resonance imaging. *Neuron* 25, 493–500.

Kuhl, P.K., Tsao, F.M., Liu, H.M., Zhang, Y. and de Boer, B. (2001) Language/ Culture/Mind/Brain: Progress at the margins between disciplines. In A. Domasio *et al.* (eds) *Unity of Knowledge: The Convergence of Natural and Human Science* (pp. 136–74). New York: The New York Academy of Sciences.

McCardle, P., Mele-McCarthy and Leos, K. (2005a) English language learners and learning disabilities: Research agenda and implications for practice. *Learning Disabilities Research & Practice* 20, 1 68–77.

McCardle, P., Mele-McCarthy, J., Cutting, L. and Leos, K. (eds) (2005b) Special series: Learning disabilities in English language learners: Research issues and future directions. *Learning Disabilities Research & Practice* 20, 1.

National Symposium on Learning Disabilities in English Language Learners: Symposium Summary (2003) Office of Special Education and Rehabilitation Services, Office of English Language Acquisition (U.S. Dept of Education) and the National Institute of Child Health and Human Development, U.S. Dept of Health and Human Services. Available at http://www.nichd.nih.gov/crmc/cdbb/cdbb.htm Retrieved 7 Sept 2004.

Pugh, K.R., Mencl, W.E., Jenner, A.J., Katz, L., Lee, J.R., Shaywitz, S.E. *et al.* (2000) Functional neuroimaging studies of reading and reading disability (developmental dyslexia). *Mental Retardation and Developmental Disabilities Review* 6, 207–13.

Pugh, K.R., Sandak, R., Frost, S.J. and Mencl, E. (2005) Examining reading development and reading disability in ELL populations: Potential contributions from functional neuroimaging. *Learning Disabilities Research & Practice* 20, 1, 24–30.

Simos, P.G., Billingsley-Marshall, R.L., Sarkari, S., Pataraia, E. and Papanicolaou, A.C. (2005) Brain mechanisms supporting distinct languages. *Learning Disabilities Research & Practice* 20, 1, 31–8.

Waxman, S. and Booth, A. (2001) Seeing pink elephants: Fourteen-month-olds' interpretations of novel nouns and adjectives. *Cognitive Psychology* 43, 217–42.

The Contributors

Diane August is currently a Senior Research Scientist at the Center for Applied Linguistics located in Washington, DC. Her research focuses on the development of literacy in language minority children. She is the Principal Investigator for a large federally funded study investigating the development of literacy in English-language learners, Co-Principal Investigator for a five-year Department of Education-funded randomized evaluation of English immersion and transitional bilingual programs, and Co-Principal Investigator for the National Research and Development Center on English-Language Learners. She has written articles and book chapters on the development of literacy in English-language learners.

Ellen Bialystok, PhD, FRSC, is Distinguished Research Professor of Psychology at York University in Toronto, Canada. Her primary research is in the development of language and cognition in preschool children and the effect of bilingualism on that development. Currently she is extending these models to examine the impact of bilingualism on aspects of cognitive processing across the lifespan, with particular attention to the changes in those effects with aging. She has published widely on issues in cognitive development, language proficiency, and second-language acquisition. Her most recent book is *Bilingualism in Development*, published by Cambridge University Press.

Margarita Calderón, a native of Juárez, Mexico, is a Research Scientist at Johns Hopkins University's Center for Research on the Education of Students Placed at Risk (CRESPAR). She is co-principal investigator with Robert Slavin on the five-year IES randomized evaluation of English immersion, transitional, and two-way bilingual programs. Through a series of other grants from OERI/IES, the Texas Education Agency, the Texas Workforce Commission, and the Department of Labor, she is conducting longitudinal research and development projects in El Paso, Texas, regarding teachers' learning communities, bilingual staff development, and adult English language learners. She conducts research on reading programs for the Success For All Foundation and is collaborating with the Center for Applied Linguistics in a longitudinal study investigating the development of literacy in English-language learners.

María Carlo is a psychologist studying bilingualism in children and adults. Her research focuses on the cognitive processes that underlie reading in a second language and on understanding the differences in the reading processes of bilinguals and monolinguals. She is co-principal investigator on an NICHD funded project that investigates the transfer of reading skills from Spanish to English among primary schoolchildren. This research seeks to understand the role played by the native language in the development of second-language literacy. Carlo has written articles and book chapters on the role of mother-tongue literacy in second-language literacy, and on the literacy assessment of bilingual learners. She is an Assistant Professor in the Teaching and Learning program in the School of Education at the University of Miami.

Alan Cobo-Lewis is an associate professor of psychology at the University of Maine. He received his PhD in experimental psychology in 1992 from the University of Wisconsin and undertook postdoctoral training at the Mailmain Center for Child Development at the University of Miami. Dr Cobo-Lewis's research interests are in language development, visual perception, developmental disabilities, and computational and statistical methodology. He has recently worked with the state government to help bring data and quantitative analysis to bear on questions of special educational policy. He is also developing software for rapid assessment of infant and toddler communicative development.

Martha Crago is a Professor of Communication Sciences and Disorders, Dean of Graduate and Postdoctoral Studies at McGill University. Her research in language acquisition focuses on cross-linguistic studies across a variety of learners, including bilingual children and children with impaired language. Her publications include numerous articles, books and book chapters.

Rebecca Eilers is Presidential Professor of Psychology at the University of Maine. She received her PhD in 1975 from the University of Washington in Developmental and Educational Psychology. She has published extensively in the areas of language development, speech perception, artificial hearing and bilingualism and is developing a new research focus in parenting.

Anne Fernald, PhD, is on the faculty of Stanford University in the Department of Psychology and the Program in Human Biology. In their current research on the early development of speech processing efficiency, she and her co-workers use real-time measures of spoken language under-standing by monolingual English-learning children and by bilingual children learning both Spanish and English at the same time.

Fred Genesee has carried out extensive research on alternative approaches to bilingual education, including second/foreign language immersion programs for language majority students and alternative forms of bilingual education for language minority students. His current work also focuses on language development in international adoptees and simultaneous bilingual preschool children.

Erika Hoff is Professor of Psychology at Florida Atlantic University. She holds a PhD from the University of Michigan. Dr Hoff's research interests include the process of early word learning, bilingual development, the role of input in early language development, and the relation of family socio-economic status to mother–child interaction and children's language development. She is the author of *Language Development*.

Tamar Keren-Portnoy is Marie-Curie Intra-European Fellow at the School of Psychology in the University of Wales at Bangor. Her primary areas of research are phonological development, the transition into language and the development of syntax. She has studied language development in children acquiring Hebrew and English.

Judith F. Kroll is Liberal Arts Research Professor of Psychology and Lin-guistics at Penn State University. Her research concerns the acquisition, comprehension, and production of words in two languages during second language learning and in proficient bilingual performance. She and Annette de Groot edited *Tutorials in Bilingualism* (Erlbaum, 1997) and *Handbook of Bilingualism* (Oxford, 2005).

Jarrad Lum is a post-doctoral research officer at the University of Wales at Bangor; he has recently been appointed lecturer at the School of Psycholog-ical Sciences at the University of Manchester. His main areas of research include language acquisition in typical and atypical populations.

Peggy McCardle, PhD, MPH, directs the research program in Language, Bilingual and Biliteracy Development and Disorders at the National Institute of Child Health and Human Development. She is co-editor of *The Voice of Evidence in Reading Research* (Brookes Publishing, Baltimore, MD) and of various thematic journal issues addressing research needs in English language learning/literacy.

Satsuki Nakai is a Research Fellow at the University of Edinburgh. Her research interests include acoustic and auditory phonetics, cross-linguistic phonetics and phonology, and first and second language acquisition.

Michelle N. Nuttall obtained her MA in clinical psychology and is currently completing her doctoral degree at the University of Houston. She obtained her BS in psychology from Brigham Young University.

Barbara Pearson is a Research Associate at the University of Massachusetts Department of Communication Disorders. She has a Masters degree in TESOL from Florida International University and an interdisciplinary PhD in Applied Linguistics from the University of Miami. Her research has focused on first and second language learning with a special emphasis on developing bilinguals. With the University of Miami Bilingualism Study Group, she collaborated on a longitudinal study of 25 bilingual infants and toddlers, and a large-scale cross-sectional study detailed in the book *Language and Literacy in Bilingual Children* (Oller & Eilers, 2000). She is currently Project Manager for the interdisciplinary team that developed a dialect-sensitive test, Diagnostic Evaluation of Language Variation (DELV) published in 2003 (and forthcoming, 2005) by The Psychological Corporation.

Guillaume Thierry is a Lecturer at the University of Wales at Bangor. He is in charge of the Language Electrophysiology Laboratory in the School of Psychology. His main areas of research include language processing at different levels, verbal and nonverbal conceptual processing, language acquisition, developmental dyslexia, bilingualism, laterality and emotion.

Marilyn Vihman is Professor of Developmental Psychology at the University of Wales at Bangor. In addition to her primary areas of research, phonological development and the transition into language, she has published a number of papers based on the acquisition of Estonian and English by her two children.

Dr Sandra Waxman, BS, PhD, University of Pennsylvania, is Professor of Psychology at Northwestern University. Funded by NIH and NSF, Waxman's research focuses on early language and conceptual organization. She adopts a developmental, cross-linguistic approach to identify infants' early capacities and the shaping role of the linguistic and cultural environment.

Whitney Weikum, BSc Honours in Psychology, is currently a PhD student in neuroscience. Her research, funded by the Michael Smith Foundation for Health Research, focuses on visual speech perception in both monolingual and bilingual language acquisition.

Janet F. Werker, FRSC, BA, Harvard University; PhD University of British Columbia, is a Professor and Canada Research Chair in Psychology at UBC. With funding from NSERC, SSHRC, and the Human Frontier Science Program, Werker's research focuses on speech perception and language acquisition, including children growing up bilingual.

Katherine A. Yoshida, MA, University of British Columbia is currently a PhD student. Her interests lie in the speech perception abilities of infants and adults in their first and second languages, and her work is funded by the BC Medical Services Foundation.